Nuclear Energy in India's Energy Security Matrix : An Appraisal

Nuclear Energy in India's Energy Security Matrix : An Appraisal

by

Major General Ajay Kumar Chaturvedi,

AVSM, VSM (Retired)

Published in Association with

Rajiv Gandhi Institute of Petroleum Technology

Vij Books India Pvt Ltd

New Delhi (India)

Published by

Vij Books India Pvt Ltd
(Publishers, Distributors & Importers)
2/19, Ansari Road
Delhi – 110 002
Phones: 91-11-43596460, 91-11-47340674
Fax: 91-11-47340674
e-mail: vijbooks@rediffmail.com
web : www.vijbooks.com

The views expressed in this book are of the author in his personal capacity. These do not have any official endorsement.

Index

List of Tables and Figures

Tables

Foreword

Energy consumption by a nation is a measure of its economic strength and as such a very important indicator of the Comprehensive National Power of a nation. Its importance can easily be discerned in its absence, because such a state enhances the vulnerability of the nation and as such jeopardizes national security. India is a very energy diverse country, which has many challenges to exploit these resources, en-route to her attaining status of Energy Secured. Mismatch between available resources and the desired conversion technologies for those resources, fragmented energy management system, restrictive regimes and poor infrastructure are some of the important challenges among others. A long term perspective needs to be envisioned when a plan is to be drawn to attain Energy Security, because the gestation period for a technology to mature and become economically sustainable is substantial. Therefore identification of technologies which lent themselves for exploitation in short medium and long term context are essential with a provision for a periodic review as a system and it should be a process which seamlessly fits into the planning process. Technology identification should logically be followed by a system's analysis to evolve a frame work wherein all elements of the national power contribute to work out a strategy which aims to enhance supply, both; using indigenous resources and also through international cooperation including acquisitions abroad. The strategy should also aim to reduce demand by an effective demand side management. This will call for stipulating a comprehensive policy, a strict enforcement mechanism and efficiency improvement of the systems and processes entailed. Finally to ensure sustainability of the energy availability, establishing of a strategic reserve should be an integral part of any effective energy management system.

Centrality of the energy security cannot be over emphasized. Energy is absolutely essential for an economically strong and assertive India. The mismatch between resource available and technology desired cannot be allowed to come in the way of the nation to claim its place at appropriate position in the comity of nations. Therefore sustained availability of energy at affordable cost is absolutely essential. This sets the agenda for the government, strategic community, scientific/ research institutions and the industry to collectively evolve solutions which not only address the situation presently but cater for the challenges in future also.

It would be stating the obvious; that the energy availability or lack of it, affects the economic growth substantially. In case of India the gap between demand and supply with economic growth is increasingly widening because of a number of reasons including; non availability of indigenous resources in adequate quantity, quality of available resources and lack of desired technologies. There is a related problem of administered prices which instead of being market driven are government controlled with a huge subsidy element built into it. Such a pricing not only affects the profitability of the concerned sourcing organizations but also affect their capability to respond to emerging energy scene due to reduced financial muscle. Therefore a collective response to the challenge of attaining Energy Security is the need of the hour, wherein all stake holders; government, research fraternity, academia, industry and users need to work in an integrated manner with the principle of 'unity of decision making', which is considered; a critical activity.

Nuclear Energy is said to form an important element in the future energy basket of India, though it also entails a technology based challenge to utilize locally available resource like thorium. Secondly; public protests post Fukushima have assumed almost a debilitating impact on the new installations coming up. Whether safety issues are critical or are a case of deliberately planted perception by the anti nuclear energy lobby? This issue needs serious examination. Next issue that needs deliberation is financial management of the programme. One of the important challenges is to meet the enormous financial demands which implementation of the nuclear energy plans would entail. One of the option to deal with this challenge is by involving the private sector in the implementation of the plan. In such a contingency the logical question would be, "How much is too much", ie., the limit to which this cooperation with private sector in a highly classified domain can be extended to? This book makes an attempt to analyze all these issues with a view to appraise the role which Nuclear Energy is going to play in the future Energy Security matrix of India.

Rajiv Gandhi Institute of Petroleum Technology, though dedicated to capacity building in the field of petroleum and related disciplines, but realizes in the field of monolithic nature of energy and therefore, it is my considered view that energy security would have to be addressed in an integrated manner. That is why we are committed to look at other forms of energy too.

Major General AK Chaturvedi, AVSM, VSM (Retired), has been looking at Energy Security as a system and has been examining various elements which contribute to enhance the energy supply and reduce the energy demand. After having examined the efficacy of water and natural gas in his earlier books, in this book, he has attempted to flag the issues related to nuclear energy with due analysis of resources, technologies and international cooperation to recommend a course of action to address present vulnerabilities. I am sure that it will generate adequate discussion to work out options for the strategy which nation needs to adopt for the sustained availability of the energy over all times to come.

New Delhi

31 January 2014

(D. M. Reddy)

President RGIPT

Preface

Post 1991, when India took a conscientious policy decision to open its economy, India became one of the fastest growing economy of the world (average GDP growth rate (between 2000 and 2012: 7.31 percent). However during the same period the use of energy demand has grown at an average rate of 7.02 percent since 1990, with the average growth rate of energy production at 6.71 percent. This yawning gap between energy demand and energy production, needs to be bridged to sustain economic growth, using all possible resources which are indigenously available and also those which can be commercially imported/ acquired through interdependence developed based on geopolitical/ geo-economic interests/ energy bearing equities acquired abroad and transporting the produce of these equities. An analysis needs to be done with respect to each of the resources for the economic viability of the available resources, technical feasibility for their efficient conversion and the qualitative assessment of the resource for an environmental impact.

To have a focused examination of each of the energy bearing resources there is a need to analyze each one of them across the entire spectrum of supply chain and the end use related to that particular resource. With abundant availability of thorium and now reasonable availability of low grade natural uranium, the nuclear energy is said to be having a potential to meet the future energy needs of India in a sustained manner to a large extent. This book attempts to examine the feasibility of such a possibility and the status of the contribution of the nuclear energy on the supply side in 2030?

While conceptually exploitation of nuclear energy appears to be a plausible solution to energy shortages in India, but to comprehensively analyze its relevance in the Indian context, the entire spectrum of following issues need to be examined:-

- Availability appraisal of resources capable of nuclear energy conversion.

- Appraisal of current conversion technologies and their trajectory of growth to meet future challenges of optimal utilization of resources.

- Infrastructure needed to convert theoretical principles of nuclear energy to its commercial utilization in Indian context.

- An appraisal of safety and hazard mitigation related to the use of nuclear energy.

- An appraisal of the capacity of Indian industry, training institutions and research organizations to support the introduction and sustenance of the

- Cost benefit analysis of utilization of nuclear energy vis-à-vis other available energy conversion options in Indian context.

The development of the research is being done in following parts:-

- A worldwide Energy Overview in general and narrowing it down to India with a particular emphasis on following issues:-

  o Overall Energy Scenario now and its extrapolation to 2030 in terms of demand and supply.

  o System of Supply Chain Management.

  o Challenges in the domain of energy.

  o Identification of the areas which need to be addressed to augment the supply and the policy initiatives to reduce the demand.

- Growth trajectory of nuclear energy:-

  o Technological appraisal.

  o Economic appraisal.

  o Infrastructural appraisal.

  o Present capacity status of industry& academic institutions, HR gaps and remedial measures.

- Comparative study of nuclear energy Vis a Vis other forms of energy

- Decision making loop of nuclear power in India

- Integration of growth of nuclear power in the overall energy management in India

- Recommendations

- Conclusion including identification of areas for further research.

Acknowledgement

"I am honoured and privileged for having been part of the Indian Army for major part of my adult life and I dedicate my work to Indian Army which has prepared me to continue working, even after hanging my uniform, on issues of national importance".

In my journey to explore the possible solutions to the Energy Security of the Country this is the third research which I am taking forward where last, "Role Pakistan in India's Energy Security" ended. In that I had attempted to analyze the importance of the Natural gas for India, to meet its energy needs. The research concluded that for short and medium term, natural gas would continue to remain an important element in the energy security matrix of India; probably only next to coal. However it is not a day too late to look beyond short and medium term to find energy solutions. It is felt that nuclear energy and the renewable energy, along with clean coal technologies, will play the most crucial role in long term. In this book, I have attempted, to do an appraisal of the efficacy of the nuclear energy to meet the future energy challenges. Role and scope of Renewable energy is planned to be taken up subsequently.

I am not re-inventing the wheel and I am quite sanguine that a lot of useful work, in this field by a large number of researchers, research establishments and academic institutions has already been done in past. I hereby acknowledge their contribution and have quoted extensively from their work with due credit being extended to each one of them. In case some names have been missed, I would like to state with due responsibility that it is not deliberate and my sincere apologies in advance for the slip up, if any.

I am thankful to Dr R Chidambaram, Principal Scientific Advisor to Government of India & the former Chairman of AEC, Shri BK Chaturvedi, Member Planning Commission & the former Cabinet Secretary and Shri Shyam Saran, Chairman National Security Advisory Board (NSAB), Chairman of the Research & Information System for Developing Countries

(A Think Tank), Senior Fellow at the Centre for Policy Research, New Delhi & Former Foreign Secretary; for their most valuable inputs which helped me to steer my research in the right direction. I also extend my thanks to Professor Rajaram Nagappa of the National institute of Advanced Studies, Bangalore and Lieutenant General Gautam Banerjee, PVSM, AVSM, YSM (Retired) for very meaningful interactions on the subject and the useful suggestions they gave, which have helped me to enhance the quality of my research. Finally, very special thanks are due to Brigadier (Dr) PS Siwach, my PhD guide for helping me at every stage of the research.

As always my wife; Mrs Renu Chaturvedi and my two daughters; Medha and Pragya helped me in IT and supporting me emotionally through this journey. I am indebted to them, for their support.

Lucknow

03 October 2013

(AK Chaturvedi)

Major General (Retired)

Abbreviations

ADB	Asian Development Bank
ADS	Accelerator Driven System
AEC	Atomic Energy commission
AECL	Atomic Energy of Canada Limited
AERB	Atomic Energy Regulatory Board
AHWR	Advanced Heavy Water Reactor
AMD	Atomic Minerals Directorate for Exploration and Research
APFSDS	Armoured Piercing Fin Stabilized Discarding Sabot
ASME	American Society of Mechanical Engineers
ASSOCHAM	Associated Chamber of Commerce and Industry of India
BHAVINI	Bharatiya Nabhikiya Vidyut Nigam Limited
BARC	Bhabha Atomic Research Centre
BAU	Business as Usual
BCS	Best Case Scenario
BHEL	Bharat Heavy Electrical Limited
BTG	Boiler Turbine Generator
BEE	Bureau of Energy Efficiency
BWR	Boiling Water Reactor

CAD	Current Account Fiscal Deficit
CAT	Centre for Advanced technology
CAGR	Compound Annual Growth Rate
CANDU	Canada Deuterium Uranium: This refers to the Canadian design of the pressurized heavy water reactor.
CBM	Coal Bed Methane
CEA	Central Electricity Authority (India)
CHTR	Compact High Temperature Reactor
CMIE	Centre for Monitoring Indian Economy
CNP	Comprehensive National Power
CTBT	Comprehensive Test Ban Treaty
¢	US Cent
DAE	Department of Atomic Energy
DGH	Directorate General Hydrocarbon
DU	Depleted Uranium
EBR	European Breeder Reactor
EIA	US Energy Information Administration
ECIL	Electronics Corporation of India Limited
EfW	Energy from Waste
EPR	Evolutionary Power Reactor or European Power Reactor
EPA	Environment Protection Agency
ERDA	Energy Research and Development Administration
EJ	Exa Joules= 1018 Joules

FBR	Fast Breeder Rector
FICCI	Federation of Indian Chamber of Commerce and Industry
Gg	Giga gram
GRIHA	Green Rating for Integrated Habitat Assessment
GW	Giga Watts
HDI	Human Development Index
HEPA	High Efficiency Particulate Air: It is a kind of air filter
HWB	Heavy Water Board
IAEA	International Atomic Energy Agency
ICC	Integrated Combined Cycle
IGCAR	Indira Gandhi Centre for Atomic Research
IISc	Indian Institute of Science, Bengaluru
INR	Indian National Rupee
IREL	Indian Rare Earth Limited
IST	Indian Standard Time
ITER	International Thermonuclear Experimental Reactor
JV	Joint Venture
KAMINI Reactor	Kalpakkam Mini Reactor
kgOe	Kilogram of Oil Equivalent
kWe	Kilo Watt (electric)
kt	Kilo Ton
KVA	Kilo Volt Ampere

LE	Life Extension
LEAP	Long range Energy Alternatives Planning: IT based energy management system.
LENR	Low Energy Nuclear Reactions
LEU	Low Enriched Uranium
LNG	Liquefied Natural Gas
LT	Low Tension Line
MEA	Ministry of External Affairs
MoU	Memorandum of Understanding
MOX	Mixed Oxide
MoP&NG	Ministry of Petroleum and Natural Gas
MoEF	Ministry of Environment and Forests
MSW	Municipal Solid waste
mtoe	Million Tons of Oil Equivalent
MT	Million Tons
MW	Mega Watts
MWd/tHM	Mega Watt Days/ Metric Ton of Heavy Metal
NIAS	National Institute of Advanced Studies
NFC	Nuclear Fuel Complex
NPP	Nuclear Power Plant
NPS	Nuclear Power Station
NPT	Nuclear Nonproliferation Treaty
NSG	Nuclear Suppliers Group
NSAB	National Security Advisory Board

OECD	Organization for Economic Co-operation and Development
OEM	Original Equipment Manufacturer
PFBR	Proto type Fast Breeder Reactor.
PHWR	Pressurized Heavy Water Reactor
PJ	Penta Joule=1015 Joules. 210 PJ= 50 Mega Tons of TNT
PV	Photo Voltaic
PLF	Plant Load Factor
PWR	Pressurized Water Reactor
PNE	Peaceful Nuclear Explosion
PPP	Public Private Partnership
REC	Renewable Energy Certificate
RES	Renewable Energy Sources
R&M	Renovation & Modernization
RPV	Reactor Pressure Vessel
RPO	Renewable Procurement Obligation
Tcf	Trillion Cubic Feet
TCM	Trillion Cubic Meters
TWh	Tera Watt Hour
T&D	Transmission & Distribution
USGS	US Geological Survey
UCG	Underground Coal Gasification
UCIL	Uranium Corporation of India Limited
VVER	Vodo-Vodyanoi Energetichesky Reactor (Water-

	Water Power Reactor)
WDI	World Development Indicators (World Bank)
WMD	Weapons of Mass destruction
WNA	World Nuclear Association
WtE	Waste to Energy

1

Introduction

"The energy produced by breaking down the atom is a very poor kind of thing. Anyone who expects a source of power from the transformations of these atoms is talking moonshine."

Lord Ernest Rutherford, 1933.

"The unleashed power of the atom has changed everything save our modes of thinking............".

Albert Einstein, 25 May 1946

"It is not too much to expect that our children will enjoy in their homes [nuclear generated] electrical energy too cheap to meter."

Lewis Strauss, Chairman, US Atomic Energy Commission, 1954.

General

In a major technological breakthrough, just a little over 20 years after the statement of Lord Rutherford, On June 27, 1954, the then USSR's Obninsk Nuclear Power Plant, in today's Russian Federation, became the world's first nuclear power plant to generate electricity for a power grid, and produced around 5 MW of electric power (World Nuclear Association, dated 24 July 2013). It was indeed a land mark which changed the contours of the energy supply in the world for all times to come.

It is therefore evident that within a period of just over one decade of the discovery of the nucleus of an atom, the immense power that the nucleus of an atom holds for harnessing, was realized. It is a separate issue, that initially it was used with a devastating effect for destruction- more about it a little later. Within two decades of the discovery of the power of the nucleus, it was realized that the nuclear energy can be a source of clean and inexpensive power. Thereafter there was no looking back and within a period of next half a century, planners started planning to build infrastructure to seamlessly integrate this form of clean energy in the existing energy utilization framework of the world which has been gasping for additional cleaner sources of energy. There are presently two main clean sources of energy which show plenty of promise for future. These are; nuclear energy and the renewable sources of energy (RES).

Thus for the future energy supply basket, nuclear energy has potential to be an important element, provided research and development can continue to find more efficient and cost effective technological solutions, to harness this form of energy safely in an integrated energy utilization framework.

Centrality of Energy for the Economic Development

Energy Consumption: A Function of Economic Growth. Growth in the energy consumption is an important indicator of the economic growth. Electrical power is an essential element in determining the quality of life. It is a well established fact that the growing industrialization, growth in sectors like services, agriculture, transportation and information management, the need of energy is growing steadily and the trend is likely to continue.

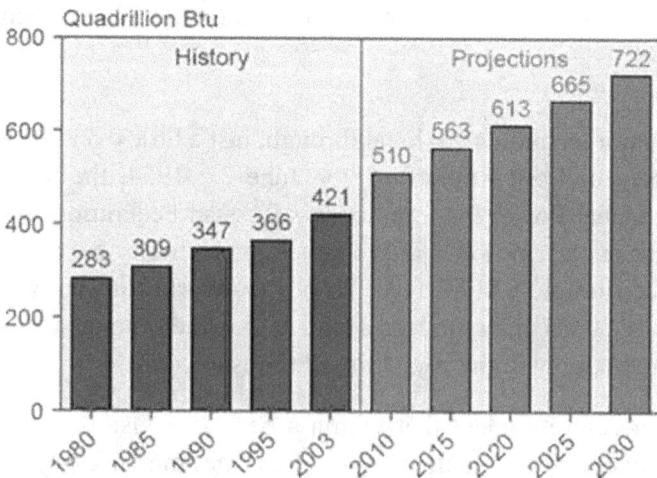

Sources: **History:** Energy Information Administration (EIA), *International Energy Annual 2003* (May-July 2005), web site www.eia.doe.gov/iea/. **Projections:** EIA, System for the Analysis of Global Energy Markets (2006).

Figure 1.1: World Marketed Energy Consumption- 1980-2030

Energy Consumption: A Changing Pattern of Consumers

Another interesting feature which is emerging is the changing profile of the energy consumers. Earlier the growth in the energy demand was driven by the organization of Economic Cooperation and Development (OECD) countries, but recent recession in Europe and USA has resulted into a slower economic growth of these countries and accordingly energy consumption in these countries, has been slowing down. While growing population of the under developed/ developing nations may be, to an extent, driving the energy demand but it is their growth on economic scale, which is spurring the demand substantially. In this connection; countries like India and China, which were not so badly affected by the global recession (especially India where the economic growth was largely driven by the internal consumption rather than international trade), led to non OECD countries overtaking OECD countries in energy consumption and as such; have now assumed the role of the growth drivers since 2008. It may be noted that China and India are steadily showing growth in the energy consumption. Combined energy consumption of India and China; in 1990 was 10 percent of the total energy consumption of the world, which became 21 percent in 2008 and likely to become 31 percent by 2035 (EIA 09 September 2011).This phenomenon corroborates the hypothesis that energy consumption is a good indicator of the economic growth. It has been observed that during the period 2008-35 world economy is likely to grow by 53 percent overall and during the same period energy usage is likely to rise by 85 percent in non OECD countries and only 18 percent in the OECD countries (EIA," International Energy Outlook-2011)

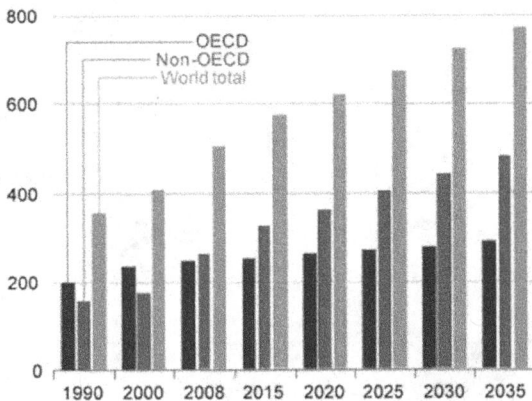

Figure 1.2: World Energy Consumption- OECD and Non OECD Countries (in Quadrillion Btu)- 1990-2035

Source: EIA, "International Energy Outlook 2011" dated 09 September 2011, uploaded on www.eia.gov/forecasts/ieo/world.cfm

Quality of Life: A Function of Energy Consumption

Human Development Index: A Function of Energy Consumption.

Improvement in the quality of life, due to the need of automation makes it imperative for the use of energy based systems. However if the economic growth is required to be an inclusive one (non inclusive growth results into a large section of society being dissatisfied and that state gives rise to fissiparous tendencies which is not conducive for national security), it becomes absolutely essential that an indicator/ combination of indicators is found, which brings out the well being of its citizenry; within the overall economic growth framework. In more measurable terms, use of energy by its citizen is one such good indicator of the growing prosperity of that nation. However while it (per capita energy consumption) is necessary, but it may not be sufficient, because per capita energy is a very simplistic way of understanding a complex problem by just dividing the overall energy demand of a country by its population. A better system of measurement will be to link human development index (HDI) with energy consumption. The relationship between per capita energy consumption and HDI is as follows:-

BARC

Perspective of a country on nuclear energy depends on domestic realities

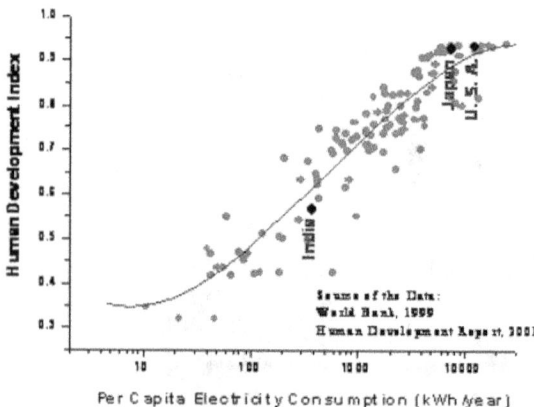

"In general, the perspective of a country on nuclear energy – and degree of public acceptance – could depend on where you are on these curves, on the availability of fossil and hydro resources, and on technological development capacity."

- R. Chidambaram, 2003

2005-05-27 (Delhi, Petrofed) RKS - India's Energy Security - The Role of Nuclear Energy   14

Figure-1.3: HDI versus Energy Consumption

It can be seen that increase in energy consumption per capita has a bearing on the improvement in HDI, which has been improving with the growth in the energy consumption, over the years. Another aspect which emerges is that the developed nations occupy higher flatter portion of the curve which means higher level of power consumption per capita is highly correlated with the improved HDI.

Correlation between Life Expectancy and Energy Consumption

Figure-1.4 below illustrates the correlation between life expectancy and the power consumption per capita. It may be appreciated that the life expectancy is a function of prosperity, health, education and mortality-reduced infant.

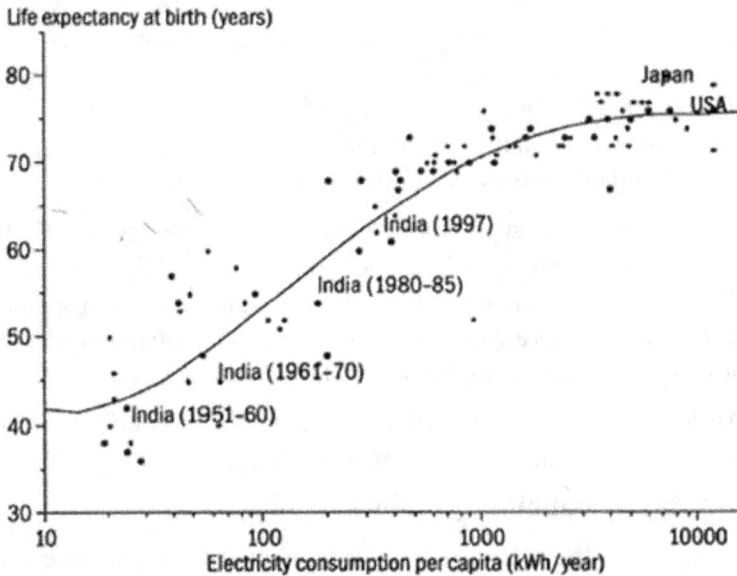

Figure 1.4: Life Expectancy at Birth with Per Capita Electricity Consumption: World and India

Source: World Bank.1999. World Development Report 1999/2000.

Analysis of the Curves at Figures-1.3 and 1.4:

- With the increase in the per capita power consumption, the HDI has been improving steadily. Improved HDI can easily be ascertained in more measurable term like; life expectancy. Life expectancy in India has increased from a dismal 31 years in 1947 to 65.48 years in 2011. The life expectancy can also be correlated with the literacy rate. Because literacy rate, especially that of women results into reduced child mortality, reduced birth rate, better health support and as such enhanced life expectancy rates and better utilization of available power per capita. Literacy rate in India has improved from a low of 12 percent (figure for female literacy is not available) in 1947 to 74.04 percent (female literacy is 65.46 percent) in 2011.

- An aspect that emerges (by implication) is that the developed countries like Japan and USA which are major consumers of the per capita power have a life expectancy in excess of 70 years (85.59 years for Japan and 78.64 years in case of USA in 2011). In other words, the quality of life improves with an access to energy, with attended implication for the national security.

- Life expectancy is substantially linked to adult literacy rate (in that female literacy rate would be a better measure) and therefore higher literacy rate, lower infant mortality rate and higher energy consumption rates considered as a whole are more comprehensive measures of the growth of a nation in tangible terms (Dr R Chidambaram).

- An implied interpretation of energy is that it is as critical for the survival of life; as food, water and fresh air.

Energy Supply: Changing Contours

The vast majority of the world's energy is generated from non-renewable sources, specifically oil, coal and gas (Figure-1.5). Just over 13 percent of global energy is derived from renewable sources, 10.6 percent of which is from combustible renewable energy sources based and renewable municipal waste. The remainder of renewable energy comes from hydro, geothermal, solar, wind, tidal and wave sources. Projections of total global energy consumption show that between 2004 and 2030, fossil fuels would provide bulk of increase, with nuclear and other sources providing relatively minor contributions in absolute terms (Figure 1.6). In percentage terms, gas and coal are likely to show the greatest change with an increase of 65 and 74 percent respectively. Oil consumption is expected to increase by 42 percent while nuclear and energy from renewable sources, starting from a much lower baseline, are expected to increase by 44 and 61 percent respectively. The ultimate contributions from different sources will be highly dependent on policy directions. In this analysis what has not been taken into account are the new sources for which technology has not yet been hardened but quite a few of those like Gas Hydrates, biomass/ algae conversion, Coal Bed Methane (CBM), breeder based nuclear technology and shale gas are likely to become commercially viable and will influence the supply substantially in years ahead.

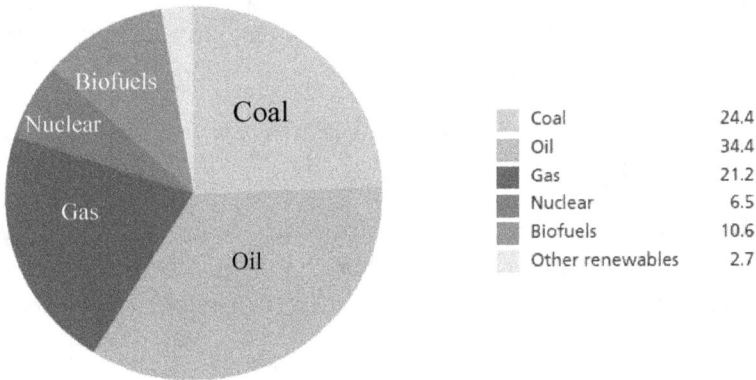

Coal	24.4
Oil	34.4
Gas	21.2
Nuclear	6.5
Biofuels	10.6
Other renewables	2.7

Source: IEA 2007a

Figure-1.5: Fuel Shares of World's Total Primary Energy Supply (in percent) in 2004

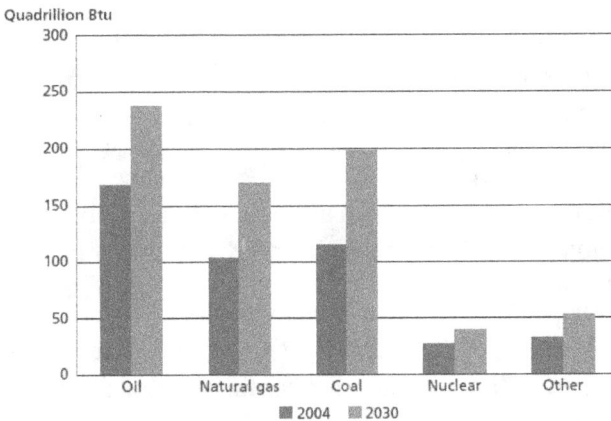

Source: EIA 2007

Note: Does not include traditional biomass.

Figure-1.6: Total Global Marketed Energy Consumption by Source in 2004 and Projected for 2030

Energy Security and the National Security

Energy Security can be explained as *a capacity of a nation to ensure sustained supply of energy in the form; it is required to be used for economic activities across the entire spectrum of the needs of the environment at an affordable cost by the entire citizenry of the nation for all times without any disruption.*

Based on above definition, the important elements which contribute to the energy security of a nation are as follows:-

- **Adequacy of the availability** of indigenous energy bearing resources.

- **Quality of indigenous resources** to ensure cost effective conversion.

- **Diplomatic muscle of the nation** to obtain resources from other resource rich countries to bridge the gap between demand and supply by creating adequate interdependence with source countries.

- **Financial strength** to acquire energy equities abroad.

- **Logistic capability to transfer the energy bearing resources** from where these equities are located

- **Capability to ensure the safety and security of these assets** is an important part of the effective energy security management mechanism.

- Equally important is the need for adequacy of funds to **create infrastructure** for optimal utilization of the usable form of energy generated, across the entire length & breadth of the country.

- Nations cannot allow themselves to be surprised by adverse geopolitical developments and therefore **creation of adequate storage facilities** to cater for contingency of a sudden disruption is necessary.

- Capacity for the continuous **raising of technological threshold** in terms of R&D establishment to exploit resources at the disposal of the nation is an essential element in the energy security matrix.

- A scientific **capability to forecast**; future requirements and technological growth trajectory should be put in place.

- As energy needs increase so should be the '**capacity build up**' across the entire spectrum of activities and desired capabilities..

- Energy is a multi faceted and multi-disciplinary subject therefore an **integrated energy management system** should be in place to manage the affairs relate to energy.

National Security entails; preservation of the core values of a nation, its security against an external threat and internal dissensions through the coercive/ cooperative measures, which include use of economic power, diplomatic leverage, capability of the defence forces to project national power, capacity of the country to project its soft power and finally the strength of the political system which the country follows. It, therefore; encompasses a broad range of facets, all of which impinge on the non military or economic security of the nation and the values espoused by the national society. Accordingly, in order to strengthen national security, a nation needs to possess economic security, energy security, environmental security, etc. Security threats involve not only conventional foes such as other nation-states but also non-state actors such as violent non-state actors, narcotic cartels, multinational corporations and non-governmental organizations; some authorities include natural disasters and events causing severe environmental damage in this category. Thus there is a strong complementarity between national security and energy security. In fact energy security is an important subset of the national security.

Control of Resources. Future conflicts between the nations are substantially going to be for the control of resources; rather than direct confrontations alone. Of all the resources; energy bearing resources are some of the most important resources because of their impact on the utilization of other resources. For example quantity of fresh water per capita is reducing for a variety of reasons and water which is essential for the survival of life and contributes towards the food security, needs to be augmented. To augment quantity of water; energy would be needed for desalination of the sea water/ treatment of the sewage/ storm water. Likewise economic prosperity of a nation depends on manufacturing, agriculture, transportation and growth of service sector. All these, as can be realized, are the functions of energy consumption. Therefore directly, as well as, indirectly energy is critical for the country and a shortage of it, results into a vulnerability of the nation which can very easily be exploited by countries who are rich in energy resources.

Energy is also an important ingredient in the defence preparedness of a nation. Thus, dependence for its energy needs by a nation makes it vulnerable to external pressures. Therefore energy plays a crucial role in the measurement of the comprehensive national power (CNP).

In view of the above; sustained availability of energy at affordable price with the optimal utilization of all available indigenous resources is one of the most important elements (in terms of both tangible and intangible repercussions) of the security matrix of a nation.

Need for Sustained Availability of Energy

The objective of an energy management plan is always to ensure that the energy availability is sustained and is independent of geopolitical and environmental development. Thus strategy which needs to be adopted has to be two pronged. Firstly augmentation of existing resources through leveraging of technology for more efficient exploration, making use of the diplomatic influence of the country; to acquire resources from resource rich countries and improving the efficiency of the current technologies for energy conversion systems. Secondly; widening the net for newer sources and quickly developing commercially viable technologies for their exploitation. This strategy brings out the centrality of a well developed forecasting system which is highly sensitive to the geopolitical developments, highly dynamic environmental factors and the economic strength of the country. In addition a strong research and development establishment is a prerequisite to respond to existing/ envisaged future demands. Equally important is the need to appreciate the time lines which need to be adhered to. It is felt that such a strategy will help the country to quickly graduate to the top flatter portion of the curve at Figures 1.3 and 1.4 where most of the developed countries are presently perched. The strategy also needs to have provisions to help the country to stay there continuously. For this; there is a need to have adequate capacity redundancy within the system. A word of caution; that while looking for newer sources one need to go for cleaner sources like nuclear energy and renewable energy to offset the ill effects of pollution, global warming and other environmental issues. It can be seen that with such an objective, a strategy will have to be worked out which entails a highly coordinated response of; government, research organizations, industry and academic institutions.

Based on the availability of the natural energy bearing resources, the world can be classified into energy-rich and energy-poor countries. Statistically; the world's population is about 6.7 billion, out of that over 5 billion people live in the economically poor countries and about 3 billion in rural areas.(SK Jain) A little deeper analysis brings out that most of these people on one hand; face natural calamities like droughts and floods with attended triggers like scarcity of resources which further enhances their poverty (in the absence of availability of resources at affordable cost) leading to a state of social instability; and on the other hand; their life is made more miserable due to lack of affordable oil and gas prices. It is a matter of fact that one-third of the population of the world does not have access to modern energy services (World Energy Council, 2001: Living in One World).

An analysis of energy resources world over; brings out that in years ahead, it will be oil, coal and natural gas, which will dominate the energy supply in the world market in short (around five years) to medium term (around twenty years). The contribution from renewable sources and nuclear energy, although will increase, but may not be in the same proportion. The share of energy from renewable sources in the total energy use increases from 10 percent in 2008 to 15 percent in 2040 (EIA: International Energy Outlook 2011). As far as nuclear energy is concerned; in the aftermath of Fukushima incident, though a certain kind of uncertainty is being felt, however; there is no evidence to support that any nuclear power plant which was planned prior to the above referred incident has been abandoned, and as such; it can easily be inferred that the nuclear energy's future as a driver of energy supply is still intact (Dr Chidambaram in an interview with the author on 31 May 2013). Though shrouded in a number of uncertainties; nuclear energy will be contributing about 7 percent of the world energy basket.

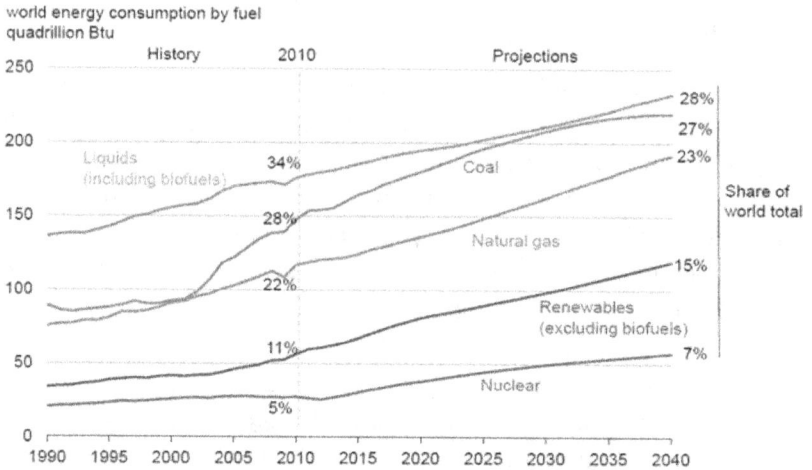

Figure 1.7: World Energy Consumption by Fuel Type: 1990-2040

Analysis: The reasons for slower growth of nuclear energy and energy from renewable sources is basically due to poor efficiency of the conversion systems (in case of solar particularly Photo Voltaic systems, solar cell efficiencies vary from 6 percent for amorphous silicon-based solar cells to 40.7 percent with multiple-junction research lab cells and 42.8 percent with multiple dies assembled into a hybrid package (U Daily, 23 July 2007) and similarly for systems based on other RES) Another reason is the lack of availability of safe technologies to harness nuclear energy at affordable cost.

Importance of Regular Review of Energy Policies

Due to criticality of the energy in the life of a nation, the energy policies of that nation need to be planned by the concerned country, depending upon the availability of the energy resources; indigenously or through assured international collaborations. Energy policies should also take into account the efforts that the concerned nation needs to make to reduce the demand through conservation, efficiency improvement and other measures of enforcement. It can therefore be appreciated that depending on typical environmental conditions of a nation, she will be required to have policies which would meet the 'felt needs of the environment'. In case of India, where the per capita energy consumption, presently is abysmally low, all resources of energy locally available in small or large quantities are required to be developed, and thereafter sustained to bridge this huge gap, through a well thought through and a comprehensive plan and a policy mechanism. The economic model to exploit various local resources will have to be given a thought to meet the economy of scales. In this connection what Dr Homi Bhabha said once, sums up the situation quite well; *"No power is costlier than no power"*, meaning thereby that whatever may be the cost of the power produced, it will always be less than the cost, which non availability of power will cause to the nation..

Need for Investments in the Energy Sector

It has been reported by a World Bank report, that as many as 1.2 billion people in the world; equivalent to almost the current population of India, don't have access to electricity and 2.8 billion have to rely on wood or other forms of biomass, to cook and heat their homes. This report is first in a series of reports, to monitor the progress of three objectives, which are as follows; firstly; full energy access, secondly; doubling energy efficiency and thirdly; optimum exploitation of the renewable sources of energy to arrive at a technological model which can guarantee provision of sustainable energy (An UN Initiative). The multi agency report has called on the public and private sectors to step up energy investments by at least US $ 600 billion a year until 2030, more than doubling the current estimated investments of US $ 409 billion. The additional US $ 600 billion would include; US $ 45 billion for electricity expansion; US $ 4.4 billion on modern cooking; US $ 394 billion in energy efficiency and US $174 billion on renewable energy. In this connection India's power report card reads as follows:-

- **100 percent Energy Access**- rate of access to electricity and primary non solid fuel by the percentage of population, will have to increase from 83 percent and 59 percent respectively in 2010 to 100 percent in 2030. In this connection following table gives a comparison of India with China, OECD countries and the world average. It clearly brings out that slowly the access to power in India is increasing from a rather lower base and though the rate of the growth is substantial yet she has a lot of catching up to do:-

Table-1.1

Country	1990	2000	2010
Access to Electricity (In Percentage)			
India	51	62	75
China	94	98	100
OECD Countries	99	100	100
World Average	76	79	83
Access to Non Solid Fuel (In Percentage)			
India	13	29	42
China	36	47	54
OECD	99	100	100
World Average	47	54	59

Source: World Bank, pub in The Economic Times, 30 May 2013, Page13

- **Doubling Energy Efficiency-** Energy intensity is a measure of the energy efficiency of a nation's economy. It is calculated as units of energy per unit of GDP. Rate of improvement of energy intensity will have to double from -1.3 percent for 1990-2010 to -2.6 percent for 2010-30.

Table-1.2: Rate of Primary Energy Intensity Improvement, CAGR (%)

Country	Rate of Intensity Improvement (%)			Cumulative Energy Saving (PJ)
	1990	2000	2010	1990-2010
China	-7.07	-2.18	-4.65	1,319,738
India	-1.72	-2.98	-2.35	114,220
World	-1.61	-0.99	-1.30	2,275,646

- **Doubling Renewable Energy-** Renewable energy share in the global energy mix will have to get doubled from an estimated starting point of at the most 18 percent in 2010, implying an objective of up to 36 percent by 2030. However the Revised Estimated share (percent) in electricity generation in 2010 of selected countries (BRIC) along with world's average was as tabulated below:-

Table-1.3: Growth of Renewable Energy

Country	Actual Growth Rate in 2010 (%)
Brazil	84.8
Russia	16.1
India	14.2
China	40.2
World	19.4

Source: World Bank, pub in The Economic Times, 30 may 2013 page13

Analysis: The data indicates that except for India, other BRIC Countries have been able to achieve the projected growth rate and also it is lower than the world's average. Therefore it is essential that a review of implementation be done and also a mechanism be evolved to continuously review the progress so that mid course corrections can be made.

Relevance of Nuclear Energy

Nuclear power is yet another of the options for providing safe, environmentally clean, reliable and economically competitive energy services. However; nuclear energy is one form of energy which either evokes a very strong support or else equally strong condemnation. One of the strongest arguments against nuclear energy is; its capacity to cause wide spread damage if conversion goes out of control. From a safety stand point, nuclear power, in terms of lives lost per unit of electricity delivered, is comparable to and in some cases, lower than many renewable energy sources. Therefore this argument does not hold ground. Another argument against nuclear energy is that it is far more expensive than some other forms of energy. It is true that the cost of nuclear power has followed an increasing trend whereas the cost of electricity is declining in case of wind power (Ryan Wiser et al). In 2011, wind power became as inexpensive as natural gas, and anti-nuclear groups in 2010 had suggested that solar power had become cheaper than nuclear power (Miranda Marquit). However data from the EIA had estimated in 2011 that in 2016, solar would have a levelized cost of electricity almost twice that of nuclear (21¢/kWh for solar, 11.39¢/kWh for nuclear), and slightly less for wind based power (9.7¢/kWh). Next issue which merits consideration is that both wind power and photo voltaic (PV) based energy conversion are variable renewable energy sources, meaning they are neither suitable for getting dispatched nor are steady for a grid. Both, unlike nuclear, require buffering, with pumped hydro storage (US EIA, November 2011). The requirements for pumped storage, in case of nuclear energy, are much less than those needed for wind power. Finally, it needs to be taken into account that the capacity factor of a typical nuclear power plant is in the range of 80-90 percent, in comparison to intermittent wind power's 30-40 percent.

No wonder, starting with a single nuclear power plant in 1950, Nuclear power, world over, has grown to 440 nuclear power plants in 56 countries (SK Jain) with a total installed capacity of 361.582 GW (as of January 2004), producing about 16 percent of electricity. In real terms it works out to be about 2574 TWh (IAEA PRIS Data). According to IAEA, economic growth, national resource scarcity and increasing population are the major factors in this tilt from the developed to the developing countries. The potential growth of nuclear power is seen more in the developing countries, especially in the Asian region. Today, twenty-two of the last 31 nuclear power plants connected to the world energy grid have been built in Asia. (SK Jain)- While it is a new found realization in these countries, in India it was envisaged long back and as such efforts to find ways and means to exploit nuclear energy commenced since early fifties. Today, India has a sound R&D base, well developed industry and a fast-expanding nuclear power programme.

2

An Overview of India's Current Energy Scene

Uniqueness of India: Technology-Availability and Quality Trap

India is a unique country which is endowed with a variety of energy bearing resources which are theoretically enough, to meet the energy requirements of its teeming millions. However; it is strange that the biggest component of the import pie of the country is on account of energy (Eric Yep)[1]. A quick appreciation reveals that its energy sector suffers from a three pronged trap consisting of technology, availability and quality of resources. An analysis of the energy sector of India brings out following:-

- India has adequate quantity of coal but that coal has very high ash content and a low calorific value. Clean Coal Technologies are still not fully matured.

- India has fully matured technologies for the exploitation for gas and oil but these resources are not available in adequate quantity.

- In the field of nuclear energy, while India has fully operational technology to use natural uranium for energy conversion using Pressurized Heavy Water Reactor (PHWR) but India has uranium only for 10000 MWe. Even the grade of Indian uranium is also quite low. On the contrary India has adequate thorium but the breeder technology is still couple of years away from becoming commercially viable.

- In case of renewable energy conversion the story is no different. In case of PV conversion, issue is that of efficiency of the Cell. In case of other solar systems, besides efficiency seasonal variations render conversion to be useful for local usage rather

---

1 By 2030, India's dependence on energy import is expected to exceed 53 percent of the Country's total energy consumption with attended problems of current account deficit. In 2009-10 India imported 159.26 million tons of crude oil which amounted to 80 percent of the total domestic crude consumption. Further that year 31 percent of country's total import were on account of oil import.

than transmission through grid. Wind power has similar issues. India has huge potential for Waste to Energy but commercially viable technology is still not available.

This state of gap between available resources and available technologies is the biggest hurdle en-route to India's quest for energy security. There is another dimension of the problem that is; low consumption of energy per capita which is well below the world average. Following table highlights the comparative state of India:-

Table: 2.1: Per Capita Energy Consumption

Country	Per Capita Energy Consumption (kgOe/ Annum)
Bangladesh	208.8
People's Republic of China	1806.8
India	**565.6**
Trinidad & Tobago	15913.3
USA	7164.5
Average in the world	**1750**

Source: "Energy Use Per capita" World development Indicators. World Bank, 2012

It is ironical that India; which ranks in the lower half of the countries as far as the energy consumption per capita per annum is concerned, is the fourth largest over all energy consumer after USA, China and Russia (12th Five Years' Plan Document) and its overall energy consumption is, in fact, increasing; probably due to growth in manufacturing and service sector. Year to year increase in consumption of energy with the growth of the GDP is; as depicted in the Figure-2.1 below. What is of concern is that there is a wide gap between availability of the energy from indigenous resources and the demand of the energy. In fact it is the direct outcome of a lack of progress on the development of technologies to harness the indigenous energy bearing resources to produce usable form of energy in response to the needs of the environment.

India's gross domestic product and energy consumption

billion 2005 U.S. dollars

quadrillion Btu

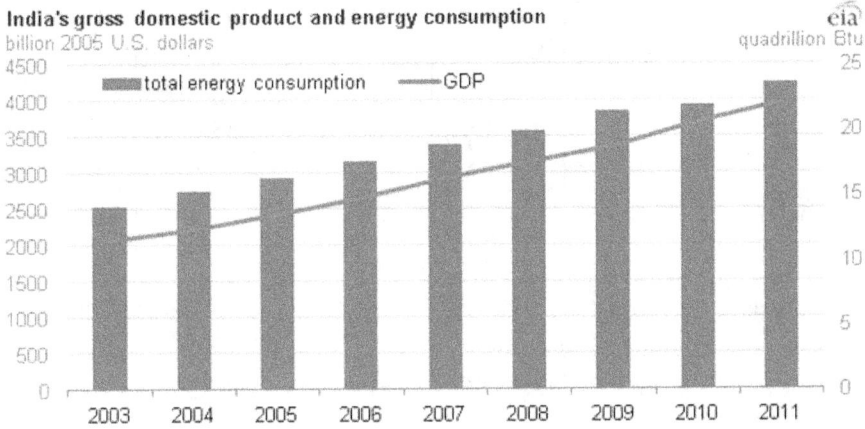

Figure-2.1: India's GDP versus Energy Consumption

Issues: Demand versus Supply. Table-2.2, below; brings out that the gap between the demand of the energy to sustain growth and the supply is ever widening. In fact even the import has not been able to reduce this yawning gap. Causes for such an imbalance need to be identified an analysis needs to be done to evolve an effective strategy to address this issue.

Table- 2.2: Trends in Supply of Primary Commercial Energy (in mtoe)

	2000-01 (Actual)	2006-07 (Actual)	2011-12 (Provisional)	2016-17 (Projected)	2021-22 (Projected)
Domestic Production					
Coal	130.61	177.24	222.16	308.55	400
Lignite	6.43	8.76	10.64	16.80	29
Crude Oil	33.40	33.99 (1.76 %)	39.23 (15.4 %)	42.75 (8.97 %)	43 (0.58 %)
Natural Gas	25.07	27.71 (10.5 %)	42.79 (54.4 %)	76.13 (77.9 %)	103 (35.29 %)
Hydro Power	6.40	9.78 (52.78 %)	11.22 (14.72 %)	12.90 (14.97 %)	17 (31.78 %)

Nuclear Power	4.41	4.91 (11.33 %)	8.43 (71.6 %)	16.97 (101.3 %)	30 (76.78 %)
Renewable energy	0.13	0.87 (569.2 %)	5.25 (503 %)	10.74 (104.5 %)	20 (86.2 %)
Total: Domestic commercial Energy	206.45	263.28	339.72	481.84	642.00
Non Commercial Energy	136.64	153.28	172.20	187.66	202.16
Total	**343.09**	**416.56**	**513.92**	**669.50**	**844.16**
Import					
Coal	11.76	24.92	54.00	90.00	150.00
Petroleum Products	77.25	98.41	129.86	152.00	194.00
LNG	0	8.45	12.56 (48.6 %)	24.8 (97.45 %)	31 (25 %)
Hydro Power	0	0.26	0.45	0.52	0.60
Total net Imports	89.01	132.04	196.87	267.76	375.60
Total Commercial energy (Growth Over Previous Five Years)	295.46	396.32 (5.01 %)	536.59 (6.25 %)	749.60 (6.91 %)	1017.60 (6.30 %)
Total Primary Energy	**432.01**	**549.60 (4.09 %)**	**710.79 (5.28 %)**	**937.26 (5.69 %)**	**1219.76 (5.41 %)**

Source: 12th Plan document, Section 14th, Volume II

Note: Figures in brackets are annual average growth rates over the previous five years' period.

Analysis of the Issues highlighted by the Table-2.2:-

- The gap between demand and supply is increasing. The gap is being bridged with import and the increasing import bill on account of this ever widening gap is adding to the current account deficit (CAD) of the country with adverse impact on the economy of the country.

- Contribution of the nuclear energy on the supply side is steadily increasing at a fairly rapid pace and with Indo US Nuclear Deal in place, NSG waiver in hand (Kranti Kumar and Deepal Jayasekera) and second stage of nuclear energy production plan likely to become a reality in near future (by 2015), situation is likely to further improve. However; despite all the anticipated growth, it needs to be noted that its contribution to total energy supply will be only 2.5 percent by 2017 and with an equally dismal figure of 3.6 percent by 2022. May be a concerted bid to accelerate indigenous Fast Breeder Reactor programme and early operationalization of Indo US Civil Nuclear Agreement and other related agreements to enhance supply of the nuclear energy is the need of the hour.

- Identical is the case with the RES based energy generation, which is also rising steadily, but its contribution to over all supply of energy is going to be just 1.6 percent by 2017 and not so encouraging figure of 2.4 percent by 2022. Exploration of energy from newer resources like garbage based energy extraction, exploitation of geothermal energy for local uses and use of biomass for energy generation needs to be taken up. However bigger issues in exploitation of RES will be following:-

  o Improving the efficiency of the equipment used for energy harnessing.

  o Use of composite systems to cater for the fluctuations in the weather with a view to ensure grid stability.

- Liquefied Natural Gas (LNG) is going to be an important element in the energy supply basket for next two decades. In this connection; new geopolitical developments like US breakthrough in Shale Gas (USA has become now a net exporter of the Natural Gas) and consequently plenty of Natural Gas in the international market becoming surplus, is assuming great importance. A proactive response of the Ministry of External Affairs (MEA) to emerging geo-political and geo-economic situation, with timely decision making by the Ministry of Petroleum & Natural gas (MoP&NG) is likely to fetch in good results. However; capacity building in terms of more number of LNG import terminals, early finalization of gas pipeline projects and creating a pool of well trained professionals; are some of the areas which need to be addressed on priority. Also a cost effective and environment friendly strategy to exploit; indigenous shale gas needs to be evolved.

- Indian coal is an important element in India's energy basket but it suffers from inefficiencies, poor quality and is a great source of pollution. It is estimated that the Carbon Dioxide (CO_2) produced in thermal power conversion in a 'Business As Usual' (BAU) scenario, has steadily risen from 32374.85 Gg to 498655.78 Gg in 2009-10 and is likely to grow to 914680 Gg by 2020-21 (Moti L Mittal et al). Because of the poor quality of Indian coal more and more emphasis is now on import of coal. As can be seen from the above table the import content of the coal had gone up from 7.9 percent of the total demand in 2000-01 to 11.8 percent in 2006-07 and is further projected to become 25.9 percent by the end of the 13th Plan (2021-22). An all out effort, therefore, needs to be made by the R&D Community of the country to develop implementable, indigenous, efficient and cost effective technologies in the sphere of Integrated Combined cycle (ICC), Underground Coal gasification and Coal Bed Methane (CBM). In this connection Coal to Liquid (CTL) one of the best clean coal technology. South Africa, who has similar type of coal as India, has already developed technology for its commercial exploitation. India my consider collaborating with South Africa to acquire this technology (Integrated Energy Policy of the Government of India: Expert Committee Report-2006). Technological agreement signed between Japan and India during the recent visit of the Prime Minister Dr Manmohan Singh's to Japan from 27-30 May 2013 about research in the field of energy (Press Release: Joint Statement on Prime Minister's visit to Japan) is a good initiative and needs to be leveraged. Japan is a de-facto leader in the research on gas hydrates. India needs to develop collaboration with Japan to achieve a break-through in the field of gas hydrates. Recently an initiative has been taken to acquire coal field blocks abroad by private players and PSUs on the lines of oil and gas equities. This initiative needs to be sustained and in fact encouraged.

- Growth in the exploitation of the hydro energy is almost stagnating. It is mainly because of two reasons, firstly; due to long gestation periods of the large hydro projects which take long time for construction and secondly; public protest on account of poor rehabilitation policy and even worse implementation strategies for the rehabilitation of the displaced persons. To improve the contribution of hydro energy a two pronged strategy may be explored; firstly; the indigenous production from this source, which has presently been plateaued, needs to be enhanced (notwithstanding the recent deluge in Uttarakhand, a solution to exploit hydro resources of the country within the rules of the environment protection set by the Ministry of Environment and Forest (MOEF) needs to be found. May be, construction of small hydro plants would be a better way ahead). Incidentally India has one of the lowest storage capacity, 207 CUM per capita (Integrated Energy Policy-2006) therefore this sector needs immediate attention. Secondly; a diplomatic initiative needs to be progressed, to enhance the supply of hydro energy through international cooperation with Nepal and Bhutan. Possibility of cooperation with China and Myanmar needs to be explored. With technological breakthrough in storage systems and transmission (existing/ desired), in fact, international cooperation with Tajikistan (a country which is extremely rich in hydro resources) and Sri Lanka can also be explored.

- Crude oil production is another area, which has been stagnating. Reasons are probably, firstly; decline in the yield of the existing oil fields which have become quite old. It may be noted that the Mumbai High oil field[2], with the exception of Mangla in Rajasthan, is the latest oil field (1974 vintage). If Mangla had

---

2 Bombay High field was discovered by a Russian and Indian oil exploration team operating from the seismic exploration vessel Academic Arkhangelsky during mapping of the Gulf of Khambhat (earlier Cambay) in 1964-67. The naming of the field is attributed to a team from a survey run in 1965 analyzed in the Rashmi building in Peddar Road, Cumballa Hill, Mumbai (erstwhile Bombay). The first offshore well was sunk in 1974. As of 2004, it supplied 14 percent of India's oil requirement and accounted for about 38 percent of all domestic production.

not been discovered in 2004, dependence on import would have gone through the roof. However; it is also relevant to note that presently less than 30 percent of the sedimentary basin has only been explored, notwithstanding the implementation of New Exploration Licensing Policy (NELP) since 1997-98 and nine rounds of it having gone through. (India has 26 sedimentary basins with an area of 3.14 million square kilometers. Considering the entire 3.14 million square kilometers of sedimentary area, on land as also shallow and deep offshore in the country, the resource base of hydrocarbons is estimated to be about 29 billion tons of oil and oil equivalent gas (O+OEG). Out of this, only 6.8 billion tons of 'in-place' hydrocarbons have so far been established through exploration (internet down load: http://www.geologydata.info/ petroleum_03.htm). Probably a review of the terms and conditions of this policy needs to be done at the earliest (present policy is such, that it is highly loaded against international players and, as such, not many big players are coming forward). Exploration, in newer areas (both, on and off shore), needs to be accelerated with a view to increase the exploration area. Government has gone for an Open Acreage Licensing Policy (OALP) with effect from 2011. As against NELP it is more flexible system wherein contract can be concluded at any time of the year. Also an effort to acquire newer oil equities, abroad needs to be taken up with vigour and with due aggression (ONGC Videsh Limited has 32 oil equities in 16 countries (PTI in The Economic Times dated 02 September 2013). Similarly life extension (LE) works and restoration & modernization (R&M) works in respect to existing oil fields need to be taken up (present rate of recovery is about 33.5 percent). Finally newer areas related to petroleum for energy extraction need to be identified. Some of the identified areas are; Pet Coke and Tar Sands[3]. R&D in areas of pet coke and tar sands need to be accelerated. A little more is discussed subsequently about the Pet

---

3 Tar sands (also referred to as oil sands) are a combination of clay, sand, water, and bitumen, a heavy black viscous oil. Tar sands can be mined and processed to extract the oil-rich bitumen, which is then refined into oil. Oil sands represent as much as 66 percent of the world's total oil reserves, with at least 1.7 trillion barrels in the Canadian Athabasca tar sands and 1.8 trillion barrels in the Venezuelan Orinoco oil sands. As of Mar 2009, there are no data available regarding availability / reserves of tar sands in India. India, with increasing energy needs, has also announced plans to invest $1 billion in the Athabasca Tar sands in 2006. Four different Indian companies are involved in this investment.

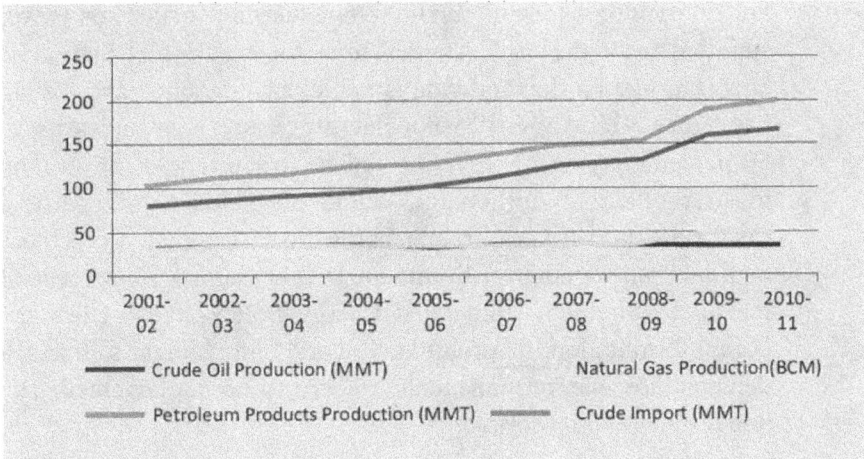

Source: Report by Indian Member Committee published in "India Energy Book 2012", pp-32, published by World Energy Council, uploaded on www.wecimc. org/

Figure-2.2: Stagnation in Indigenous Crude Production

- There is a growing import element in the energy supply in almost all forms of energy. Probably decision makers have realized the importance of availability of the energy bearing resources, at this point in time, to maintain the tempo of the economic growth rather than develop technological capacities to exploit local resources which could be highly time consuming and may not help to meet the need for energy demand at this point in time. However; at no point in time effort on R&D to develop technologies, to exploit local resources, should slow down, because such a strategy would be highly counter-productive in long run.

- Notwithstanding an all out effort to enhance supply, necessity of improving the demand side management (improved efficiency of systems, reducing the energy demands by using more energy efficient systems and following building norms which lend themselves to energy saving) with an improved enforcement mechanism, assumes great importance[4]. In this connection an innovative strategy to optimally utilize energy would be to consider introducing differential time zones. Such a strategy will

---

4 GRIHA (Green Rating for Integrated Habitat Assessment), the green rating system developed by The Energy Resources Institute (TERI), is promoted by the Ministry of New and Renewable Energy (MNRE) as the National rating system.

help in optimizing use of sun light to reduce dependence on power supplied from the grid. Another area for ensuring reduction of energy usage on demand side is vehicular efficiency and freight passage by railways. If vehicular efficiency goes upwards of 50 percent, saving by 2031-32 will be to the tune of 86 million tons. Another 36 million ton would be added to this kitty if railways can win back freight battle by 50 percent. Both these methods put together will amount to a saving of 25 percent of the oil requirement (Integrated Energy Policy-2006). Clear cut policy formulation, its promulgation and enforcement to manage demand side energy management needs to be implemented with due firmness and priority.

Status of Energy Supply in India

The energy supply in India is steadily increasing, as is evident from the Table-2.2 above. The growth is not only in the traditional sources of supply but newer areas are being explored to add to the energy basket of the country. To further add to these measures, induction of more efficient technologies is essential. A continuously evolving process needs to be strengthened in such a way, so that even well before the flatter portion of the S curve of technology, during the journey of the technology growth, is reached, a new technology is introduced. Though energy generation in India is getting affected in a number of cases due to public activism but the progress has been substantial as evident from the Table-2.2. As on 31 July 2012 following was the status of various forms of energy:-

Table-2.3: Status of Power Generation

Type	No of Plants	Total Capacity (in MW)
Nuclear	21α	4780.00#
Thermal	102	87093.38*
Gas	161	17,706.35*
Diesel	27	1,199.75*
Hydroelectric	204	30017.00*
Wind		9587.00*
Solar		1686.44@

Source:

*-	Central Electric Authority dated 31 July2012
#-	Atomic Energy Commission
@-	MNRE: Achievements as on 31 March 2013
α -	Including Kudankulam-1, which has become critical wef 13 July 2013

but so far power produced from this has not been integrated with the grid.

ENERGY MAP OF INDIA

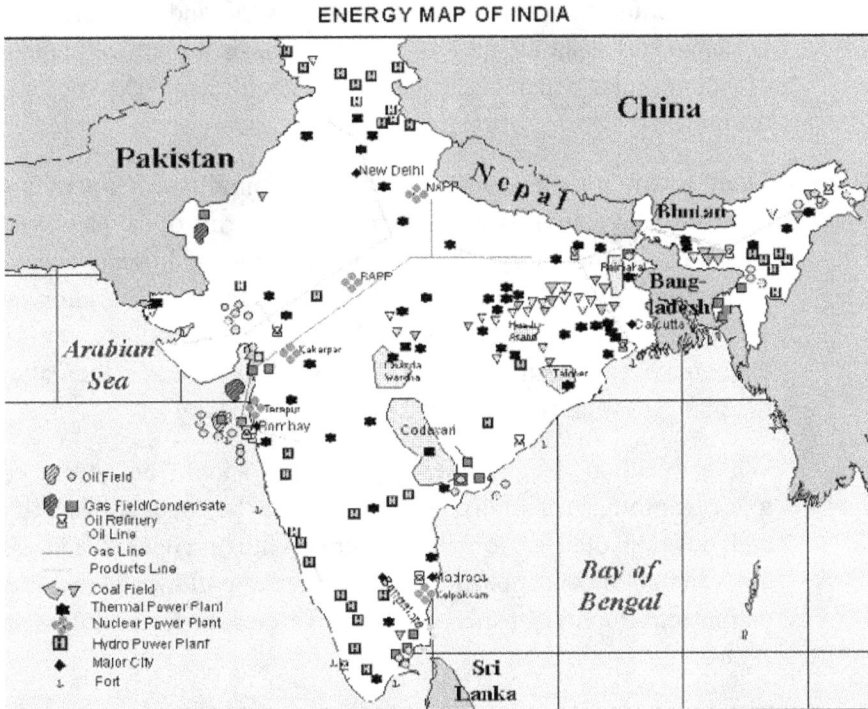

Figure-2.3: Energy Map of India

Strategic Shift

Comprehensive National Power (CNP) is a function of the economic strength of a nation. A sustained GDP growth rate of 8-9 percent of is essential to make a positive perceptible change to the CNP. India is transforming and the economy of India is gradually getting geared up to cater for fast burgeoning manufacturing and Service sector. To build up the more sustained availability of those forms of energy which are less damaging to the environment and are available at affordable cost, will be the need of the hour. Some of the relevant issues to enhance the energy supply are as follows:-

- One of the most important inputs into this transformation would be the need to create additional capacity for energy generation. In recent times there has been a policy shift. Earlier emphasis was on indigenous capacity building, however inhibitions to refrain from resorting to import appear to have now gone, which is quite evident from table 2.2. Such a development clearly indicates about a policy shift in overall context of the energy management. While it could be a very useful strategy in short and medium term, but in no way it should take away the emphasis from development of technologies which can effectively and efficiently exploit local resources.

- There is also a requirement to ensure that simultaneous planning is done to develop; related infrastructure in terms of capital assets and trained human resources to handle the additional energy generation. Also an infrastructure to do scenario building to envision future requirements needs to be created so that an all encompassing planning can be done well in time and thereafter the plan is executed to achieve necessary capacity.

- While existing sources of energy supply should be continued to be exploited optimally, efforts need to be made to identify and develop cleaner forms of energy with a view to address environmental concerns and problems due to pollution at the time of the introduction of the cost effective cleaner technologies in future.

- There should always be an endeavour to develop only cost effective measures to exploit indigenous resources to make those measures sustainable.

- There should be a comprehensive national endeavour to utilize indigenous resources and create mechanisms to make up the deficiency through import through international cooperation, acquisition, research, improve efficiency of existing systems/equipment and a mechanism for continuous monitoring.

New Emerging Sources to Augment Energy Supply in India

Petroleum coke (abbreviated as Pet coke or pet coke) is a carbonaceous solid derived from oil refinery Coker units or other cracking processes (International Union of Pure and Applied Chemistry Gold Book). Unlike other types of coke; which have traditionally been derived from coal, this coke can either be of fuel grade (high in Sulphur and metals) or of anode grade (low in Sulphur and metals). The raw coke directly out of the Coker is often referred to; as green coke. In this context, "green" means unprocessed. The further processing of green coke by subjecting it to calcination in a rotary kiln removes residual volatile hydrocarbons from the coke. The calcinated pet coke can be further processed in an anode baking oven in order to produce anode coke of the desired shape and physical properties. The anodes are mainly used in the aluminum and steel industry. Some of the relevant issues which need to be taken note of, before it is included in the future energy plan of India are as follows:-

- **Relevance for India**- India is gradually emerging as a mega hub of refining and pet coke is a major by product of the reefing process. Pet coke is essentially a by-product, derived from the refining of crude. Currently, in India, the cement industry is the largest end user segment of pet coke. The cement industry is able to use high volumes of pet coke as the presence of high sulphur content in pet coke is neutralized by the use of limestone in the clinkerization process. Pet coke is also used in boilers, though; on a limited scale. Typically coal meets approximately 80 percent of the total energy requirement of the cement industry; other fuels fill the remaining 20 percent requirement. The majority of pet coke demand in the cement industry is from the Northern region of the country, which is estimated to be about 75 percent. The demand for pet coke from the cement industry is estimated to grow at a rate of 24 percent. Following Figure -2.4 provides the demand and supply outlook for pet coke till 2011-12. It can be discerned from the above discussion read in conjunction with the trend displayed by Figure-2.3 that the indigenously produced pet coke in India is just about enough to be absorbed in the domestic market alone.

Demand supply balance of Pet coke

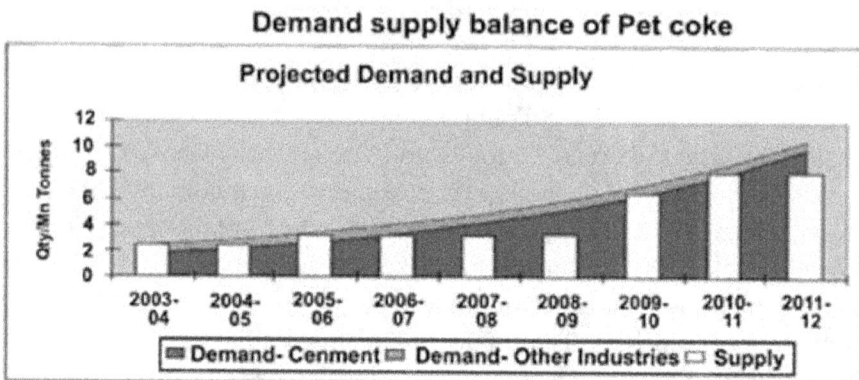

Fig: 3 Ref: CALS Refineries internal data

Figure-2.4: Demand and Supply- Pet Coke

Source: Market Analysis of Indian Refining Sector, posted on http://www. chemtech-online.com/events/chemtech/2010/01/market-analysis-of-indian-refining-sector.php dated 21 January 2010

- **Environmental Impact of Pet Coke-** Pet coke is over 90 percent carbon and emits five to 10 percent more carbon dioxide (CO_2) than coal when burnt on a per-unit-of-energy basis. As pet coke has a higher energy content, pet coke emits between 30 and 80 percent more CO_2 than coal per unit of weight (Donald Lawson Turcotte and Gerald Schubert). The differences between coal and coke in CO_2 production per unit energy produced are small and depend upon the moisture in the coal (increases the CO_2 per unit energy -- Heat of combustion) and volatile hydrocarbon in coal and coke (decrease the CO_2 per unit energy). Fluidized bed combustion is commonly used to burn petroleum coke. Gasification is another of the process, which is increasingly being used with this feedstock (often using gasifiers placed in the refineries themselves). Therefore it needs to be remembered that, though the Pet coke looks and acts like coal, but it is dirtier and. has even higher carbon emissions than already carbon-intensive coal. Pet coke, on a per-unit of energy basis, emits five to 10 percent more CO_2 than coal. As a comparison; a ton of pet coke yields on an average 53.6 percent more CO_2 than a ton of coal. However its capacity to produce energy is substantial. In a study it has been concluded that only the proven tar sands reserves of Canada will yield roughly 5 billion tons of pet coke – enough to fully fuel, 111

U.S. coal plants by 2050. One of the reasons, why its propensity to adversely impact the environment has not been fully appreciated, because it is considered a refinery by product and the emissions on its (pet coke) burning are not included in most assessments of the climate impact of tar sands or conventional oil production and consumption. Thus the climate impact of oil production is being consistently under counted (Lorne Stockman). Therefore it is essential that before jumping to a policy of using pet coke as part of a future energy matrix, its environmental impact is taken seriously.

Gas Hydrates. Clathrate hydrates (or gas clathrates, gas hydrates, clathrates, hydrates, etc.) are crystalline water-based solids physically resembling ice, in which small non-polar molecules (typically gases) or polar molecules with large hydrophobic moieties are trapped inside "cages" of hydrogen bonded water molecules. In other words, gas hydrates are compounds in which the host molecule is water and the guest molecule is typically a gas or liquid. Without the support of the trapped molecules, the lattice structure of hydrate clathrates would collapse into conventional ice crystal structure or liquid water. Most low molecular weight gases, including oxygen, hydrogen, nitrogen carbon dioxide, methane hydrogen sulphide, Argon, Krypton and Xenon as well as some higher hydrocarbons and Freon, will form hydrates at suitable temperatures and pressures. Clathrate hydrates were first documented in 1810 by Sir Humphrey Davy (Ilem Thomas). Naturally on earth; gas hydrates can be found on the seabed, in ocean sediments (Kvenvolden, K. A.; McMenamin, M. A. (1980)), in deep lake sediments (e.g. Lake Baikal), as well as in the permafrost regions. The amount of methane potentially trapped in natural methane hydrate deposits may be significant (1015 to 1017 cubic meters(CUM)) (Michael Marshal), which makes them of major interest as a potential energy resource. Some of the relevant issues are as follows:-

- **Indian Endeavour and International Cooperation-** The Directorate General of Hydrocarbons in India (DGH) has done pioneering work for initiating gas hydrate exploration in the country. Reconnaissance surveys carried out by DGH in the East Coast and Andaman Deepwater areas in 1997 discovered the most promising areas for Gas Hydrates. The surveys have indicated the presence of several Gas Hydrate leads/ prospects. The total prognosticated gas resource from the gas hydrates in the country is placed at 1894 TCM. Gas hydrates have still not become commercially viable energy source and most of the work on it is being done, world over, is presently in the research stage. There is still no proven technology, world over, to exploit methane from Gas hydrates on a commercial scale. There is a divergence between the Indian needs and the present experience of researchers' world over. Since much of the gas hydrate reserves worldwide are found trapped in sandstone, thrust of the research being done all over the world, is towards the extraction of gas from hydrates and also it focuses on disseminated deposits in sands. This research is unlikely to help India in addressing the gas hydrates likely to be available in the KG basin's offshore area. Therefore there is a need to develop 'India specific' technology to exploit off shore gas hydrates in Indian context which are massive in nature and found in fractured shale. DGH has been able to delineate and sample some of the best finds (DGH Site). These are as follows:-

o   Krishna Godavari Basin-one of the richest marine gas hydrate accumulations as yet discovered anywhere in the world.

o   Andaman Islands- one of the thickest and the deepest gas hydrate occurrence (volcanic ash bearing gas hydrates as deep as 600 meters below the sea floor).

o   Mahanadi Basin of the Bay of Bengal- has been confirmed as the fully developed gas hydrate system.

• **Recommended Strategy**

o   Indian Scientists to work in association with that of the USA & Japan, the two other countries besides India who have contributed largely in this field. Undertaking joint R&D studies for knowledge sharing and information exchange will pay rich dividends. This can also include holding of joint seminars and conferences in the area of Gas Hydrate R&D.

o   An attempt should be made to evolve a plan for the Indian agencies to work in close coordination and work association with leading scientists globally, with a view to remain updated with the recent developments and device methodologies in a real time frame so that as and when it is required the same (the ongoing research work) can be incorporated to suit national requirements.

o   Take up joint exploration & exploitation programme in offshore areas with US and Japan on cost sharing basis. Form a tripartite consortium of Hydrate R&D taking USA and Japan as a consortium partners. This would enable worldwide hydrate experts to work jointly on projects and gain expertise & experience which would be useful to all the three countries.

o   Establishing a national Gas hydrate R&D Center / Directorate in India, to look into the exploration & exploitation aspects of Gas Hydrates. This would help extract the best from the intellectual resources present in our country.

Shale Gas in India. Shale is a common sedimentary rock and extensively found across different sedimentary basins in the country. Gas is trapped in little bubbles in the near-impermeable thick shale formations, running over miles. Though the world always knew about its potential to produce fuel, but the shale gas became popular only in the last decade. This was after the introduction of new technologies, such as; hydraulic fracturing and horizontal drilling by American companies, and the rise in natural gas prices which made such extraction viable. The new technology uses a lot of water mixed with sand and large number of chemical additives at high pressure, to fracture the hard rock and free the gas bubbles. Following issues merit consideration in the context of India:-

•   **Status in India**- Current research has identified a potential of 63 tcf of shale gas stretched across six main basins that could be successfully exploited once the Indian government reveals its national shale oil and gas policy (policy has since been promulgated vide Ministry of Petroleum & Natural Gas, Government of India vide F.No- 32011/41/2009-ONGC-I dated 14 October 2013). The six identified Indian basins are; Cambay (Gujarat), Assam-Arakan (North-East), Gondwana (Central India), Krishna Godavari onshore (East coast), Cauvery onshore, and Indo-Gangetic basins (Elliot Brennan & Silvia Pastorelli). In 2010 the government signed a MoU with the U.S. in order to cooperate in developing Indian shale gas resources. Exploration and assessment of the potential of shale gas are part of the objectives of the MoU and, under the agreement, in 2012 the U.S. Geological Survey (USGS) assessed the resources in a number of basins (the Cambay, Cauvery, and Krishna-Godavari basins), estimating the total of recoverable resources to be 6.1 tcf. This figure contrasts with the estimates suggested by the U.S. Energy Information Administration (EIA) in 2011 of 63 tcf (IBID).

Map 2. Shale Gas Basins and Natural Gas Pipelines of India/Pakistan

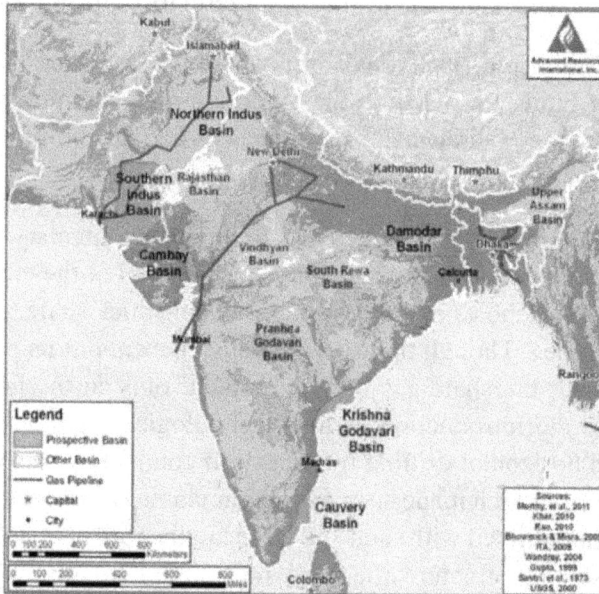

Source: Jane Nakano et al, "Prospects for Shale Gas Development in Asia-Examining Potentials and Challenges in China and India"- A Report of the CSIS Energy and National Security Program dated August 2012

Figure-2.5: Areas Potentially Rich in Shale Gas

- **Environmental concerns**- These continue to shroud shale gas production worldwide. Such concerns contributed to the postponement of the first shale asset auction in India to 2013, with a view to allow for further environmental analysis before a decision about the auction could be taken. Indeed, India cannot escape the global debate on the possible risks posed to water aquifers, ecosystems, and public health, as well as the issue of flow back water disposal, by the shale gas exploration. Water, in particular, will represent a major challenge for Indian shale gas development programme. The large amount of water required in the process of hydraulic fracturing[5] is a considerable obstacle in a water stressed country such as India, which continues to suffer from chronic shortages. The bad news is that the basins in India which are rich in Shale gas are likely to become water scarce by 2030 (RK Batra).

• **Other Problems**- there are some other issues which are typical of India. These are as follows:-

o Land acquisition- most of areas which have been identified as prospective areas having shale gas, are having very high density of population and also the land use in those areas is basically for agriculture and that makes the land acquisition extremely difficult and recovery extremely technically complex.

o Relocation/ rehabilitation of displaced people will be highly problematic. Violent protests over land acquisition are common in India. Case in point is West Bengal, where the Oil and Natural Gas Corporation completed its first shale gas test well in March 2007 and post that West Bengal exploded (Jane Nakano et al).

o Location of shale gas bearing rocks being close to CBM bearing rocks which have already been allocated and as such problem of ownership exists which needs to be resolved.

o Policy of control is still not clear; whether it will be Central Government or some other specially designated agency.

Biomass. Biomass is biological material derived from living, or recently living organisms. It most often refers to plants or plant-derived materials which are specifically called lignocelluloses biomass. As a renewable energy source, biomass can either be used directly via combustion to produce heat, or indirectly after converting it to various forms of bio fuel. Conversion of biomass to bio fuel can be achieved by different methods which are broadly classified into: thermal, chemical, and biochemical methods. Among the biomass energy sources, wood fuels

---

5   In USA from a minimum of 2.5 million gallons to a maximum of 13 million gallons of water is needed per well/ fracking (RK Batra)

are the most prominent. With rapid increase in fossil fuel use, the share of biomass in total energy declined steadily through substitution by coal in the nineteenth century and later by oil and gas during the twentieth century. Despite its declining share in energy, global consumption of wood based energy has continued to grow. During 1974 to 1994, global wood consumption for energy grew annually by over 2 percent/ annum. Presently, the biomass sources contribute 14 percent of global energy and 38 percent of energy in developing countries (Woods and Hall, 1994). Globally, the energy content of biomass residues in agriculture based industries annually is estimated at 56 Exa Joules, nearly a quarter of global primary energy use of 230 Exa Joules (WEC, 1994). Specific Issues pertaining to India are as follows:-

- Biomass contributes over a third of primary energy in India. Biomass fuels are predominantly used in rural households for cooking and water heating. In addition it is also used for heating by traditional and artisan industries particularly by brick kilns. Quantitatively biomass delivers most energy for the domestic use (rural - 90 percent and urban - 40 percent) in India (NCAER, 1992). Further analysis reveals that within the overall context of biomass, wood fuels contribute 56 percent of total biomass energy (Sinha et. al, 1994). It has also been noticed that the consumption of wood has grown annually at two percent rate over past two decades (FAO, 1981; FAO, 1986; FAO, 1996).

- **Potential and Status**- The current availability of biomass in India is estimated at about 500 million metric tons per year.   Studies sponsored by the Ministry have estimated surplus biomass availability of about 120 – 150 million metric tons per annum covering agricultural and forestry residues exists. This quantum of biomass corresponds to a potential of about 18,000 MW (EAI). This is apart from about 5000 MW of additional power which could be generated through bagasse based cogeneration in the country's 550 Sugar mills, if these sugar mills were to adopt technically and economically optimal levels of cogeneration for extracting power from the bagasse produced by them (Internet down load from MNRE site). Presently biomass contributes 1200 MW as cogeneration and a meager 180 MW from other sources of biomass. The potential and the sources with capacity to produce biomass are as tabulated below:-

Table-2.4: Source with Potential (in MW) of Biomass

Biomass Type	Realistic		Optimistic		Pessimistic	
	2014-20	Beyond 2020	2014-20	Beyond 2020	2014-20	Beyond 2020
Agro Potential	20687	21743	30506	38934	16937	16107
Live stock	9767	10470	19126	20639	7356	7938
Fruits	963	1165	1084	1392	570	627
Vegetables	1481	1633	208	2578	960	1008
Industrial Waste	2289	2857	2918	3998	1722	1926
Subtotal	**35187**	**37868**	**53842**	**67541**	**27545**	**27606**
Urban Waste						
Municipal Solid Waste (MSW)	6773	9781	7818	12098	4181	5057
Municipal Liquid Waste (MLW)	492	574	622	794	404	436
Sub Total	**7265**	**10355**	**8440**	**12892**	**4585**	**5493**
Grand Total	**42452**	**48223**	**62282**	**80433**	**32130**	**33099**

Source: EAI, "Potential for Biomass Power in India", uploaded on http://www.eai.in/ref/ae/bio/pot/biomass_power_potential.html

Note:

- It can be seen that even in the most pessimistic case, there is a substantial scope for biomass based energy generation during the period beyond 2020.

- Areas particularly of great potential in India are; agro based biomass, live stock and MSW.

- **New Initiatives**- Ministry of New and Renewable Energy has realized the potential and role of biomass energy in the Indian context and hence has initiated a number of programmes for promotion of efficient technologies for its use in various sectors of the economy to derive maximum benefits. Biomass power generation in India is an industry that attracts investments of over Rs.600 crores (MNRE Site) every year, generating more than 5000 million units of electricity and yearly employment of more than 10 million man-days in the rural areas. For efficient utilization of biomass, bagasse based cogeneration in sugar mills and biomass power generation have been taken up under biomass power and cogeneration programme. In recent times another initiative is gathering momentum and that is use of algae for power generation. Although; algae cost more per unit mass (as of 2010, food grade algae costs ~$5000/ ton), due to high capital and operating costs (F. David Doty), yet, it is claimed to yield between 10 and 100 times more fuel per unit area than other second-generation bio-fuel crops (H. C. Greenwell et al). It is felt that once use of algae becomes commercially viable, it will revolutionize the concept of power generation. Thus it can be concluded that the biomass is definitely an extremely promising source of energy for future energy basket of India.

Solar Energy. Intensity of solar radiation on India is estimated to be 200 MW/ km^2. In more practical terms it works out to be 6kWh/ metre^2/day. However keeping of all disallowances into account theoretical potential in India is 8000 million MW which is equivalent to 5909 mtoe. In normal course large areas would be needed to harness this potential. An innovative approach to tackle this issue will be to enforce GRIHA norms and also an amendment to the building codes be thought so that certain equipment based on the concept of solar energy exploitation are incorporated into the buildings. When the innovative approach is discussed one example that comes to mind is what has been done in recent times in Gujarat, where Solar PV panels have been placed on top of a canal. Such an approach has resulted into space optimization and also has given an idea that building designs be modified in such a way that solar based systems are fully integrated into the building design. Another area where

SPV systems can be of great help in reducing dependence on petroleum products is rural electrification and the electrification of slum areas in urban areas. A small study of the existing statistics will reveal its potential. India has 67.6 million rural and 3.7 million urban house hold which use kerosene oil for lighting. A large number of them can get at least one bulb to provide light and save a large quantity of kerosene oil. Thus, in future energy matrix of India, solar energy will play a very important role.

Geo-thermal Energy. The adjective geothermal originates from the Greek roots γη (ge), meaning earth, and θερμος (thermos), meaning hot. It is the thermal energy generated and stored in the crust of the Earth. The geothermal energy of the Earth's crust originated from the original formation of the planet (20 percent) and from radioactive decay of minerals (80 percent) (Clean Energy uploaded on Internet). The geothermal gradient, which is the difference in temperature between the core of the planet and its surface, drives a continuous conduction of thermal energy in the form of heat from the core to the surface. Geothermal power is cost effective, reliable, sustainable, and environmentally friendly (Glassley William E.), but has historically been limited to areas near tectonic plate boundaries. Recent technological advances have dramatically expanded the range and size of viable resources, especially for applications such as home heating, opening a potential for widespread exploitation. Geothermal wells release greenhouse gases trapped deep within the earth, but these emissions are much lower per energy unit than those of fossil fuels. As a result, geothermal power has the potential to mitigate global warming if widely deployed in place of fossil fuels. The Earth's geothermal resources are theoretically more than adequate to supply humanity's energy needs, but only a very small fraction can be exploited profitably. Drilling, exploration and transmission of energy from deep sources is very expensive. Forecasts for the future potential of the geothermal energy depend on certain assumptions which are; availability of technology in certain time frame, energy prices, subsidies, and interest rates. Till 2010, geothermal power plants were being operated in at least 24 countries and it was being used directly for heat in at least 78 countries. Currently; the geothermal power plants in these countries have a total capacity of 10.7 GW of which about 88 percent is being generated in just seven countries and these countries are; the USA, Philippines, Indonesia, Mexico, Italy, New Zealand, and Iceland (EAI, Internet download). Certain aspects with respect to geo thermal energy, in the context of India, which merit special mention are as follows:-

- **Environmental Effects** - Fluids drawn from the deep earth carry a mixture of gases, notably carbon dioxide , hydrogen sulfide, methane and ammonia. These pollutants contribute to global warming, acid rain, and noxious gases; if released in the environment. Existing geothermal electric plants emit on an average of 122 kilograms (270 lb) of CO_2 per megawatt-hour (MWh) of electricity, which is a small fraction of the emission intensity of the conventional fossil fuel plants (Bertani, Ruggero; Thain, Ian)

- **Potential of Geo-thermal Energy in India** - India has reasonably good potential for geo-thermal energy exploitation. The identified areas; which have potential for the geothermal energy extraction can produce theoretically 10,600 MW of power (but experts are confident that only a maximum of about 100 MW can be produced). However an enquiry reveals that so far no geo-thermal power projects have yet been established, owing to a variety of reasons (EAI, Internet download). It is appreciated that till such time the exploitation of geothermal energy becomes commercially viable and inescapable due to energy needs of the country, it will continue to remain confined to off grid local use only. The resources of India are as shown in the Figure 2.6:-

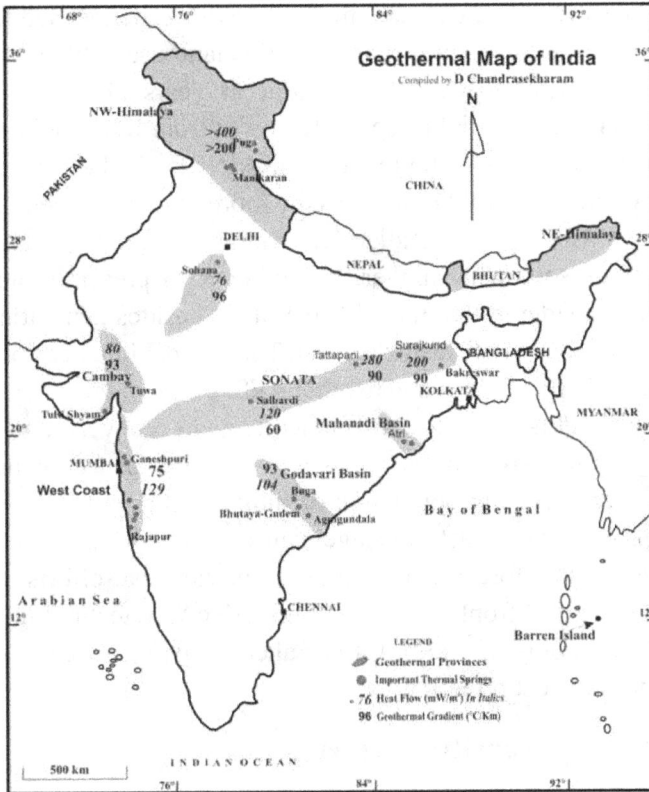

Figure-2.6: Geothermal Energy Resources of India

Garbage based Energy- Waste-to-energy (WtE) or energy-from-waste (EfW) is the process of generating energy in the form of electricity and/or heat from the incineration of waste. WtE is a form of energy recovery from waste. Most WtE processes produce electricity and/or heat directly through combustion, or produce a combustible fuel commodity, such as methane, methanol, ethanol or synthetic fuels (Perinaz Bhada-Tata). The Ministry of New and Renewable Energy (MNRE) in its annual report of 2009-10 had estimated that approximately 55 million tons of MSW is getting generated in urban areas of India annually. It is estimated that the amount of waste generated in India will increase at a rate of approximately 1-1.33 percent annually (Ibid). The Ministry of Environment and Forests (MoEF) promulgated the MSW Management and Handling Rules in 2000 requiring municipalities across India to adopt sustainable and environmentally sound ways of processing MSW, including incineration. WtE is perceived as a means to dispose MSW, produce energy, recover materials, and free up scarce land that, otherwise is being used for landfill presently. It needs to be appreciated that this land use is likely to increase exponentially, with growing population, in years ahead. The MNRE estimates that the potential to generate power from MSW will more than double in next ten years. The report from MNRE further adds that from industrial waste it is likely to increase by more than 50 percent during the same period. Although, the Indian Government's figures suggest that the cost of WtE is somewhat higher than other RES presently, however, it needs to be considered that the WtE facilities, besides generating energy, also serve the purpose of waste disposal. Therefore, higher cost per MW of capacity from WtE as compared to other RES, gets more than compensated through the benefits of waste management, metals recovery, and reduction of Green House Gas (GHG) emissions. Another aspect which merits attention is the growing population of India; which will further magnify the twin problems of waste management and the shortage of energy in coming years; therefore it is extremely important that efforts need to be accelerated on R&D front to find a cost effective WtE technology. It is also felt that the economy of scales in years ahead may, in any case, render the WtE technology cost effective.

India's Energy Security: Challenges

Energy security of a nation is a function of a large number of tangible and intangible parameters. All these parameters are required to be monitored/ matched/ progressed and reviewed for mid course corrections simultaneously. Some of the more important challenges are as discussed in succeeding paragraphs (Internet upload: Emerging opportunities and challenges India Energy Congress – 2012, 23 January 2012 uploaded on http://www.pwc.com.au/asia-practice/india/assets/publications/Opportunities-Challenges-India-2012.pdf).

Low Per-Capita Consumption. The average per capita consumption of electricity in India is a mere 565.5 kWh (2010), compared to the world average of 1750 kWh (CEA load balance report on CIA Fact Book). The other comparable countries, like other BRIC nations, have significantly higher per capita consumption as compared to India. The average rate of per-capita consumption has been growing steadily at 1.3 percent of CAGR (IBID) over the last 10 years. It, indeed, is too less and thus has two effects, namely; quality of life of the population leaves much to be desired and thus tends to become a source of growing discontent among the people and secondly; a lower base of energy consumption results into a lower figure for the energy forecast demand, which, with overall high energy consumption figure, may result into a mismatch between demand and supply forecasts with attended implications. Therefore; it needs to be enhanced for which additional energy will be required to be added to the kitty. Government of India had targeted a per capita consumption of 1,000 kWh by 2011-12 (IBID), which has not happened. Such a state makes energy consumption growth skewed; because while India has grown up to be fourth in overall energy consumption, the consumption per capita has continued to be low, with obvious implications on national security. There is definitely a need to improve this state. Thus the issue for the planners is to find ways and means to improve this state. As can be appreciated that the plan to execute will be fairly complex and It would indeed be a challenge for the executing agencies to execute that kind of a plan. A linked issue with this is the need to cater for an increase in the demand in absolute terms, due to population growth and the bigger issue will be to identify means that would be needed to tackle it.

Table-2.5: Projection of Population

Year	Population
2011	1,189,172,906
2020	1,326,093,247
2030	1,460,743,172

Source: United States' Census Bureau: International Programme, "Midyear Population Density- Custom Region- India, updated up to 2013 and uploaded on http://www.census.gov/population/international/

Note: This increase in population will further enhance the demand. A sizeable population increase is likely to be in areas not well covered by the grid and therefore besides increasing the penetration of the grid, a strategy based on off grid energy supply will pose challenge in terms of selection of correct source of energy and the related cost effective technology, development of desired infrastructure and other coordinating/ monitoring issues.

Industrial Capacity. There is a gap between the manufacturing capacity of the industry, particularly that of Private Sector and the envisaged power requirement. The capacity addition envisaged under 12th

Five Year Plan is 75 GW (excluding renewable energy) and almost double under the next five year plan (13th Five Year Plan). In addition, it is also expected that close to INR 33, 839 crores would be invested on Restoration and Modernization (R&M) and Life Extension (LE) works with respect to aging oil fields, where production is steadily going down, during the 12th Five Year Plan. The demand for Boiler, Turbine and Generator (BTG) equipment is expected to rise with a view to enhance overall capacity of these categories of equipment to touch 35 GW by 2013-14. The domestic equipment major Bharat Heavy Electricals Limited (BHEL) is already loaded with bulk orders for next two to three years and is unlikely to have capacity to absorb any more orders and hence there is a need to enhance/ encourage private sector investment in Original Equipment Manufacturers' (OEM) space.

The Core Capacities of Players in India's Energy Sector. It needs to be improved substantially, particularly of energy companies. For this one of the important steps would be reviewing policy measures and thereafter adopting a policy of strict implementation of the policy in letter and spirit. The policy landscape in India has progressively evolved since Independence and has led to radical changes in the power sector, commencing with the passing of the Electricity Act 2003. The environment and the approach; especially in terms of competition, private sector involvement and focus on green energy over the last decade has transformed the landscape substantially. Till early 1990s', the power sector was shielded from any private sector involvement; however, the mounting pressure on Government resources to support capacity additions, repeated delays encountered by the state utilities and the growing demand supply gap, has led the Government of India to open the power sector to private participation along with the country's globalization policy. However, most of the participation by the private investors has happened in the generation sector, driven by; de-licensing of generation, fiscal incentives for large scale capacity additions and the system of competitive procurement of the power. However, addressing the generation related problems is only first step in the direction of tackling the challenge. Transmission, distribution and enforcement of policies are equally big challenges. Despite all these, the Indian power sector has achieved a lot, over the last decade in the areas of policy reforms, private sector participation in generation and transmission, new manufacturing technologies and capabilities. The momentum needs to be continued as there is still a lot to be achieved and a number of challenges are to be overcome before the opportunities can be leveraged.

Acquisition of Land and Obtaining Clearances. Land is a basic necessity when it comes to taking up establishment of power generation projects. Past experiences bring out that there are a number of hurdles for land acquisition and securing clearances besides issues which may affect connectivity or supply chain. A lot of projects remain either still born or get delayed or finally get cancelled due to non-availability of land or difficulties in land acquisition. Next major hurdle, post identification and acquisition of land, is securing the required clearances. There are a number of clearances required from the Ministry of Environment and Forests (MoEF), Ministry of Civil Aviation, Department of Forests and other government bodies. The enormity of problem can easily be appreciated by noting the fact that for 12th Plan, still about 1300 acres more are required to be acquired and for 13th Plan for which planning has already commenced, a total of 64000 acres of land will be required to be acquired for various energy related projects. Certain other reasons are as follows:-

- Social reasons like opposition from local population due to concerns over loss of land, water and pollution which they feel would result into, if the project is executed.
- Resettlement and rehabilitation of displaced persons.
- Regulatory delays.
- Compensatory Afforestation.
- Infrastructural and related logistics Issues specific to affected state.
- Financial constraints resulting from rising costs of the land, planning project, building design/ construction, incorporating safety norms and finally project management including supervision and monitoring.

Project Execution. The major players in India's Power Sector have shown strong operational capabilities but have fared poorly in project management and execution. A capacity addition of 41,110 MW was planned in the 10th five year plan period, against which only 21,180 MW could be achieved, i.e., an achievement of merely 51.5 percent against the set target. Though; there may be many reasons; operational, environmental, public opposition, effect of international pulls and pressures, bureaucratic red tapism and many more reasons, but the bottom line is that the capability to do project planning and execute projects is nothing to be proud of. In fact ever slipping dead lines of major projects is a clear indication of the prevailing state of affairs.

Rising Import Bills: Impact on Economy. As mentioned earlier, the increasing import of energy bearing resources (crude oil, Natural Gas, Coal and natural uranium) contributes in increasing the import bill and with that the gap between expenditure on procurement of resources far out strips the income earned through exports. This inevitable negative income expenditure gap results into a very high current account fiscal deficit (CAD). Though presently India has a large foreign exchange reserve of the order of $ 290.66 billion (Reuters India 14 June 2013), but rising import bill is a cause of worry. If the currency fails to appreciate despite colossal efforts by the Reserve Bank of India in recent times, this reserve will not take long to reduce to alarming levels (Lydia Powell). The list of negative impacts and their cascading secondary impacts is long and troubling. In fact widening CAD will result into a cascading spiral where INR will continue to go down and the import bill will keep spiraling up with all its negative impacts. To begin with it will increase 'under-recoveries' and subsidies. The share of crude in India's total imports (in terms of value) has fluctuated in the last four decades reflecting changes in the global and local economy. In 1970, it was less than 10 percent but increased to more than 40 percent during the oil crises of the late 1970s. It has remained above 25 percent over the last ten years (ibid) (refer figure 2.6). Though this partly reflects increase in consumption of oil due to transformation of economy from a consumption base to manufacturing and service base. As a recent paper from the IMF (IMF Country Report No 13/37) warns, scarcity induced high oil prices could constrain economic growth and current account imbalances. India's oil import bill is estimated to increase by INR 100 billion for every rupee depreciated against the US dollar. This means that the depreciation of INR 10 against the dollar over the recent past will translate into an increase of INR 1 trillion in India's oil import bill if the depreciation of the currency is sustained and all other factors remain constant. It needs to be appreciated that, in real term, it would be about a tenth of the tax and non tax revenue raised by the central government in 2010-11. Further for every rupee depreciation 'under-recoveries' on oil products are expected to increase by close to INR 80 billion and the subsidy bill by about INR 50 billion. This will widen the fiscal deficit. This will cause inflation which will have, besides economic, political and social ramifications.

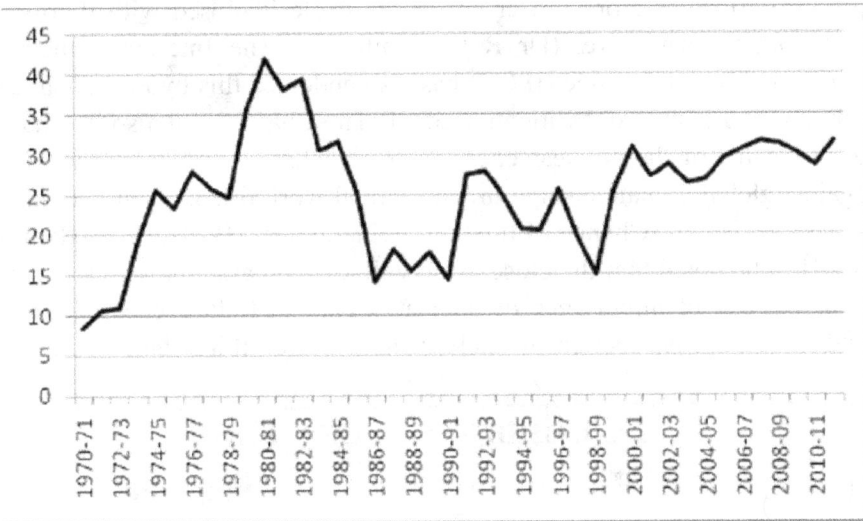

Source: Reserve Bank of India

Figure-2.7: Oil Import as a percentage of Total Import

Climate Change. Given our energy mix, and fast growing demand, there is a need to pay equal attention to the challenges of climate change. Climate change is going to affect supply side of energy (hydro energy will reduce because of high floods during monsoons and lesser water levels during lean periods) and will also affect demand side because of the need for enhanced efficiencies, a need for power conservation and above all increased power requirement to cater for enhanced demand due to climate change. A small example which can sum up the impact of the global warming is that buildings account for about 30 percent of the electricity needs which is exponentially growing as more and more number of malls and energy intensive buildings are coming up and rise in ambient temperature will call for more power which would pose a challenge to the demand side management. By an estimate according to McKinsey & Company, India can save $42 billion every year just by reducing energy waste in buildings (Peter Lehner). World scientific community has acknowledged that technology for exploiting nuclear energy is a mitigating factor in the context of climate change threat. In that the close cycle which reprocesses waste is even better and more sustainable. India consciously went for close cycle for exploitation of nuclear energy to make it sustainable, by closing the nuclear fuel cycle with Plutonium, the same amount of Uranium can produce 50 times more power and if the cycle is closed with thorium, it becomes even more. (Dr R Chidambaram) The Intergovernmental Panel on Climate Change (IPCC) has also endorsed this hypothesis in an official report entitled, 'Mitigation of Climate Change' and also it alludes to the status of the Nuclear energy's range that contribute to the fight against global climate change in a a seminal work titled, "Commercially Available Climate Change Mitigating Technologies" (B Metz et al). It also needs to be noted that the close cycle will keep on assuming greater role with the rise of importance of nuclear energy in India's energy matrix and increasing production of nuclear energy when third stage of India's

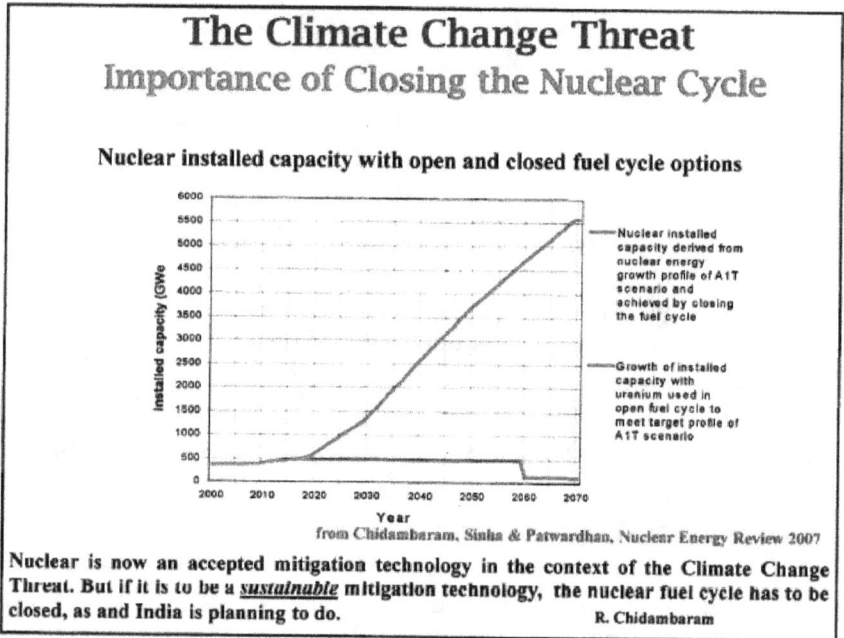

Figure-2.8: Importance of Closed Nuclear Cycle

Tariff and Subsidy. Pricing mechanisms in the energy sector must ensure commercial viability. The welfare oriented well intentioned policies in democratic polity of India, aim to provide energy access to the entire population at tariffs which are as per the paying capacity of the population in general rather than governed by the market forces. The overall impact of these unrealistic tariff calls for giving subsidies to poor and not so poor consumers as well as, energy producers who become unintended beneficiaries. However such subsidies do not help the energy sector to grow because; it is the profit earned by the producers, which helps the industry to grow and in a subsidy driven market, it is the oil PSUs which suffer the losses or the government who bears the cost of subsidy. Though, in recent times there had been some reforms in the energy sector, however, in combination with the recently introduced industrial policy, that aims to protect the indigenous manufacturing industry through import substitution, India now finds itself trapped halfway along the transition towards an open and well-performing energy sector. India's energy sector is increasingly becoming inadequate to deliver a secure supply of energy amid growing demand and fuel imports. In conjunction with a rising subsidy level and systemic failure to ensure proper revenue collection along the value chain, the financial capacity of energy sector players is getting significantly undermined. Lack of sufficient capacity, to make timely and adequate investments, gives reason to fear that India is heading towards energy crisis. Increasing import dependency exposes India to greater geopolitical risks, fluctuating world market prices and intensifying international competition. Indian energy policy cannot be set in isolation and needs to account for rising global interdependence, while simultaneously communicated appropriately to the public and reflected in policy debates. The energy efficiency initiatives introduced by the BEE (Bureau of Energy Efficiency) and others are necessary to reduce our energy intensity, but for them to bear fruit, we also need to redesign tariff structures in such a way that they become cost effective. The Renewable Energy Certificate (REC) mechanism is a major step forward to bring renewable energy into market pricing in a way that helps it to move away from administrative feed-in tariffs. However it needs to be noted that the REC market cannot get formed if the Renewable Procurement Obligation (RPO) is not mandatory.

Fragmented Energy Management Mechanism. In India the energy management is highly fragmented wherein a number of different ministries/ departments/ organizations, deal with the subject area as it pertains to their respective ministry/ department/organization as per their own understanding of the energy for the growth of the area they deal with. Starting from PMO these are; Planning Commission, National Security Advisory Board (NSAB), Ministries of; Coal, power, water resources, petroleum & natural gas, rural development, Non Conventional & Renewable Energy,

Environment & forest, External Affairs, Departments of Atomic Energy, space and Oceanography. Besides perceptual incongruence, a competitive response to emerging needs to grow independently. In the present system PMO, Planning Commission and NSAB do perspective planning and assume the role of the agency which provides higher direction. However there is a need to evolve a coordinating mechanism to plan, execute, monitor and finally review the energy plans of India.

Financial Management. India requires significant investment to meet its growing energy demand and provide access. As an example it has been suggested by an Asian Development Bank (ADB) Report that India up to 2020 will need US $ 67,830 million to reduce emissions intensity of the GDP by 20-25 percent (ADB Report). Similarly the Working Group constituted by the Planning Commission has estimated that the total fund requirement during the 12th Plan, considering each aspect of the power sector, is expected to cost about Rs 14 lakh crores. It is indeed going to be a major exercise to generate these kinds of Funds.

Sector Specific Challenges

Coal Sector. India's power requirement over the years has largely been dominated by coal based generation, with close to 55 percent of the 182 GW of the installed capacity being coal based power plants, accounting for over 80 percent of the total units generated in the country. However, more stringent rules and norms brought about recently by the MoEF for the award of the coal blocks have left many developers short of coal. Even state Generating companies are reportedly coming under pressure due to lack of adequate and timely supply of the coal. It has been estimated by the Working Committee Group on coal of the Planning Commission that the country will have a shortfall of coal of 238 MT/annum by 2016-17, if current trend of fuel utilization continues (Planning Commission). As the demand for electricity grows, the role of coal would remain undiminished. Many of the Indian companies are now relying on supply of coal via import route; especially from Indonesia and Australia. However there have been some changes in the international markets recently, which are impacting the supply from the import route. Most notable change has been an enactment of a new mining law in Indonesia, which has significantly affected the cost of imported coal for Indian companies. This new development has put Indian power companies in a dilemma. While cleaner imported coal has become more expensive, the Indian coal has a high ash and mineral content. In view of these developments, now the strategy has to be revised. The revised strategy will have three prongs. Prong one; is to strengthen the infrastructure for coal washing, prong two; is to go for expensive imported coal for short to medium term and finally; make an effort to develop clean coal technologies which will be beneficial in long term and hence are of paramount importance for a country like India (India Energy Book 2012). Currently there are a number of existing technologies like coal beneficiation, coal combustion, coal conversion, coal gasification, coal to liquid and carbon capture. India has made some progress in implementing super critical, pulverized coal combustion and coal gasification technologies. Such technology choices would have a long term impact (life of the plant) and need to be chosen carefully, though on priority, to cater for technology void. Power plant technology also needs to graduate to super critical technology. In this connection it is understood that an effort is being made to suitably modify nuclear reactor technology for power generation in thermal power stations (Dr Chidambaram in an interview with the author, 31 May 2013). More favourable policy initiatives are also needed to overcome any economic hurdles (issues of pricing and subsidy), which investors and consumers might face. In fact the falling rupee will otherwise further squeeze the margins of these plants as they are heavily dependent on imported coal. The import of coal has to be in accordance with the requirement of the power, steel, cement and other user industries. Current estimates are that the total imports will be around 165 MT and about 70 percent of this will be for power plants (Interview of Shri BK Chaturvedi, Member Energy Planning Commission with Yogima Seth Sharma of ET dated 16 July 2013).The planning Commission of India is pitching for higher tariff revision for power plants in coastal areas, arguing that a long term goal is envisaged to provide a larger quantity of domestic coal to user industries to ensure that they stay competitive and increase their production accordingly. Lastly a policy review is needed with a view to establish power plants near pit head or near ports so that cost of transportation can be minimized and the power wasted in transportation is saved. This policy review's scope can further be enlarged so that power generated is transmitted through the enlarged grid.

Gas Supply to Power Sector. Gas supply has been lower than the requirement and gradually over the last 10 years; the gap has been increasing. CEA reports that "The total loss of generation in FY10 was 3.24 billion units due to shortage of the gas supply." Due to certain recent geopolitical developments (US , the biggest consumer has changed from net importer to net exporter of the gas due to technological breakthrough in the field of exploitation of shale gas), the deficit for gas has reduced from 45 percent in FY-2000- 01 to 20 percent in FY-2010-11. In fact a new kind of challenge is emerging due to discovery of huge reserves of natural gas, estimated to be 24.4 trillion cubic metres (TCM) in the USA. With such a glut in the international gas market, the gas price has fallen from US $ 8-12 to US $ 2-3 per million metric British thermal units (mmbtu), a cost that makes other forms of energy generation particularly; nuclear power, uncompetitive. However; it needs to be noted that though shale gas production is encouraging but the issues of safety and environmental protection need to be taken into account. It is the considered view of the policy makers in the US that the USA should not be putting all its eggs in one basket; either nuclear, natural gas or coal. They feel that their best bet in the unfolding energy scenario would be to spread its resources. This is where India can benefit by having a good working relationship with the USA, which can help India to have access to cheaper natural gas from the USA through an arrangement which can be sustained over a long period of time. Still there are some actions which can be taken to improve the gas supply situation. These are as follows:-

- Go in for early international tie ups, to make use of emerging glut of gas in international market which has come about due to USA becoming Gas surplus.

- Build up of infrastructure for LNG terminals (a highly expensive proposition: each terminal costs $ 10 billion) on priority.

- Early progress on international pipelines to enhance supply of gas from Turkmenistan, Iran and Myanmar.

- Aggressive acquisition of gas bearing equities be speeded up despite competition from China, for which a strategy at highest level be formulated. A diplomatic initiative to evolve a cooperative approach in conjunction with China to enhance supply to both the countries can aggressively be progressed. Establishment of a national sovereign fund would be another good option.

- Extra effort should be put in to enhance indigenous exploration effort. Improving of NELP to attract bigger international players into the field of exploration is an option which needs to be looked at seriously. Another important initiative which is the need of the hour is early promulgation of policy on LNG and tariff issues with a view to encourage private players' enthusiastic participation.

Alternate Sources of Energy. While Indian companies are largely focused on traditional sources of energy, global investments in RES has jumped 32 percent, reaching a record high of US $ 211 billion in 2010, which is over 5 fold increase since 2004. (India energy book- 2012). Even developing countries like China have ramped up their investments in alternate sources of energy. Steadily, India too is looking at building a strong renewable energy portfolio in coming years. Government of India is offering a number of incentives to renewable energy developers to accelerate investments in renewable energy space. The National Solar Mission plans a capacity addition of 22,000 MW by 2022. Government of India targets a growth in renewable energy consumption of over 6 percent CAGR and a capacity addition of 18500 MW during the 12th Five Year Plan period (Draft Policy Report by MNRE on JNNSM Phase -2; targets 10 GW of Utility solar installations dated 03 December 2012). Some of the other challenges are as follows:-

- Need to enhance efficiency of solar systems.

- Single technology based systems are inadequate to deal with seasonal variations- Systems should be designed to tackle seasonal variations. One recommended approach is to plan hybrid systems Instead of single technology based energy harnessing system, so that the supply remains continuous irrespective of the weather conditions.

- Modern concept of building designs is increasingly becoming global in nature, which, many a times, is not in conformity with the prevailing weather conditions and comfort in these designs is provided by leveraging technology which invariably is energy intensive- Best option to tackle such a situation is to go for either vernacular architecture (which caters for local weather conditions) or strictly enforce green building norms (GRIHA Norms).

- Normally alternate sources are land intensive, which are increasingly becoming scarce. Therefore the need is to design a building in such a way that requirement of large surface areas can be enmeshed into the building designs itself by suitable innovations/ design modification/ use of material which lend themselves for use in green buildings.

- Systems and equipment exploiting alternate sources of energy are Capital intensive. Therefore generation of funds will be a major challenge. The enormity of funds requirement can be appreciated by only one figure that a sum of $19 billion will be needed for 20 GW of power that MNRE has planned to add by 2020 (Draft Policy on JNNSM)

Hydro Energy. In last 30 years, the share of hydroelectric energy in the Indian power basket has been going down steadily. It has dropped from about 46 percent in 1970 to 40 percent in 1980, 29 percent in 1990 and 25 percent in 2003. Although, India has a very large potential for hydro energy but as is evident from the Table- 2.6, exploitation is quite less, as compared to other countries:-

Table-2.6: Hydroelectric Energy: Potential versus Installed Capacities

Country	MW		Percentage
	Potential	Installed	
Norway	47,000	27,360	58
Canada	160,000	65,378	48
Brazil	170,000	52,427	31
China	310,000	56,000	18
India	150,000	27,000	18

Source: RV Shahi, Secretary, Ministry of Power, Government of of India, "Hydroelectric Projects Development: Challenges and Response" up loaded on http://www.powermin.nic.in/whats.new/pdf/cold.doc.

Some of the challenges are as follows:-

- Longer gestation period of the construction of the hydro energy plants. Technology needs to be leveraged to reduce it and also small hydro plants (up to 25 MW capacity) could be considered as a possible solution (G. Baidya), which, besides reducing the gestation period, will also be less damaging to the environment.

- Other challenges are environmental degradation due to deforestation/ submergence of large areas, rehabilitation and resettlement (R&R) of displaced persons.

- Design based safety of dams- as a large number of dams are located in seismically sensitive areas and need to be taken care of. Another related issue is the security of dams; as most of them are located in areas which are generally affected by internal disturbance. Safety and security of these assets against damage due to sabotage in today's environment is of paramount importance.

Nuclear. Although the next two chapters are fully devoted to issues pertaining to nuclear energy but there are few important challenges that are pertinent for examination when energy challenges of India are considered holistically. These are with a view to establish; whether nuclear energy can be an adequate source of energy in future and if so in what time frame. Following challenges are some of those which may act as impediments in the implementation of the plans to introduce nuclear energy as a main stay for future energy needs:-

- **Technological challenges**- so far only PHWR based technology has been hardened in India. Commercially viable fast breeder reactor based technology (second stage of three stage programme) is unlikely to be ready before 2015. Third stage of the 'Three Stage Nuclear Energy Programme' of India ie., thorium based nuclear energy production is still only in conceptual/ pilot project stage. An extremely concentrated endeavour needs to be made to progress technology hardening, so that by 2030 energy generation reaches a stage where nuclear energy assumes the role of leading contributor to the energy basket of India. Presently nuclear programme is all set for a boost in the months ahead, because Kudankulam-1 is likely to begin operations (the plant attained criticality on the night of 13-14 July 2013 and power generation has partially commenced). This will add, when fully functional 1,000 MWe of additional capacity to overall kitty. The coming on stream of this plant will be a big boon to the power-deficient Tamil Nadu, the present deficit being of the order of 4,000 MW. The adverse publicity from the Fukushima disaster and the orchestrated but misinformed campaign against the plant has however now died down. Kudankulam-2 unit is also likely to come on stream next year, while the 500-MWe prototype fast breeder reactor (PFBR) at Kalpakkam is also set to begin operations by 2015 (indications are there that it might slip to 2017). Six additional nuclear power reactors with 4,300 MWe capacity are expected to be operational by 2016-end, adding to the 21 reactors currently operating with a capacity of 5,780 MWe [6]. Meanwhile, new reactor projects are envisaged, in collaboration with AREVA of France, Russia and other partners. Eight more reactors would be put under the safeguards of the International Atomic Energy Agency by 2014, in addition to six already under the plan for civil-strategic separation. A bright feature is that the capacity factor of operating NPCIL reactors has shot up from a low of 50 percent in 2008-09, to 83 percent in the current year. One of the possible reasons for this improved PLF is due to the increased availability of fuel as a result of India being given the Nuclear Suppliers' Group (NSG) waiver. The new projects envisaged include a mix of the traditional pressurized heavy water reactors (PHWRs) of 700 MWe (10 units to be set up by NPCIL), and foreign-supplied pressurized water reactors (VVERs/ PWRs), of 1,000-MWe-plus capacity from Russia (Kudankulam 3-6) & France (Jaitapur 1-2), and finally two fast breeder reactors of 500 MWe to be set up by BHAVINI (Bhaskar Balakrishnan).

- **Availability of Resources-** this is the biggest constraint to the implementation of stage-one, because despite NSG waiver and IAEA safe guard agreement, the supply of natural uranium is still not fully operationalized. One of the nagging issues is; India's Nuclear Liability Act which foreign vendors are finding stringent. As an alternative if indigenous sourcing is considered for the supply of natural uranium then it emerges that the Indigenous discoveries are still mired in controversies of various kinds due to perceptual incongruence between public and NPCIL/ Uranium Corporation of India (this public sector undertaking is responsible for mining/ milling of uranium in India) with respect to safety issues. Thus, if the supply from external sources is not facilitated expeditiously, and a focused awareness campaign is not launched at the earliest, the entire nuclear energy programme may get derailed.

- **Human Resources Capacity-** The expansion of India's nuclear programme will require sufficient human resources with skills in nuclear technology, engineering, health, physics, safety, security and regulatory matters. There is little evidence of any strategic

---

6   21st Reactor is Kudankulam-1 which has now started contributing to the grid.

plans to make an inventory of the personnel required for our nuclear programme and build up this capacity. As in any other area of high technology, skilled personnel are a valuable asset and it takes considerable time to get them prepared. However, suffice to say at this stage that much more needs to be done to attract young students into a scientific career, such as nuclear science and nuclear engineering. Training courses and programmes, offered by institutions should be of high standard. An appraisal suggests that the quality and the number of institutions which impart training in subjects related to nuclear energy are not too many and it would be a challenge for the planners to work out future requirements and initiate cases to enhance capacity. In the interim the training programmes run by the BARC, TIFR, NIAS, IISc, Bengaluru and IITs need to be increased. This capacity building needs to be proliferated to junior supervisor levels and also skill development programme for lower level be introduced and progressed. This kind of capacity addition will also help industry to have adequate people in the field which will help nuclear energy market to grow and will help to reduce dependence on pure government funding in future.

• **Cost-** The average costs of the indigenous PHWRs is around $1,200 a kWe for an indigenous plant. For a foreign supplied plant, the cost would be in the range of $2,000 a kWe, although the Department of Atomic Energy has set a benchmark for capital cost of $1,600 per kWe (IBID). Apart from higher costs, the foreign-supplied reactors are of the PWR type. These require low-enriched uranium as fuel and water as the coolant. The reactor has to be shut down for refueling and spent fuel has to be accounted for, according to the fuel-supply agreement. These units require a massive steel reactor pressure vessel (RPV) weighing over 500 tons, and can only be manufactured in a few countries such as Japan, whose consent will be necessary for the supply. This equipment is very expensive and specialized. Presently no Indian Company manufactures it and thus it will remain a challenge for the Indian Industry for a long time to enhance its indigenous content. The life of RPVs in PWRs is at present limited to around 40 years, after which the entire plant has to be closed down and decommissioned. These imported reactors are subject to international safeguards. Such a state enhances the affected nation's vulnerability to external pressures. Though the research is going on to find a technology to extend their (RPVs) lifespan but it still has not reached a logical conclusion. These issues have gained importance in recent years as many of the world's PWRs are reaching the 40-year limit. These factors need to be kept in view while going in for imported PWRs.

- **Significance of PHWR**- On the other hand, the CANDU types PHWRs being used in India today have several advantages. They do not have to be shut down for refueling and can use natural uranium as fuel instead of enriched uranium. They further have flexibility in fuel use, including use of thorium and mixed fuels. They do not require the massive pressure vessel, and the technology and know-how is already available in India for fabricating the components. India has had considerable experience in manufacturing and operating these types of reactors with a very high capacity utilization and availability. The main drawback of these reactors is the requirement of using heavy water as coolant as well as moderator. However in case of India it is not such a major issue because it is being produced indigenously. Probably at some point of time in future, the capacity of the country to produce heavy water will have to be scaled up to meet the growth in the requirement due to additional reactors coming up. The PHWRs have been discouraged by some Western countries, as they apprehend that India will use these reactors to produce fissionable material for possible military use. Although, theoretically true, but India has been following this technology for a different reason. Plutonium produced in these reactors is critical because it is essential for operationalizing of the second stage of the India's nuclear programme.

- **Safety Issues**- In India Safety audit is done by Atomic Energy Regulatory Board (AERB). Though it is an independent body but it draws its personnel from Atomic Energy Commission (AEC) and its HQ is collocated with AEC in Anushakti Bhawan. In this connection it is pertinent to note that India is the only country which has such a huge nuclear programme but the regulatory body is not strictly independent. It is also contrary to international practice as well as the treaties that India has signed on the need to have separate regulatory and operational functions for the management of the nuclear energy. This remains the single biggest obstacle for a safe nuclear energy programme in the country. It is not the best kept secret in the world that Indian plants have had problems at different points in time, though may not have been so serious. The collapse of the Kaiga dome and the fire in Narora which caused all controls to be lost are cases in point. In Narora, again workers, facing very heavy odds, managed a safe shut-down of the reactor manually. A former Chairman of AERB, Dr. A. Gopalakrishnan has commented that AERB has no serious disaster management oversight and does not have the ability to address serious design and safety issues. (Mail Today). The opening up of the nuclear sector to foreign collaboration has brought in PWR/ LWE type of reactors whose safety record is suspect, to say the least, and therefore, need for an independent body to do safety audit is not a day too soon. It is therefore necessary that the challenge of making AERB truly independent be taken up at the earliest (Prabir Purkayastha).

- **Carbon emissions**; in case of nuclear reactors, as compared to other forms of energy, are quite low. The mean value of emissions over the course of the lifetime of a nuclear reactor (reported from qualified studies) is 66 g CO_2e/ kWh, due to reliance on existing fossil-fuel infrastructure for plant construction, decommissioning, and fuel processing along with the energy intensity of uranium mining and enrichment (Benjamin K. Sovacool). Thus, nuclear energy is in no way "carbon free" or "emissions free," even though it is much better (from purely a carbon-equivalent emissions standpoint) than coal, oil, and natural gas electricity generators, but worse than renewable and small scale distributed generators. For example, it has been found that coal, oil, diesel, and natural gas generators emitted between 443 and 1050 g CO_2e/ kWh, far more than the 66 g CO_2e/ kWh attributed to the nuclear lifecycle (Gagnon et al. (2002)). Therefore though the main stay of India's energy supply is presently dominated by coal, yet case for increasing reliance on relatively clean/ totally clean sources of energy becomes highly desirable and needs to be factored in all future energy planning arrangements.

Carbon emissions from nuclear power
Sovacool life cycle study survey, 2008

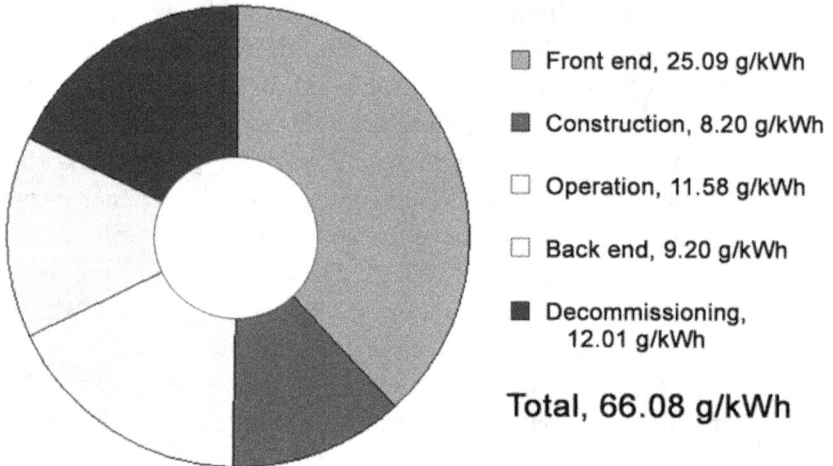

- Front end, 25.09 g/kWh
- Construction, 8.20 g/kWh
- Operation, 11.58 g/kWh
- Back end, 9.20 g/kWh
- Decommissioning, 12.01 g/kWh

Total, 66.08 g/kWh

Figure- 2.9: Assessment Carbon Dioxide Emissions during Nuclear Power Generation

Source: Leightonwalter, own work, dated 30July 2009 uploaded on en.wikipedia. org as part of Nuclear Power

- Life cycle analysis (LCA) of carbon dioxide emissions, show nuclear power as comparable to renewable energy sources. Emissions from burning fossil fuels are many times higher (Benjamin K Sovacool) and also lethal (Nuclear Energy Institute upload).

Issues with respect to Transmission. Size of the pan India grid is 100,619 circuit km (www.powergridindia.com). Plans are there to add another 100,000 circuit km during 12th Plan and 130,000 Circuit km during 13th plan. Funds required during 12th Plan will be INR 180,000 crores and INR 200,000 crores during 13th Plan (Transmission and Distribution in India: A Report). Average T&D losses, in the Indian Grid system, are 28 percent while the global standards are as low as 05-10 percent (Mrinalini Prasad). In this area China, Pakistan and even Bangladesh are doing better than India (World Bank Data). Though losses have reduced from 33.98

percent in 2002 to present state but a lot of ground is yet to be covered. It has been assessed that In terms of capacity, 25 percent of T&D losses would account for about 50,000 MW capacity, with the total energy generation in India reported to be 2,07,006 MW (IBID). Therefore efforts need to be made to reduce AT&C loss. Some of the other challenges that impede the growth of this essential segment of energy management in India are as follows:-

- **Funding for projects**- for grid line as well as terminal equipment which are enormous in quantum is to be organized. World over; the norm for investment in case of generation to T&D infrastructure is 1:1. But in India it is 1:0.45.

- Hap hazard growth of the transmission and distribution lines.

- Large scale rural electrification through 11 KVA line/ Low Tension line (LT)

- Improper load management

- Many stages of stepping down and poor quality of equipment.

- **Power Theft**- is another challenge in India. Inefficiency in the power distribution system has led to a failure in checking of power theft and this leakage continues to plague the sector. According to the Economic Survey of 2006-07, loss due to theft and pilferage is estimated to be about Rs.20,000 crore annually. As per the provisions of the Electricity Act, 2003, special courts to deal exclusively with cases of electricity theft have been set up in 23 states except Bihar, Goa, Jharkhand, Kerala, Arunachal Pradesh and Mizoram. In addition to this, special police stations have also been set up in 11 states viz. Andhra Pradesh, Delhi, Gujarat, Karnataka, Madhya Pradesh, Maharashtra, Orissa, Rajasthan, West Bengal, Himachal Pradesh and Tripura. Considering the High AT&C losses in various states, it is proposed that Special Courts may be set up in all districts together with police stations (IBID).

- **Integration of the Grid with the Source of Generation in Foreign countries**- Cross border electricity transaction particularly with Nepal and Bhutan may be facilitated through Inter Governmental framework agreements. There is also a need to develop, coordinated procedures for scheduling and dispatch of cross border power and for financial settlement of electricity transactions. With plans of exporting power to Pakistan, such an arrangement will have to be designed at Indo Pak border also.

- **Right of Way (ROW)** - issues when transmission line passes across the road. In the absence of a good coordination mechanism between NHAI, NHPC, state; PWD & irrigation departments and Power Grid Corporation of India, planning of power grid lines along with proposed new road construction, crossing of the road along the culverts/ bridges and realignment of power lines during road widening pose tremendous amount of technical and financial challenges.

- **Low Operational Efficiency**- the AT&C losses in case of India are 31 percent (Planning commission-2011 (b)), which costs nation almost 1.5 percent of the GDP amounting to $ 17 billion (CEA-2010). These are astronomically high figures as compared to other comparable economies. This would be quite evident from following table:-

Table-2.7: AT & C Losses

Country	AT & C Losses (in percent)
Brazil	17
China	5
India	**31**
Indonesia	10
Japan	5
South Korea	4

Source: WDI-2012, http://www.databank.worldbank.org/

Besides technical reasons during transmission, other relevant reasons are theft, non-payment by the consumers and incorrect classification of the consumers leading to lesser recovery of the dues (Planning commission -2006). There is a need to go in for SMART GRIDS to improve the efficiency of the grid. Smart grids are transmission network that utilize information and communication technologies to make the transmission infrastructure more efficient and resilient. It enables developers and operators to carry out real time monitoring and controlling the systems.

This helps in reducing AT&C losses, peak load management, outage management, power quality management and also channeling power from renewable energy resources.

- **Regional Imbalances-** Demand in India is basically concentrated in North, South and Western regions (27-33 percent), whereas East and North Eastern regions in their present state of industrialization, contribute only 11-12 percent of the electrical demand. It is interesting to note that a large number of sources of supply are located in those regions where demand, presently is comparatively lesser. To enhance cost effective supply in overall context these areas will have to have power producing centers and such a state will call for the development of either a stronger grid covering larger area or a faster industrialization of the areas which are presently underdeveloped. An analysis of economics of the two competing options will suggest the need for a more comprehensive but swifter development of the power grid.

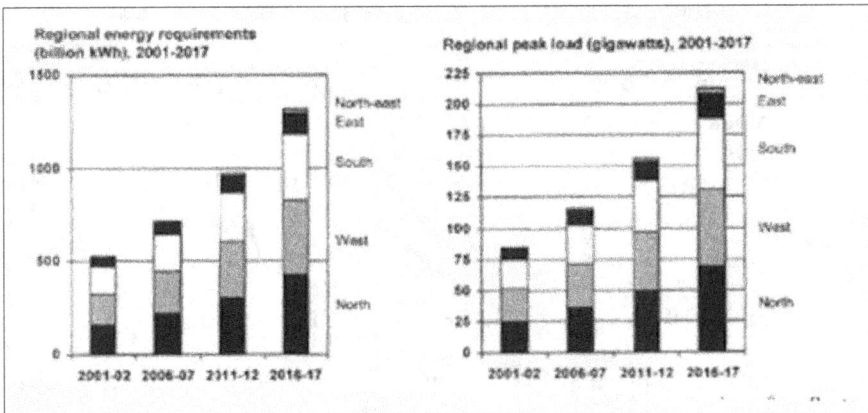

Figure- 2.10: Geographical Imbalance

Source: Kakodkar, Dr Anil, "Nuclear Power in India: An Inevitable Option for Sustainable development of a Sixth of Humanity," World Nuclear symposium, 4-6 September 2002, London.

Note: The regional imbalance of the energy requirement is not closing and as such may call for a review of the strategy.

Agenda to Enhance State of Energy Security

Based on the challenges enumerated above a national agenda needs to be evolved to address the inhibitors to the growth of energy sector and thus by implication contributing towards the energy security of the nation. Some of the issues which need to be included in this agenda are as discussed hereafter.

- **Research and Development.** Future belongs to clean technologies and as such effort needs to accelerate research and simultaneously develop market with the involvement of industry to make following technologies cost effective based on indigenous resources:-

  - Nuclear

  - Renewable

  - Pet coke

  - Coal- ICC, CBM, underground coal gasification.

- **Complete deregulation of the coal sector**, with view to allow private investments and move to market based pricing and promote PPP model of sector development with Coal India. Hereafter coal block allocation should be through competitive bidding.

- **Strategic storage and strengthening the logistic chain** for an efficient and effective transportation of energy and energy bearing resources to power generation plants/ usage points

- **Faster clearances** based on single window clearance.

- **Enhance availability of natural gas/ LNG**, which will be the main fuel to meet the industrial, power and transport sector requirements in short and medium term. It should be done through accelerated local exploration/ international tie ups including trans-national gas pipelines and increasing the local pipeline network for distribution.

- **Enlarge scope of exploration for crude oil** and improve yield through LE works and R&M projects.

- **Process of acquisition of energy bearing properties** of; coal, oil and gas located abroad be accelerated- safety and security of assets in location of acquisition and security of assets during transit should be factored in the planning. Ways and means to improve interdependence with the host country, with a view to ensure uninterrupted supply, should also be part of the agenda.

- Steps be taken to strengthen and enlarge transmission and distribution net work by using smart grid technique that uses information and communications technology to gather and act on information with respect to behaviors of suppliers and consumers, in an automated fashion to improve the efficiency, reliability, economics, and sustainability of the production and distribution of electricity. Such an system will also help to reduce power theft and AT&C losses.

- **Demand side management** through right sizing of energy expenditure, enhance efficiency, reduce demand through better green buildings, introduce more efficient equipment, better and standard vehicle efficiency norms and finally there is a need to examine whether there is a case for introducing different time zones in the country to optimize use of sun light and thereby reduce need for energy for lighting and cooling.

- **Improve financial management** through innovative measures so that fund supply for erection of necessary infrastructure for generation and transmission of energy is ensured at all times.

- **Review policy guidelines** to improve demand side management, enforcement, better coordination between various ministries/ departments/ organizations, better future scenario build up and improved efficiency of the equipment.

3

Growth of Nuclear Energy

Introduction

Nuclear energy, in general terms is referred as the energy which is produced during the exothermic reactions involving; fission/ fusion/ decay of the nucleus in case of a radioactive element. On further examination of the energy produced, it emerges that it is in the form of useful heat (generated during the exothermic reaction), which can be converted to electricity. Fission is the process when a large nucleus gets split into smaller nuclei and is accompanied with the release of energy. Fusion is the process when two or more, smaller nuclei get fused and in the process energy is generated. Radioactive decay, also known as nuclear decay or radioactivity, is the process by which a nucleus of an unstable atom loses energy by emitting particles of ionizing radiation. A material that spontaneously emits this kind of radiation—which includes the emission of energetic alpha particles, beta particles, and gamma rays—is considered radioactive. Decay continues over a long period of time till it transforms into a smaller and stable nucleus of a different element. These elements are from the actinide series[1] of the periodic table. Radioactive decay process is more relevant in the case of geothermal energy, and finally through radioisotope thermoelectric generators; in niche uses. The fission process often produces free neutrons and protons (in the form of gamma rays), and releases a very large amount of energy even by the energetic standards of

---

1 The actinide series encompasses the 15 metallic chemical elements with atomic numbers from 89 to 103. These are actinium, thorium, protactinium, uranium, neptunium, plutonium, americium, curium, berkelium, californium, einsteinium, fermium, mendelevium, nobelium and lawrencium. All actinides are radioactive and release energy upon radioactive decay; naturally occurring uranium and thorium, and synthetically produced plutonium are the most abundant actinides on Earth. These are used in nuclear reactors and nuclear weapons. Uranium and thorium also have diverse current or historical uses, and americium is used in the ionization chambers of most modern smoke detectors.

radioactive decay.

This energy released in a fission reaction is both; in the form of electromagnetic radiations and also as the kinetic energy of the fragments (heating the bulk material where fission takes place). In order to produce energy during the fission, the total binding energy of the resulting elements must be greater than that of the starting element. The amount of free energy contained in a nuclear fuel is millions of times the amount of free energy contained in a similar mass of chemical fuel such as gasoline. This makes nuclear fission a very dense source of energy. It should however be remembered that the products of a nuclear fission are on an average far more radioactive than the heavy elements which originally are subjected to fission reaction. It also needs to be noted that these resultant radioactive products remain so for significant amount of time before becoming stable thus giving rise to a nuclear waste problem with the associated need for its safe disposal. The flow chart of the reaction is as given in the Appendix- A attached.

Historical Perspective

The pursuit of nuclear energy for electricity generation began soon after the discovery of the structure of the atom in the early 20th century. It was discovered that radioactive elements, such as radium, released immense amounts of energy, according to the principle of mass–energy equivalence. However, means of harnessing such a form of energy was considered impractical, because intensely radioactive elements, by their very nature, were short-lived (high energy release is correlated with short half-lives).

The concept of harnessing of energy contained in the nucleus got a boost in the late 1930s, with the discovery of nuclear fission. In 1932, James Chadwick discovered the neutron (Internet download: atomicarchive. com/History/mp/p1s1.shtml), which was immediately recognized as a potential tool for nuclear experimentation because of its lack of an electric charge. During the experimentation with the bombardment of materials with neutrons, led Frédéric and Irène Joliot-Curie[2] to discover induced radioactivity in 1934, which allowed the creation of radium-like elements

---

2 Frederic Joliot-Curie and Irene Joliot-Curie were both French scientists. Husband and wife, they were jointly Nobel laureates in 1935 for their joint discovery of new radioactive isotopes which they prepared artificially. They are also known for their contribution towards the discovery of the neutron.

at much less the price of natural radium (Internet download: thebigger. com). Further work by Enrico Fermi[3] in 1930s focused on using slow neutrons to increase the effectiveness of induced radioactivity. In 1938, German chemists, Otto Hahn (Internet download: nobleprize.com) and Fritz Strassmann, along with Austrian physicist Lise Meitner and Otto Robert Frisch, determined that the relatively tiny neutron could split the nucleus of a massive uranium atom into two roughly equal parts (Internet download: Vanderkrogt.com). This was an extremely significant result because all other forms of nuclear decay involved only small changes to the mass of the nucleus, whereas this process—dubbed "fission" involved a complete rupture of the nucleus. Subsequently a number of scientists, including Leó Szilárd, who was one of the first to have recognized the significance of the fission reaction observed that the fission reactions released additional neutrons, resulting into a self-sustaining nuclear chain reaction. Once this observation was experimentally confirmed and announced by Frédéric Joliot-Curie in 1939, scientists in many countries (including the United States of America, the United Kingdom, France, Germany, and the USSR) petitioned their respective governments for support of their research on nuclear fission, just on the cusp of World War II. In most cases the research was aimed to finally develop a nuclear weapon (Internet download: atomicarchive.com 22 June 2013).

In the United States, where both Fermi and Szilárd had emigrated; Fermi in 1938 and Szilard in 1943, this led to the creation of the first man-made reactor, known as Chicago Pile-1. It consisted of uranium embedded in brick like blocks of graphite to serve as the moderator. The reactor achieved criticality on 02 December 1942. This work became part of the Manhattan Project, which made enriched uranium and built large reactors to breed plutonium for use in the first two nuclear weapons, which were used on the cities of Hiroshima[4] and Nagasaki[5] in Japan with a devastating effect which was without a precedence and actually hastened the process of surrender by Japan to Allied Forces.

---

3 Enrico Fermi (1901-54) was an Italian Physicist who is best known for controlled nuclear chain reaction. He was awarded Nobel Prize for physics in 1938. He migrated to the USA in 1944 where he worked on Manhattan project during World war-II.

4 Bomb codenamed, "Little Boy" was dropped over Hiroshima, on 06 August 1945. In next two to four months the acute effect of the bombs killed 90,000 – 160,000 people with half of them having perished on first day itself.

5 Bomb codenamed, "Fat Man" was dropped over Nagasaki on 09 August 1945. The casualty figures were 60,000-80,000 people with similar pattern as in the case of Hiroshima.

Atom for Peace. The devastation of Hiroshima and Nagasaki by Nuclear Bombs shocked the international community. A large number of thinkers started a campaign to ban the nuclear weapons, but a lot of positive minded people among those thinkers went a step ahead and tried to argue the case for use of nuclear energy for peaceful purposes and wanted the scientific community to explore the possibility of using the immense power contained in the nucleus for the good of mankind. This kind of thought gradually coalesced into the idea of using "atomic energy" for power generation, rather than simply for enhancing war waging potential/ deterrence capability of the holder of atomic energy capability. This led to 'Atom for peace' movement started gathering a new momentum. In 1953, the then US President Dwight Eisenhower,[6] gave his famous and historic "Atoms for Peace" speech at the United Nations, emphasizing the need to develop "peaceful" uses of nuclear power quickly. The speech was part of a carefully orchestrated media campaign, called "Operation Candor", to enlighten the American public on the risks and hopes of a nuclear future. This was followed by the '1954 Amendments' to the 'US Atomic Energy Act' which allowed rapid declassification of U.S. reactor technology and encouraged development by the private sector. Prior to Eisenhower's 'Atoms for Peace' speech, the research and the development in the field of atomic energy was being kept, by each of those countries who were active in this domain, under the wraps of strictest of secrecies. Sharing of the information and expertise on the subject was bound by a pact of secrecy between allies (the secret Quebec agreement of 1943). The reason for such a secrecy was that- till then holders of the atomic weapons led by the USA were of the view that the atomic energy was not meant to be used for peaceful processes but as a deterrent against their adversaries. As such, each one of them were working; to refine the atomic weapons related technologies that they had acquired, to keep ahead in the development of the weapon systems as compared to their adversaries and finally to deny the same to their adversaries. With the purpose of development, at that point in time, in the field of atomic energy being weapon related capability which was mostly classified in nature, no safety protocols were documented and also no safety standards were developed. Eisenhower's speech, in fact indicated a paradigm shift in the policy of the USA in the strategic domain

---

6 Dwight David "Ike" Eisenhower was the 34th President of the United States from 1953 until 1961. He had previously been a five-star general in the United States Army during World War II and served as the Supreme commander of the Allied Forces during Operation 'OVERLORD' (Invasion of Europe)

as it brought the subject of the atomic energy, which so far was a "national security" issue, into the public domain. He urged the world to support his model of nuclear energy growth. An implied aim of the US President, as can be appreciated in the hind sight, was basically to share the nuclear technology with only selected allies/potential allies and deny the same to adversaries or those who were not with the USA, in the highly surcharged atmosphere of the Cold War. Within a year of Eisenhower's UN speech, the United States moved swiftly and began training foreign scientists at a new School of Nuclear Science and Engineering at Argonne Laboratory; declassified hundreds of nuclear studies and reports; sponsored the first UN Conference on the 'Peaceful Uses of Atomic Energy' where many of the declassified documents were released and concluded nuclear cooperation agreements with more than two dozen countries. Countries of South Asia in the mid-1950s were particularly high on the priority list in so far as Washington DC's policy to promote nuclear technology was concerned, which is evident from two of the Eisenhower administration's major policy directives; firstly, NSC 5409 ("U.S. Policy toward South Asia"), which the president approved in March 1954 to support "strong, stable and responsible governments" in a region that is "a major battleground in the Cold War" and secondly; NSC 5507/2 ("Peaceful Uses of Atomic Energy"), which he approved in March 1955 to utilize nuclear technology exports to promote the international and regional interests of the United States. The then Chairman of the Atomic Energy Commission of India, Dr Homi Jehangir Bhabha[7], recognized the opportunity and lobbied hard to make India the first recipient of the USA's nuclear material/ technology under the Washington DC's new nuclear export policy. The US Atomic Energy Commission sold India 10 tons of heavy water in February 1955 for the use in its CIRUS[8] (Canadian-Indian Reactor, US) research reactor; a facility Canada had agreed to supply with generous financing. It was done by the USA, largely because of its own regional security interests. Relentless efforts of Dr Bhabha also contributed substantially to make it

---

7   Dr Homi Jehangir Bhabha was the first Chairman of the Atomic Energy Commission of India and retained that position from 1948 to 1966 when he died in an Air Craft crash.

8   CIRUS (Canadian-Indian Reactor, U.S.) was a research reactor at the Bhabha Atomic Research Center (BARC) in Trombay near Mumbai, India. CIRUS was supplied by Canada in 1954, but used heavy water(deuterium oxide) supplied by the United States. It was the second nuclear reactor to be built in India. It was modeled on the Canadian Chalk River National Research X-perimental (NRX) reactor. The 40 MW reactor used natural uranium fuel, while using heavy water as a moderator.] It is a tank reactor type with a core size of 3.14 m (H) × 2.67 m (D). It first went critical July 10, 1960.

happen. The USA became India's leading supplier of the nuclear technology and materials related to it. The USA provided New Delhi with more than $ 93 million in loans and grants between 1954 and 1974 under the scheme of 'Atoms for Peace'. Three-quarters of these funds were utilized for the construction and operation of India's first power reactor at Tarapur (Peter R Lavoy).

Initially, most scientists were of the view that the hardening of the technology to harness nuclear energy and the related engineering to generate power will take at least a decade to fructify. In this connection a significant aspect was that almost all operating nuclear reactors were also being used to produce plutonium to fuel the nuclear weapons. This status of the Nuclear Power Plants (NPPs) meant that most national governments were also having nuclear weapons programme as part of their security apparatus (same as those in the USA, the UK, Canada, and the erstwhile USSR). Security issues led these countries to make attempts, to keep reactor research under strict government control. Work in the USA, UK, Canada (Bain, Alister S, et al), and the erstwhile USSR proceeded along this approach during later half of 1940s and early 1950s.

Electricity was generated for the first time by a nuclear reactor on December 20, 1951, at the Experimental Breeder Reactor (EBR-I) experimental station, near Arco, Idaho, which initially produced about 100 kWe (Popular Mechanics, March 52). It was enough to power the equipment in the small building where the reactor was housed. The world's first commercial nuclear power station, Calder Hall at Windscale, England, became functional in 1956 with an initial capacity of 50 MW (later 200 MW) (Kragh, Helge) (BBC News, 17 October 1956). On June 27, 1954, the erstwhile USSR's Obninsk Nuclear Power Plant became the world's first nuclear power plant to generate electricity for a power grid, and produced around 5 MW of electric power (Staff report by IAEA).

One of the first organizations other than governments which saw the immense potential of the nuclear energy was the US Navy, which decided to develop nuclear power for the purpose of propelling submarines and aircraft carriers. It turned out to be a great force multiplier, as it provided ships/ submarines the kind of sea endurance which was, hither to fore; unknown. The first test reactor was developed in 1953 (Submarine Thermal Reactor (STR) designed by Argonne National Laboratory). The first nuclear-powered submarine, USS Nautilus (SSN-571), was put to sea in December 1954 (Internet download: IAEA). Since then many military and some civilian (such as some icebreaker) ships had been using nuclear marine propulsion (Bellona, 20/06-2003). Few space vehicles (Soviet RORSAT series and the American SNAP-10A) have also been launched using full-fledged nuclear reactors. Despite few serious nuclear and radiation accidents involving nuclear submarines (*A total of eight nuclear submarines have sunk, till date, as a consequence of either accident or extensive damage: two from the US Navy, four from the Soviet Navy, and two from the Russian Navy. Only three were lost with all hands: two from the US Navy and one from the Russian Navy. All sank as a result of accident with the exception of K-27, which was scuttled in the Kara Sea when repair was deemed impossible and decommissioning too expensive.*) (compiled by Wm. Robert Johnston last updated 23 September 2007), neither the pace of research has slowed down nor its application has ebbed. Presently about 140 ships/ submarines are using nuclear energy. For this there are about 180 reactors in operation for their propulsion and to meet their power requirement.

Installed nuclear capacity initially rose relatively quickly, rising from less than One Giga Watt (GW) in 1960 to 100 GW in the late 1970s, and 300 GW in the late 1980s. Between 1970 and 1990, more than 50 GW of capacity was under construction (peaking at over 150 GW in the late 70s and early 80s). Three Mile incident in 1979 turned out to be a dampener to the growth of nuclear power as more than two-thirds of all the nuclear plants ordered after January 1970 were eventually cancelled (David Fischer). A total of 63 nuclear units were canceled in the USA alone between 1975 and 1980 (Rebecca Mcncrnay). Similarly; post Chernobyl incident in 1986, the worldwide capacity has risen much more slowly, reaching 366 GW only in 2005.

History of the Global Nuclear Power Industry

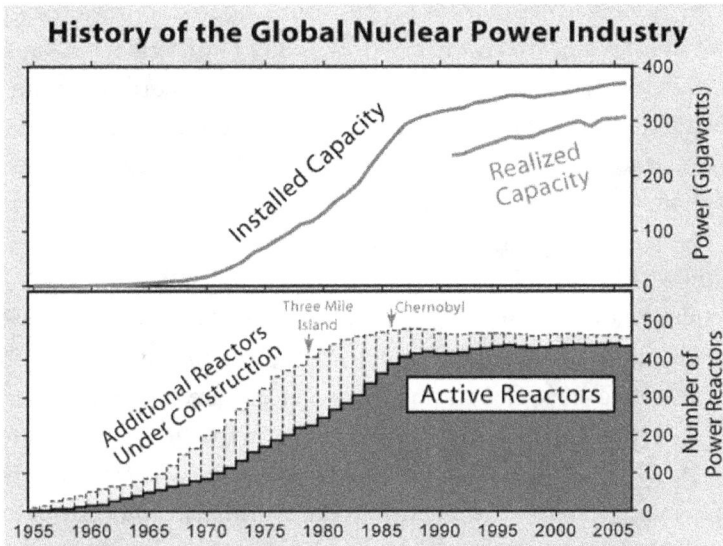

Figure- 3.1: History of Nuclear Power Industry

Note: As can be seen, in early sixties nuclear energy got a boost and a large number of new reactors world over got commissioned. Trend continued till 1979 (three Mile incident) but the real dampener came in 1986 (Chernobyl Incident).

In 2011 the worldwide nuclear output fell by 4.3 percent and nuclear power provided only 10 percent of the world's electricity (IEA, 2012). This decline in the consumption of the nuclear energy was due to sharp decline in the usage of the nuclear power by Japan (-44.3 percent) and Germany (-23.2 percent) (BP Statistical Review of World Energy, June 2012). Probably Fukushima incident in 2011 was the root cause of such a decline because post that incident a number of reactors were closed down for the assessment of the safety readiness status of those plants. May be a detailed analysis of the Fukushima incident and its impact on the growth of the nuclear energy will be in order. Nuclear power stations (NPS) using the process of fission, excluding the contribution from naval nuclear fission reactors, provided about 5.7 percent of the world's energy and 13 percent of the world's electricity in 2012 (Key World Energy Statistics 2012 by IEA). In 2013, the IAEA report states that there are 434 operational nuclear power reactors (IAEA: PRIS dated 14 June 2013), in 31 countries (WNA dated 09 June 2008), although not every reactor is producing electricity (Reuters Tokyo, 17 June 2012). In addition still there are approximately

140 naval vessels using nuclear propulsion in operation powered by some 180 reactors ("Nuclear Power in World Today" in Engineers Garage) and (WNA updated up to August 2013). As of 2012, according to the IAEA, there were 68 civil nuclear power reactors all over the world which were under construction in 15 countries (IAEA: PRIS dated 14 June 2013), approximately 28 of which are in the Peoples Republic of China (PRC) alone. The most recent nuclear power reactor (as of May 2013) which is to be connected to the electrical grid, went critical on February 17, 2013 in Hongyanhe Nuclear Power Plant in the PRC ("Worldwide First Reactor to Start Up in 2013, in China" - World Nuclear Industry Status Report). In the USA, two new Generation III[9] reactors are under construction at Vogtle. U.S. nuclear industry officials expect five new reactors to enter service by 2020, all at existing plants (Ayesha Rascoe). Today the USA produces maximum nuclear energy in the world. This works out to be 19 percent (EIA, 2010) of the total electricity which is being consumed in the USA. France, as of 2006, produced 80 percent of its electrical energy from nuclear reactors, which is highest in the world (Eleanor Beardsley, NPR 2006). In the European Union (EU) as a whole, nuclear energy provides 30 percent of the electricity (EUROSTAT, 2006).

---

9 These are Improvement on Generation-II reactors in terms of a longer operational life (60 years of operation, extendable to 120+ years of operation prior to complete overhaul and RPV replacement) compared with currently used generation II reactors (designed for 40 years of operation, extendable to 80 plus years of operations prior to complete overhaul and RPV replacement). Furthermore, core damage frequencies for these reactors are lower than for Generation- II reactors; 60 core damage events per 1000 million reactor year for the EPR; 3 core damage events per 1000 million reactor year for the ESBWR significantly lower than the 10,000 core damage events per 1000 million reactor year for BWR/4 generation II reactors. The Generation III EPR reactor was designed to use uranium more efficiently than older Generation II reactors, using approximately 17 percent less uranium per unit of electricity generated than these older reactor technologies. The first Generation III reactor to have begun was at Kashiwazaki in 1996.

Nuclear Power

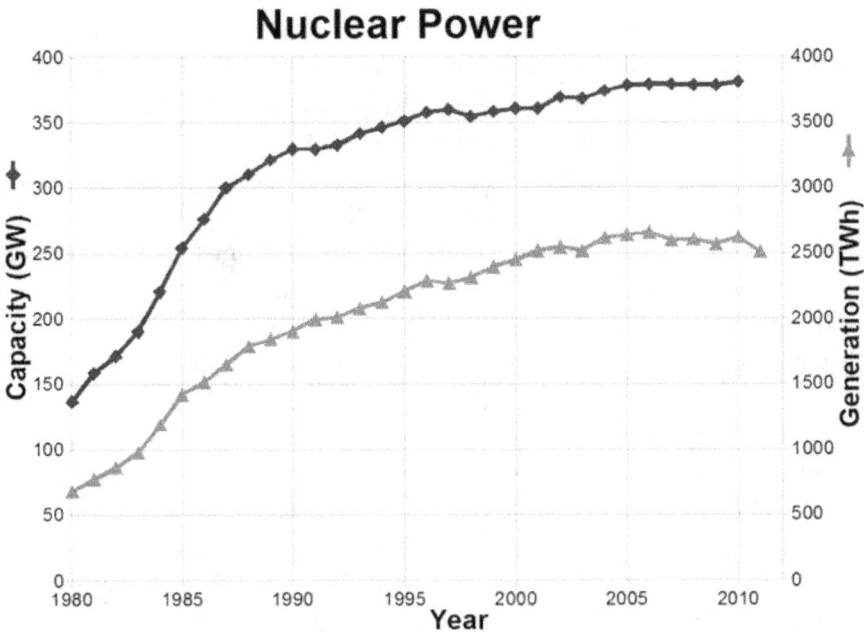

Source: Nuclear Power- Wikipedia uploaded on http://en.wikipedia.org/wiki/ Nuclear_power

Figure-3.2: Growth of Nuclear Power

Note: The graph at Figure-3.2 clearly establishes that there is a gap between the existing capacity & the production, and the gap is increasing. Maximum increase was during 1983 to1990 and post 2010 decline in production is becoming quite prominent. It was, as mentioned earlier, due to a number of working reactors getting shut down for safety assessment readiness and an overall question mark on nuclear energy post Fukushima.

Nuclear Cycle. The process starts with mining of uranium[10]. Mined uranium ore after extraction is usually converted into a stable and compact form such as yellow cake, and then transported to a processing facility. Here, the yellow cake is converted to uranium hexafluoride, which is then enriched using various techniques. At this point, the enriched uranium, containing more than the natural 0.7 percent U^{235}, is used to make rods of the proper composition and geometry for the particular reactor that the fuel is destined for. The fuel rods will spend about three operational cycles (typically six years total) inside the reactor, generally until about 3 percent

---

10 Uranium Mines are underground, open-pit or in-situ leach mines.

of their uranium has already been subjected to fission. Then they will be moved to a spent fuel pool where the short lived isotopes generated by the fission can decay away. After about five years in a spent fuel pool the spent fuel is radioactively and thermally cold enough to get handled and fit enough to get moved to dry storage casks or get reprocessed. Uranium is a fairly common element in the Earth's crust. Uranium is approximately as common as tin or germanium in the Earth's crust, and is about 40 times more common than silver (Encyclopedia.com, 26 August 2013). Uranium is a constituent of most rocks, dirt, and of the oceans. The fact that uranium is so spread out is a problem because mining uranium is economically feasible only where there is a large concentration of the uranium exists. Still, the world's present measured resources of uranium, economically recoverable at a price of US $ 130 per kg, are enough to last for a period; between 70 to 100 years (A Policy Brief-Challenges facing Asia, January 2011) (Nuclear Energy Agency, 03 June 2008). Uranium represents a higher level of assured resources than is normal for most minerals. On the basis of analogies with other metallic minerals, a doubling of price from present levels could be expected to create about a tenfold increase in measured resources, over time with a pure fast reactor fuel cycle with a burn up of, and recycling of, all the uranium and actinides. Actinides are presently the most hazardous substances in nuclear waste. There is 160,000 years worth of uranium in total conventional resources and phosphate ore is available presently (Ralph EH Sims et al).

Physics of Nuclear Fission. As seen earlier; uranium is the most important ore for the nuclear power generation. Natural Uranium has two isotopes of Uranium, namely; U^{235} which is only 0.7 percent of the quantity mined and the second isotope is U^{238} which is 99.3 percent. Of these two isotopes; only U^{235} is fissile. U^{238} on absorbing neutrons produces Plutonium (Pu^{239}). In case instead of Uranium, another naturally occurring metal, Thorium (Th^{232}) is used for fission reaction (case of Fast Breeder reactors), it produces U^{233} on absorption of neutrons. Thus Pu^{239} and U^{233} are not naturally occurring isotopes and are produced in a nuclear reactor. The fission produces following:-

- Fission products, which are radioactive- Pu^{239}/ U^{233}
- Radiations.
- Fast neutrons at the rate of 2.5 neutrons per fission.
- Heat.

Fissile material (Pu^{239} / U^{233}) is also recovered by reprocessing the spent fuel coming out of reactor. This process is known as **closed Nuclear Fuel Cycle**. In breeder reactors / fast breeder reactors more fissile material can be produced than what is consumed.

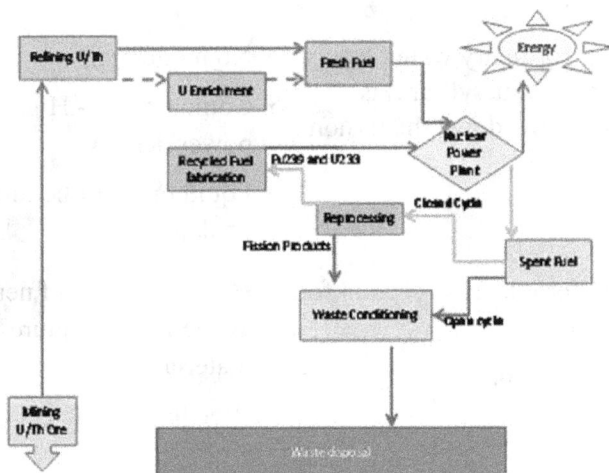

Figure-3.3: Open and Close Nuclear Cycle

• As can be appreciated that to make the nuclear power generation sustainable over a long time, especially if the availability of natural Uranium is limited, as is the case with India, 'Close Cycle' is the most viable option. It is a very interesting piece of record that when the entire world was following open cycle, India doggedly continued to work to develop closed cycle and now it is a reality. Advantage of closed cycle is that spent fuel is reprocessed to produce fissile material for breeder reactor. More on it a little later.

Type of Nuclear Reactors

There are two types of nuclear reactor systems namely Thermal Reactors and Fast Reactors. Their comparison is as per Table- 3.1

Table-3.1: Comparative study of Thermal Vs Fast Reactors

Thermal Reactors	Fast Reactors
Fission is sustained primarily through thermal neutrons (E≈ 0.025 eV)	Fission is sustained by fast neutrons (E≈1MeV)
• Moderator (ordinary water, heavy water, graphite, beryllium) is required to slow down the fission neutron.	• No moderator. • Compact core- High core power density.
• Large core	• liquid metal or helium gas as coolant.
• Very high fission cross-section for thermal neutrons.	• Higher number of neutrons available for capture in fertile material.
• Less fuel inventory	• Breeding possible.

Current fission reactors in operation around the world are second or third generation systems, with most of the first-generation systems having been retired some time ago. Research into advanced generation IV reactor types was officially started by the Generation IV International Forum (GIF) based on eight technology goals. The important parameters are as follows:-

- Better nuclear safety.

- Better proliferation resistance.

- Minimum waste.

- Optimum natural resource utilization.

- The ability to consume existing nuclear waste in the production of electricity.

- Cost viability to build and run such plants.

It may be noted that these reactors (Generation-IV) would mostly differ significantly from current operating light water reactors, and are generally not expected to be available for commercial construction before 2030 (Internet download: http://ossfoundation.us/projects/energy/nuclear).

Fast Breeder Reactors. As compared to current PHWRs and LWRs which use U^{235} (0.7 percent of all natural uranium), fast breeder reactors use U^{238} (99.3 percent of all natural uranium). It has been estimated that there is up to five billion years' worth of U^{238} for use in these power plants (John McCarthy). Breeder technology has been used in several reactors, but the high cost of reprocessing fuel safely, at 2006 technological levels, requires uranium prices of more than US $ 200 per kg before becoming economically viable (World Nuclear Association, "Advanced Nuclear Power Reactors", updated up to June 2013). Breeder reactors are still being pursued as they have the potential to burn up all of the actinides in the present inventory of nuclear waste while also producing power and creating additional quantities of fuel for more reactors via the breeding process (Fred Pearce). In 2005, there were two breeder reactors producing power; the Phénix (Phoenix in English) in France, which has since been shut down in 2009 after 36 years of operation, and the BN-600 Reactor, a reactor constructed in 1980 at Beloyarsk, Russia; which is still operational. The electricity output of BN-600 is 600 MW. Russia plans to expand the use of breeder reactors with the operationalization of next reactor in the series namely; BN-800 Reactor, which is scheduled to become operational in 2014 (World Nuclear News, 24 January 2013). Simultaneously technical design of a yet larger breeder reactor; BN-1200 reactor is being worked out. It is expected that the design is likely to get finalized during current year (2013) itself, with construction planned to commence by 2015 (World Nuclear News, 27 June 2012). Japan has a MOX fueled, Breeder Reactor, located at Monju; in the Fukui prefecture. It was lying in a state of shut down since 1995[11]. It was restarted in 2010; however it worked for just three months and once again got shut down after some equipment fell into the reactor during the reactor's checkup. It is now being planned to become re-operational during late 2013 (The Asahi Shim bun Report dated 09 November 2012). China and India are also building their respective breeder reactors. In case of India; one Fast Breeder Test Reactor (FBTR) is already operational since 1985 and a 500 MWe PFBR is under construction which is scheduled to become operational by 2015. India has further plans to build four more fast breeder reactors by 2020 (PTI, Hindustan Times

---

11 It was shut down in 1995 when Sodium which was used as coolant had leaked, resulting into a fire.

dated 20 February 2012). China appears to have made a better progress and her 'China Experimental Fast Reactor' has begun producing power since 2011 (Xinhua English News dated 31 October 2012).

Thermal Breeder Reactors. An alternative to the fast breeder reactors is thermal breeder reactor; which uses U^{233}, bred from thorium as a bye product of fission, in the thorium fuel cycle. Thorium is about 3.5 times more commonly available than uranium in the earth's crust, and has different geographic characteristics. This would extend the total practical fissionable resource base by 450 percent (World Nuclear Association, "Thorium" updated up to June 2013).

Nuclear Waste and Waste Management

Nuclear Waste. The most important waste from a Nuclear Power Plant (NPP) is spent nuclear fuel. It primarily is composed of unconverted uranium; as well as significant quantities of Trans-Uranic actinides (mostly plutonium and curium). In addition, about 3 percent of it forms fission products from the nuclear reactions. The actinides (uranium, plutonium, and curium) are responsible for the bulk of the long-term radioactivity, whereas the fission products are responsible for the bulk of the short-term radioactivity (MI Ojovan & WE Lee, 2005). The existing nuclear energy producing assets of the world, generate about 10,000 metric tons of the spent nuclear fuel each year (Benjamin K Sovacool, 2011). High-level radioactive waste management concerns disposal of highly radioactive materials created during production of nuclear power. It is a major critical issue; which needs to be addressed, as a part of an effective nuclear waste management strategy. The technical issues in accomplishing this task are challenging; because for an extremely long period of time the radioactive waste remains deadly to living organisms. Of particular concern are two long-lived fission products; Technetium-99 (half-life 220,000 years) and Iodine-129 (half-life 15.7 million years) (Environmental Surveillance, Education and Research Programme at Idaho national Laboratory of USA, 2008), which continue to dominate the radioactivity from the spent nuclear fuel even after a few thousand years. The most troublesome trans uranic elements in spent fuel are Neptunium-237 (half-life two million years) and Plutonium-239 (half-life 24,000 years) (Vandenbosch, 2007). Consequently, high-level radioactive waste requires sophisticated treatment and management to successfully isolate it from the biosphere. This usually necessitates treatment, followed by a long-term management strategy involving permanent storage, disposal or transformation of the waste into a non-toxic form (Ojovan, MI; Lee, WE, 2005). Presently, waste is mainly stored at individual reactor sites and there are over 430 locations around the world where radioactive material continues to accumulate. Some experts suggest that centralized underground repositories which are well-managed, guarded, and monitored, would lead to a vast improvement in the waste management (Montgomery, Scott L, 2010). There is an "international consensus on the advisability of storing nuclear waste in deep geological repositories" (Al Gore,2009), with the lack of movement of nuclear waste in the 2 billion years old natural nuclear fission reactor in Oklo, Gabon being cited as "a source of essential information today." (Bruno Comby, December 2005). As of 2009 there were no commercial scale purpose built underground repositories in operation (US Department of Energy Office of Civilian Radioactive Waste Management, Yucca Mountain Project, DOE/YMP-0010, November 2004). The Waste Isolation Pilot Plant in New Mexico has been taking nuclear waste since 1999 from production reactors, but as the name suggests, it is a R&D facility. A nuclear plant needs to be disassembled and removed. Much of the disassembled nuclear plant needs to be stored as low level nuclear waste (Jon Samseth et al 2012).

Waste Management. Governments around the world have been considering a range of waste management and disposal options. However, only a limited progress towards implementing long-term waste management solutions has been achieved (Paul Brown, 14 April 2004). This is partly because the time frames in question when dealing with radioactive waste range from 10,000 to millions of years (Report by the Committee on Technical Bases for Yucca Mountain standards of national research Council, 1995), according to studies based on the effect of estimated radiation doses (Environmental Protection Agency,22 August 2005). Disposal of nuclear waste is often said to be the Achilles' heel of the industry (Montgomery Scott L). There is not a single final storage facility for nuclear waste available anywhere in the world. Safe secure storage of high level waste over thousands of years remains unproven, leaving a deadly legacy for future generations. Despite this the nuclear industry continues to generate more and more waste each day. Even U.S. is having a complex situation on account of lack of storage facility which has further been compounded by the lack of consensus on how to store 68,000 tons of spent fuel lying in concrete casks on the premises of nuclear plants. Worse still is the fact that this quantity is increasing by 2,000-3,000 tons every year. Although a sum of $28 billion is available in a trust fund created to tackle this problem, a move to store the fuel in a repository in the Yucca mountains in Nevada State has already failed. Therefore new initiatives are needed to be thought of. Some of the measures which are employed or are presently in the domain of R&D are as follows:-

- **Use of Advanced Reactors** - Some proposed nuclear reactor designs such as the American Integral Fast Reactor and the Molten salt reactor can use the nuclear waste from light water reactors as a fuel, transmutating it (nuclear waste) to isotopes that would be safe after only hundreds of years, instead of tens of thousands of years. This offers a potentially more attractive alternative to deep geological disposal (Duncan Clark, 09 July 2012).

- **Use of thorium in a reactor** especially designed for thorium (rather than mixing in thorium with uranium and plutonium (i.e. in existing reactors). Used thorium fuel remains only a few hundreds of years radioactive, instead of tens of thousands of years which waste from uranium based systems remain (NWT Magazine, October 2012).

- **Nuclear fusion** reactions have the potential to be safer and are likely to generate less radioactive waste than fission (T Hamacher and AM Bradshaw, October 2001).These reactions appear potentially viable, though technically appear at this point in time quite difficult and have yet to be created on a scale that could be used in a functional power plant. Fusion power has been under intense theoretical and experimental investigation since the 1950s. Nuclear fusion, in the form of the '**International Thermonuclear Reactor**' (ITER) is predicted to achieve an energy return on investment between 2020 and 2030. With a follow on commercial nuclear fusion power station, Demonstrated Power Plant (DEMO)[12], estimated to be operational by 2030 (Internet down load: ITER Information Service, "Beyond ITER" and 14

12 DEMO is intended to be built upon the expected success of the ITER. The ITER's goal is to produce 500 MW of fusion power for at least 500 seconds and as against this the DEMO will be able to produce at least four times that much power on a continued basis. While ITER's goal is to produce 10 times, as much power as is required; for the breakeven, DEMO's goal is to produce 25 times of that kind of power quantum. DEMO will also be the first fusion plant to generate electrical power.

August 2013). Fusion powered electricity generation was initially believed to be readily achievable, as fission power had been. However, the extreme requirements for continuous reactions and plasma containment led to projections being extended by several decades. More than 60 years after the first attempts, commercial power production from fusion reaction is believed to be unlikely before 2050 (IBID).There are also suggestions for a power plant to come up, based upon a different fusion approach; that is of a Inertial fusion power plant. Bottom line is that the power generation through fusion energy route is still in the research domain and therefore cannot be counted as a waste management technique as of now.

- **Latest in Nuclear Energy Conversion Technology-**
  Hybrid nuclear power is a proposed means of generating power by the use of a combination of nuclear fusion and fission processes. The concept dates to the 1950s, and was briefly advocated by Hans Bethe during the 1970s, but largely remained unexplored until a revival of interest in 2009 happened by a number of researchers, mainly due to delays in the realization of pure fusion. When a sustained nuclear fusion power plant is built, it has the potential to be capable of extracting all the fission energy that remains in spent fission fuel, reducing the volume of nuclear waste by orders of magnitude. More importantly it will help in eliminating all actinides, present in the spent fuel, which are cause of safety concerns, (Ed Gerstner, 02 July 2009). As the name itself suggests, there is a long way before this concept takes a concrete shape and still a longer way for it to become commercially and technically viable.

Reprocessing- It involves the chemical extraction of contaminated uranium and plutonium from used reactor fuel rods. There are now over 230,000 kilograms of plutonium stockpiled around the world from reprocessing. *As an aside; only five kilograms is sufficient for one nuclear bomb, thus the world is literally sitting on the stockpile of nuclear bombs.* Reprocessing, it may be noted, is not the same as recycling.[13] Reprocessing

---

13 Entire spent fuel is not waste, as plutonium and uranium – which can be recycled – contribute to about 98 percent of the spent fuel, and thus only the remaining two to three per cent of spent fuel is waste. Therefore used nuclear fuel (UNF) has long been reprocessed to extract fissile materials for recycling to provide fresh fuel for existing and future nuclear power plants. Details are at : http://analysis.nuclearenergyinsider. com/operations-maintenance/recycling-spent-nuclear-fuel-ultimate-solution-us#sthash.

is extraction of fissile material from used fuel and recycling is converting extracted fissile material into feed for the reactor. The volume of waste, if not reprocessed, increases many tens of times and millions of litres of radioactive waste are generated which is discharged into the sea and air each day. The process also demands the transportation of radioactive material and nuclear waste by ship, rail, air and road around the world. An accident or a terrorist attack could release vast quantities of nuclear material into the environment. There is no way to guarantee the safety of nuclear waste. Current LWRs make relatively inefficient use of nuclear fuel, subjecting only U^{235} isotope present in the fuel to the process of fission and thus leave a substantial quantity of waste. Nuclear reprocessing can make this waste reusable. Also more efficient reactor designs, such as Generation III reactors,[14] which are currently under construction, might achieve a higher burn up efficiency of the available resources, as compared to the current vintage generation II reactors[15], which make up the vast majority of the current reactors worldwide (World Nuclear association, "Radioactive waste Management", updated up to April 2012). Reprocessing can potentially recover up to 98 percent of the remaining uranium and plutonium in spent nuclear fuel, putting it into new mixed oxide (MOX) fuel. This produces a reduction in long term radioactivity within the remaining waste, since this is largely short-lived fission products, and reduces its volume by over 90 percent. Reprocessing of

---

m32s5HTp.dpuf:

14 Generation –III reactors have higher operational life of 60 years, extendable to 120 plus years as compared to 40 years, extendable to 60 years of Generation II reactor. In the case of Generation- III reactors; frequency of core damage events/ million reactor year is much lower; 3 as compared to 60 for generation –II reactor. These reactors make more efficient use of uranium by using 17 percent less uranium per unit of electricity generated. The first Generation-III rector is operational since 1996 at Kashiwazaki.

15 A generation II reactor is a design classification for a nuclear reactor, and refers to the class of commercial reactors built up to the end of the 1990s. The nomenclature for reactor designs, describing four 'generations', was proposed by the US Department of Energy when it introduced the concept of generation IV reactors. The designation generation II+ reactor is sometimes used for modernized generation II designs built post-2000, such as the Chinese CPR-1000, in competition with more expensive generation III reactor designs. Prototypical generation II reactors include the PWR,CANDU, BWR, AGR, and VVER. These are contrasted to generation I reactors, which refer to the early prototype of power reactors, such as Shipping port, Magnox, Fermi 1, and Dresden. Typically, the modernization includes improved safety systems and a 60-year design life. Generation II reactor designs generally had an original design life of 30 or 40 years. However, many generation II reactors are getting their life-extended to 50 or 60 years, and a second life-extension to 80 years may also be economical in many cases.

civilian fuel from power reactors is currently done in Britain, France and Russia (Former USSR), soon will be done in China and India, and is being done on an expanding scale in Japan. Capacity of India has enhanced in recent times and it is presently 300 tons per annum (using four PHWRs). The full potential of reprocessing has not yet been achieved because it requires breeder reactors, which are not commercially available in as much quantity as desired, because so far the concept in the West was to optimally use Uranium/ enriched uranium for power generation. France is generally cited as the most successful reprocessor, but it presently recycles only 28 percent (by mass) of the yearly fuel use, 7 percent within France and another 21 percent in Russia (Peter Fairley, dated 01 February 2007). Reprocessing is not allowed in the U.S (Anthony Andrews dated 27 March 2008)[16]. The Obama administration has continued to disallow reprocessing of nuclear waste, citing nuclear proliferation concerns (Internet down load, 08 July 2009). In the U.S., spent nuclear fuel is currently treated as a waste (World Nuclear Association, "Processing of Used Nuclear Fuel", updated up to June 2013).

Safety Setup

It should be emphasized that a commercial power reactor simply cannot under any circumstances explode like a nuclear bomb because fuel of a NPP is not enriched beyond about five percent. The International Atomic Energy Agency (IAEA) was set up by the United Nations Organization (UNO) in 1957. One of its functions was to act as an auditor of world nuclear safety, and this role was enlarged substantially following the Chernobyl accident in 1986. It prescribes safety procedures and reporting of even minor incidents. The Role of the IAEA has further been strengthened since 1996. Every country, which operates Nuclear Power Plants, has a nuclear safety inspectorate which works closely with the IAEA.

Economics of Nuclear Power

Comparison with Renewable Sources of Energy. The cost of nuclear power has followed an increasing trend whereas the cost of electricity is declining in case of wind power (Ryn Wiser et al). In 2011, wind power became as inexpensive as natural gas, and anti-nuclear groups have suggested that in 2010 solar power became cheaper than nuclear power

---

16 It is a legacy of Carter years when it was considered; a route to weponization.

(Miranda Marquit). Data from the US Energy Information Administration (EIA) in 2011 estimated that in 2016, solar energy will have a levelized cost of electricity almost twice that of nuclear (21¢/kWh for solar, 11.39¢/kWh for nuclear), and wind somewhat less (9.7¢/kWh). Wind power and PV cells are variable renewable energy sources, meaning they are not dispatchable. Both, like nuclear, require buffering, with pumped hydro storage (EIA, November 2010). However due to nuclear power plant's capacity factor of 80-90 percent, in comparison to intermittent wind power's 30-40 percent, the requirements for pumped storage are much less than those needed for wind power. From a safety stand point, in terms of lives lost per unit of electricity delivered, nuclear power, is comparable to and in some cases, lower than many renewable energy sources (Internet download: David JC Mackay).

Capital Cost of Nuclear Power Plants. During the 1970s and 1980s rising economic costs (related to extended construction times largely due to regulatory changes and pressure-group litigation) (Bernard L Cohen) and falling fossil fuel prices made nuclear power plants, then under construction, less attractive. In the 1980s (U.S.) and 1990s (Europe); flat load growth and electricity liberalization also made the addition of large new base load capacity unattractive. Following the 2011 Fukushima nuclear accident, costs are expected to increase further for currently operating and new NPPs, due to increased requirements for on-site spent fuel management and elevated design basis threats (Professor Stephen Ansolabehere et al).

Cost of Decommissioning. The price of energy inputs and the environmental costs of every NPP continue long after the facility has finished generating its last bit of electricity. Both nuclear reactors and uranium enrichment facilities must be decommissioned, returning the facility and its parts to a safe enough level to be entrusted for other uses. After a cooling-off period that may last as long as a century, reactors must be dismantled and cut into small pieces to be packed in containers for final disposal. The process is very expensive, time-consuming and dangerous for workers, hazardous to the natural environment, and presents new opportunities for human error, accidents or sabotage (Benjamin K Sovacool, 2011). The total energy required for decommissioning can be as much as 50 percent more than the energy needed for the original construction. In most cases, the decommissioning process costs between US $300 million to US$5.6 billion. Decommissioning at nuclear sites which have experienced a serious accident are the most expensive and time-consuming. In the U.S. there are 13 reactors that have permanently been shut down and are in various phases of decommissioning, and none of them have completed the process (IBID).

Analysis of the Economics of Nuclear Power

- **Issue of Liability**- It must take into account as to who bears the risks of future uncertainties. To date all operating NPPs have been developed by state-owned or regulated utility monopolies (Ed Crooks) where many of the risks associated with construction costs, operating performance, fuel price, accident liability and other factors were borne by the consumers rather than suppliers. In addition, because the potential liability from a nuclear accident is so great, the full cost of liability insurance is generally limited/ capped by the government. In case of the USA it is formal and governed by an act; The Price-Anderson Act: the Third Decade, NUREG-0957 of 1983. It is the responsibility of the U.S. Nuclear Regulatory Commission to decide the quantum of the subsidy. Many countries have now liberalized the electricity market where these risks and the risk of cheaper competitors emerging before capital costs are being recovered and are borne by the plant suppliers and operators rather than consumers, which leads to a significantly different evaluation of the economics of new nuclear power plants (John Deutch).

- **NPP versus Wind Turbine**- According to Lappeenranta University of Technology, an economic life span of a typical nuclear power plant is around 40 years, while wind turbines have a life span of around 25 years (Tarjane Risto, Kivisto Aija). However, wind turbines are much easier to decommission and replace with new ones, extending the life of the wind farm indefinitely, where as nuclear facilities must be closed at the end of their useful life. The cost of both nuclear power and wind power are dominated by the construction costs of the plant. As far as operation and maintenance costs are concerned there were two views. According to the US EIA for nuclear power it was estimated to be slightly higher than wind power in 2008 (Annual energy Outlook 2013 dated 28 January 2013), however; according to Lazard it was found to be considerably cheaper. (Lazard's Levelized Cost of energy Analysis).

- Nuclear power has been compared to renewable energy as neither produce greenhouse gases in operation and both have low lifecycle greenhouse gas emissions (Internet download: WNA Report).

- **Carbon Signature** - Along with other sustainable energy sources, nuclear power is a low carbon power generation method of producing electricity. An analysis of the literature on its total life cycle emission intensity finds that it is similar to other renewable sources in a comparison of GHG emissions per unit of energy generated (Internet down Load 24 January 2013). Therefore; since 1970 when nuclear power stations became commercial, the nuclear energy has been instrumental in prevention of 64 giga tons of carbon dioxide equivalent (Gt CO_2- eq) of GHG emission as compared to enormous amount of emissions that would have been produced if the power was generated by burning fossil fuels in a thermal power station. (Pushker A Kharecha and James E Hansen).

Mean number of deaths prevented annually by nuclear power
1971-2009

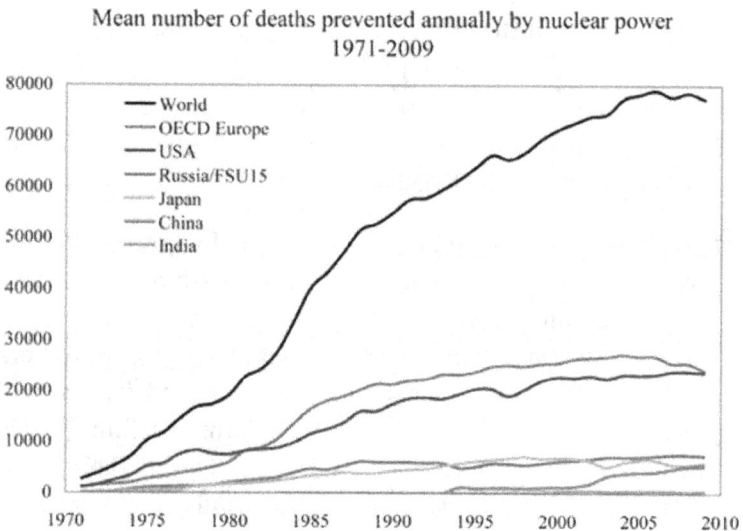

Source: Pushker A and James E Hansen, "Prevented Mortality and Greenhouse Gas Emissons from Historical and Projected Nuclear Power", published in Environmental Science & technology

Figure-3.4: Mean Number of Deaths Prevented

Analysis. In the aftermath of the accident at Japan's Fukushima Daichi NPP in March 2011, future of the nuclear power in the global energy supply matrix has become somewhat uncertain. However before drawing any hasty conclusion, certain relevant facts need to be taken into account and these are, firstly; nuclear energy is an abundant, low carbon source of base load power, which can make a major contribution to the mitigation of global climate change and prevent air pollution. An analysis of the historical data reveals that the nuclear energy has helped in prevention of on an average 1.84 million air pollution related deaths besides preventing almost 64 Gt CO_2-eq of emissions which would have been the result of the power generation following the thermal power production route. Secondly; a trend analysis of the global projection data up to 2050 with Fukushima accident factored in, brings out that on an average 4,20,000- 7.04 million deaths would be prevented and 80-240 Gt CO_2-eq of emissions would be mitigated, depending on which fuel the nuclear energy would be compared with for the time period up to 2050. For example; unrestrained use of natural gas to produce same amount of power will result into far more number of deaths on account of resultant pollution and also will not be able to address the environmental degradation due to climate change problem. (Pushker A Kharecha and James E Hansen).

Why Nuclear Energy

A report on "The Role of the IAEA to 2020 and beyond", was prepared by an independent Commission at the request of the Director General of the IAEA in 2008. The commission had following view:

"Expanded use of nuclear technologies offers immense potential to meet developmental needs. In fact, to satisfy energy demands and to mitigate the threat of climate change- two of the 21st century's greatest challenges- there are major opportunities for expansion of nuclear energy in those countries that choose to have it".

It may be noted that only about 150 tons of uranium is needed for a yearly power generation capacity of 1000 MWe as against approximately 2.6 million tons of coal which would be needed for the same quantum of power in a coal based thermal power plant and this assessment does not take into account the advantage which a relatively clean fuel like nuclear energy has over the traditional coal based power generation in terms of pollution control and logistic inconvenience on account of use of coal as a feedstock for power generation (Ratan K Sinha). By a study done by a research organization; 'Urban Emission, for Conservation Action Trust', it has been revealed that in 2011-2012, emissions from Indian coal plants (111 in number) have resulted into 80,000 to 115,000 premature deaths and more than 20 million asthma cases. From an exposure to pollution, the study quantifies the additional health impacts such as hundreds of thousands of heart attacks, emergency room visits, hospital admissions, and lost workdays caused by coal-based emissions that will take place. The study estimates that the monetary cost associated with these health impacts exceeds Rs.16,000 to 23,000 crores (\$ 3.3 to 4.6 billion) per year (Conservation Action Trust). As far as logistic load is concerned a minimum of five goods train per year would be needed to transport coal from mines to power plant per year for 1000 MWe capacity. (Ratan K Sinha).

Proponents of nuclear energy contend that nuclear power is a sustainable energy source that reduces carbon emissions and increases energy security by decreasing dependence on imported energy sources (Jay Newton-Small). Proponents further claim that nuclear power produces virtually no conventional air pollution, such as greenhouse gases and smog, in contrast to fossil fuels which cause substantial amount of air pollution. Nuclear energy can produce stable power unlike many other renewable energy sources which are intermittent in nature (as they depend on weather conditions) lacking large-scale and cheap ways of storing energy (WNA, updated up to July 2013). It is felt that unless used with due rationing, oil as a resource is likely to run out, and it has been proposed by a number of analysts that the nuclear energy could be one of the important replacement energy source (M King Hubbert). Proponents claim that the risks of storing waste are small and can be further reduced by using the latest technology in newer reactors, and the operational safety record in the Western world is excellent when compared to the other major kinds of power plants (Bernard Cohen, 1990).

Opponents of the nuclear energy argue that this form of energy exposes people to threats on account of resultant/ residual radiations and the environment degradation (Jeffrey St Clair). These threats include the problems of processing, transport and storage of radioactive nuclear waste, the risk of nuclear weapons proliferation and terrorism, as well as health risks and environmental damage from uranium mining (Global Energy Scenario Report, January 2007). They also contend that reactors themselves are enormously complex machines where many things can and do go wrong; and there have been serious nuclear accidents (Benjamin K Sovacool, 2008). Critics do not believe that the risks of using nuclear fission as a power source can be fully offset through the development of new technology. They also argue that when all the energy-intensive stages of the nuclear fuel chain are considered, from uranium mining to nuclear decommissioning, nuclear power is neither a low-carbon nor an economical electricity source (Kurt Kleiner, October 2008). Author: The fear of these people is not supported by any kind of firm evidence. After all in last sixty years there have been only three known serious accidents[17]. On the contrary the environmental degradation and medical problems on account of the use of fossil fuel/ petroleum products far outweigh the threats on account of nuclear energy.

Nuclear Power in the World Today

From the first commercial NPP of a capacity of 5 MW of grid connected electrical power at Obninsk in present day Russia in 1954, nuclear energy has come a long way. Today there are some 435 nuclear power reactors operating in 31 countries plus Taiwan, with a combined capacity of over 370 GWe. In 2011 these provided 2518 billion kWh, about 13.5 percent of the world's electricity WNA update as on 31 July 2013). As far as research reactors are concerned there are 284 reactors in 56 countries (Ratan K Sinha). According to the World Nuclear Association, globally during the 1980s one new nuclear reactor started up every 17 days on average, and by the year 2015 this rate could increase to one every 5 days (WNA, updated up to March 2013). Number of plants, all over the world, is likely to double up by 2030 (Steve Kidd).

China has 17 nuclear power reactors in operation, 28 are under construction, and more, including some of the world's most advanced ones, are being planned to give a four-fold increase in nuclear capacity to at least 58 GWe by 2020, then possibly 200 GWe by 2030, and 400 GWe by 2050. Addressing the climate change is one of the important reasons for change in the profile of China's energy basket. China has become largely self-sufficient in reactor design and construction, as well as other aspects of the fuel cycle, but is making full use of western technology while adapting and improving it. China's policy is for closed fuel cycle (WNA update as on 10 December 2010). China may achieve its long-term plan of having

---

17 Three Mile, Chernobyl and Fukushima accidents.

40,000 MW of nuclear power capacity four to five years ahead of schedule (Internet download: 21cbh.com dated 21 September 2010).

USA is the world's largest producer of nuclear power, accounting for more than 30 percent of worldwide nuclear generation of electricity. The country has 104 nuclear reactors which produce over 19 percent of total electrical output during 2011 (WNA update as on 31 Jul 2013). Although since 1977 no new reactor has been built, probably based on the safety fears, however the USA is going back to nuclear energy; while licenses of almost half its reactors have been extended to 60 years (WNA update as on 31 July 2013), there are three which are under construction presently. but by 2020, 4-6 new units are likely to come up, although falling gas prices since 2009 have put the economic viability of some of these projects in doubt (IBID) and plans, to build another dozen, are under serious consideration (Mathew L Wald). Lot of R&D work is in progress to evolve new and more efficient reactor designs as US in their National energy Policy of 2001 have set; expansion of nuclear energy as one of the objectives (James A Lake). Another interesting feature of US nuclear programme is that the basic route which US follows is enriched uranium (PWR), probably because of a large prospected holding of uranium[18]. Nuclear power capacity worldwide is increasing steadily, with over 60 reactors under construction in 13 countries (WNA update as on 31 Jul 2013). An interesting aspect is that, despite major plans for new units in the USA and Russia, most reactors on order/ planned are in the Asian region.[19] (Author: *Recent interest in Nuclear energy is not only to improve the indigenous electrical supply within USA but also is driven by commercial interests of supplying the reactors to new emerging markets like China and India. One of the major drivers for the signing of Indo US Civil Nuclear Agreement was the commercial interest of USA as it provided a large number of jobs in nuclear energy industry.*)As such in the U.S. and Europe, investment in research and in the nuclear fuel cycle has continued and new NPPs may come up in US and Europe. Some nuclear industry experts attribute it to a three fold strategy of Western powers, which is; firstly; to grab the opportunity to supply nuclear energy related equipment to developing nations, secondly; to get better prepared to tackle likely electrical shortages in future (James A Lake) and finally; to deal with global warming issues, created substantially by themselves only,

---

18 US produced 4.1 million pounds of uranium during 2012 (EIA- May2013 Report)

19 Notably in China, South Korea, Russia and India.

but now trying to address those issues with the support of the developing countries.

A group of 12 top economies was analyzed and it was found that there is a strong correlation between GDP and the electrical consumption of the country. Exception are two countries; Russia and Canada, who despite being lower on GDP Ladder (Russia is 9th and Canada is 12th) have electrical production rank as 4th and 6th respectively which is probably on account of extreme cold climate conditions prevailing in those countries. Most of the countries in this group (12 countries having highest GDP) have nuclear energy generation programme with France being highest; 80 percent and Italy presently having no nuclear programme. However Italy imports 20 per cent its power requirement from France which, as said earlier, has a very elaborate nuclear power programme (Ratan K Sinha).

There is a possible impediment to erection of NPP, as only a few companies worldwide have the capacity to forge single-piece reactor pressure vessels (Steve Kidd), which are necessary in the most common reactor designs. Utilities across the world are submitting orders years in advance of any actual need for these vessels. Other manufacturers are examining various options, including making the component themselves, or finding ways to make a similar item using alternate methods (Yoshifumi Take Moto). Other solutions include using designs that do not require single-piece forged pressure vessels such as Canada's Advanced CANDU Reactors or Sodium-cooled Fast Reactors.

4

Nuclear Energy in India

Table-4.1: Sources and their Potential

Resource	Amount	Potential (GWe-year)
Coal	38 billion Tons (extractable)	7614
Oil+ Oil Equivalent Gas	12 billion Tons	5833
Natural Uranium	61,000 Tons Metal	328 in PHWRs
Thorium	2,25,000 Tons Metal	• 42,231 in FBRs • 2,25,000 in Breeder Reactors
Hydro	150 GWe	69/year
Renewable	100 GWe	33/ year
Total Solar Insolation	6,00,000Gwe	

Source: DAE, "A Strategy for Growth of Electrical Energy in India", August 2004

Comment:

• Table 4.1 puts in perspective most of the indigenous energy bearing resources. It is of interest to note that India has huge potential for the exploitation of thorium and solar energy. However; in both these cases availability of commercially viable technology is the issue.

• As far as uranium is concerned confirmed reserves are limited but technology for its exploitation (PHWR) is available up to 700 MW[1]

---

1 Post Fukushima, none of the plants anywhere in the world have been shut down. In fact a number of new plants are being planned world over, including few in India. It however is of extreme importance that the need for a cooling of the NPP, post an event of extreme

and therefore international cooperation is the key for progressing on this route. This clearly brings out the criticality of an early operationalization of the Indo-US Civil Nuclear Agreement and other similar agreements.

- Need for a more extensive and wider exploration leveraging technology in Oil and Gas along with uranium is the need of the hour. For uranium exploration, a special drive needs to be launched to generate awareness to allay the fears of the concerned population.

- A very dynamic review system be introduced to find the technological solutions which can respond to the environmental needs in real time with respect to other indigenous resources like, coal[2] , hydro[3] and oil[4] with a view to ensure their optimum exploitation.

- R&D should be strengthened to evolve commercially viable technologies with respect to resources, like shale gas, gas hydrates, OTEC, which presently for want of commercially viable related technologies are not being utilized.

- Constant endeavour be made to leverage technology to enhance efficiency of the systems for exploitation of the resources which are the main stay of the current energy supply system.

Evolution of India's Nuclear Programme

India decided to explore the possibility of using nuclear energy for power generation as early as 1948. Accordingly; it established an Atomic Energy Commission (AEC) under the chairman ship of Dr Homi Jehangir Bhabha in 1948 vide Government of India, Notification No F-402/DSR/48 dated 10 August 1948 under the clause 13 of the Atomic Energy Act No XXIX of 1948. The commission had three members and the AEC was tasked to work under the guidance of the Prime Minister with following mandate:-

---

nature, is not to be overlooked.

2 Clean coal technologies be introduced.

3 Instead of large hydro projects, SHP can be thought off.

4 Strengthening of NELP and international cooperation should be considered.

- To take such steps as may be necessary from time to time to protect the interests of the country in connection with the Atomic Energy by exercising the powers conferred on government of India by the provisions of Atomic Energy Act.

- To survey the territories of the Indian Dominion for the location of useful minerals for their utilization for harnessing atomic energy.

- To promote research in their own laboratories and to subsidize such research in existing institutions and universities. Specific steps will be taken to increase teaching and research facilities in nuclear physics in the universities.

In August 1954, the Government of India was advised to establish a Department of Atomic Energy (DAE) for undertaking research and development in the field of nuclear technology. Accordingly a Department of Atomic Energy (DAE) was created under the Office of the Prime Minister. In March 1958 AEC was reconstituted by a special resolution by the Government of India to further strengthen the AEC with full executive and financial powers. This resolution also made the Chairman of the AEC an ex officio Secretary of the DAE (Auth: New Resolution (No 13/7/58-Adm. Bombay 01 March 1958). The resolution laid down that the Commission would have full time and part time members totaling not less than three and not more than seven according to the choice of the Chairman (Dhirendra Sharma). On 15 September 1962, Indian parliament passed the enhanced and the most powerful Atomic Energy Act ever envisaged. It replaced atomic Energy Act of 1948. From a modest beginning in 1948, nuclear establishment of the country has come of age over a period of time. The broad organization of the nuclear establishment is as given in the Appendix B attached. In addition organisation of the Bhabha Atomic Research Centre (BARC) which is a premier institution of the Department of Atomic Energy and its activities are listed at Annexure I and Annexure II respectively.

Initially the AEC and DAE received international cooperation, and by 1963 India had two research reactors and four nuclear power reactors. In spite of the humiliating defeat in the border war by China in 1962 and China's nuclear testing in 1964; India continued to adhere to the peaceful uses of nuclear energy. On 18 May 1974 India performed a 15 kt Peaceful

Nuclear Explosion (PNE).[5] The Western powers considered this test as a case of nuclear weapons' proliferation by India and cut off all financial and technical help, even for the production of nuclear power. However, undaunted by such a response, India continued its pursuit of peaceful exploitation of nuclear energy and in fact made substantial progress in mastering the entire nuclear cycle. After gaining experiences in various aspects of the nuclear cycle, India using her existing/ indigenously developed nuclear infrastructure, carried out second set of tests on 11-13 May 1998 using both fission and thermonuclear devices [6]. The international community viewed the event as a serious breach of the Non-Proliferation Treaty (NPT)[7] and the Comprehensive Test Ban Treaty (CTBT)[8]; both deemed essential by USA and other big five nuclear states; to stop the spread of nuclear weapons. India considers these treaties discriminatory and has not signed these treaties and as such is not bound by them. India

---

5 It was a high explosive implosion fission device, which had a close resemblance to American nuclear bomb code name 'Fat Man' which was dropped at Nagasaki. It was assembled at Terminal Ballistic Research Laboratory, Chandigarh and its detonation system was developed at the High Energy Material Research Laboratory, Pune. The six kilogram s of plutonium came from the CIRUS reactor at BARC. The neutron initiator was of polonium-beryllium type. The complete nuclear bomb was engineered and finally assembled by the Indian Engineers in Trombay before transporting it to Indian Army's Test Range at Pokhran in Rajasthan. The detonation was done by a team of Indian Army on 18 May 1974. Code named as 'Smiling Buddha' it was partially successful. Though claimed to be having a yield of 12 kt, but American Intelligence community estimated that the yield was between 4-6 kt.

6 Code named as Shakti-98, a series of five nuclear bombs, named; Shakti-I to V were test exploded by India at the Indian Army's Pokhran Test range on 11th and 13th May 1998. Device used in this test were both fission/ fusion. Maximum claimed yield by the BARC was 58 kt but independent estimates confirmed the yield to be 45 kt. Three laboratories of DRDO were involved in designing, testing and producing components for the bombs, including the advanced detonators, the implosion and high voltage trigger systems. These laboratories were responsible for weaponizing, system engineering, aerodynamics, safety interlocks and flight trials. On 11th May Operation Shakti was initiated with the detonation of one fusion and three fission bombs. On 13th May two additional sub kilo ton devices were detonated. Shakti-1 was a thermo nuclear device, Shakti-II was a plutonium implosion device (an improvement on Smiling Buddha Device), and Shakti- III was an experimental boosted fission device that used non weapon grade plutonium. Shakti-IV and Shakti-V were experimental devices. Significantly Shakti-V used uranium-233. This clearly indicated India's capability to deal with Thorium cycle. There was suspected to be an additional device present, but was not detonated. One of the greatest achievements of Indian project team was the camouflage with which Indians managed to hide the preparations.

7 India is not a signatory to this Treaty.

8 India is not a signatory to this Treaty.

feels that these treaties favour declared five nuclear weaponized states (USA, Russia, UK, France and China), and thus are indicative of an effort on the part of these five nuclear states to maintain a sort of nuclear apartheid. India has made it clear that she is prepared to sign if genuine nuclear disarmament is included as an integral part of these treaties. (Chaturvedi Ram)

India's Atomic Energy programme has been a mission-oriented comprehensive programme with a long-term focus. From its inception the guiding principle of this programme has been self-reliance through the utilization of domestic mineral resources, and building up capability to face possible restrictive regimes like NPT and CTBT by 'Nuclear Haves' to deny technology and the exchange of resources. The events of the last 50 years, in fact have validated this approach.

It may also be noted that nuclear energy is one area; where post PNE of 1974; India became almost an international pariah and as such growth of India's nuclear programme has practically been indigenous. It is only post Indo-US nuclear agreement of 2008 that India has started getting some sort of support from other countries. In this connection following Venn diagram explains the situation well:-

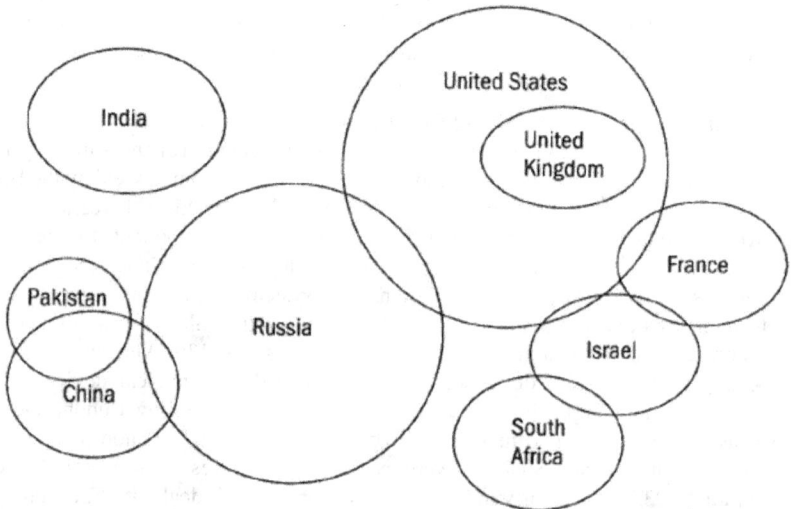

Figure-4.1: Sharing Of Nuclear Knowledge between the Nations

Source: Adopted from Christopher E Paine and Mathew G Mckinzie, Science and Global Security, 1998, Volume- 7, PP-151-193

Analysis: The interactions between various countries as indicated in the above Venn diagram clearly bring out the sources of the proliferation of the nuclear technology to various countries. As can be seen, Indian programme generally grew indigenously but post 1974 PNE, India got isolated as far as international cooperation was concerned and as such Indian nuclear programme in general and India's nuclear weaponization programme in particular evolved totally indigenously.

Development of Indian Nuclear Programme. Homi Jehangir Bhabha conceptualized the use of nuclear energy as an important element in the energy supply matrix of India nearly 60 years ago, when India possessed hardly any infrastructure to support India's nascent nuclear technology exploitation programme. It is amazing to realize that as early as 1944, Dr. Homi Jehangir Bhabha (1909–1966) had envisioned;

> *"When nuclear energy would have been successfully applied for power production, in say a couple of decades from now, India will not have to look abroad for its experts but will find them ready at home".*

Equally amazing was the understanding of the first Prime Minister of India, Pandit Jawaharlal Nehru, who understood the importance of the nuclear energy and encouraged morally and administratively Bhabha and his team to lay the foundations of the Indian atomic energy programme, with 'Self-Reliance' as the motto. In this connection a speech by Pandit Jawahar Lal Nehru on 26 June 1946 at a public gathering, even before India became independent, is relevant. Nehru said,

> *"…. I have no doubt India will develop her scientific researches and I hope Indian scientists will use the atomic force for constructive purposes….."*

Thus a highly motivated, greatly knowledgeable and fully determined scientific community led by Bhabha was encouraged to start working on the establishment of nuclear infrastructure. It needs to be noted that it was the period of Cold War and every nation who had nuclear programme was fairly secretive about their respective programme, because most of it was in security domain and not exactly in energy domain. Accordingly, a R&D establishment, named Atomic Energy Establishment, Trombay, was progressively set up post independence, which in due course of time became the premier research and capacity building institution of India.

This was renamed as the Bhabha Atomic Research Centre (BARC), after India tragically lost Bhabha in an air crash in 1966. It incorporates research reactors, basic facilities for nuclear research, supporting infrastructure, and conducts training of human power in all disciplines both; core and peripheral, which are relevant for the growth of the nuclear energy.

Six decades later, India is having one of the most extensive plans in the world which aims to add a very large number of nuclear power plants to boost the power generation capability. She has a very optimistic and ambitious nuclear power programme, perhaps the largest and the most unique among all the developing countries. The uniqueness of this programme is derived from the concept of a 'Three-Stage Nuclear Power Programme' propounded by Dr. Bhabha in November 1954 during the first National level Atomic Energy Conference. He presented a paper, *"The Need for Atomic Energy in the Under-developed Countries"* at the Second International Conference on the Peaceful Uses of Atomic Energy in Geneva in September 1958. Dr. Bhabha and Dr. N.B. Prasad presented another paper, *"A Study of the Contribution of Atomic Energy to a Power Programme in India"*. These papers argued the importance of nuclear power in the developing countries – a fact which is being realized by developing countries even today after 65 years. Utilization of abundant thorium resources in combination with moderate uranium resources through a Three-Stage Nuclear Power Programme for India was also outlined. The Three-Stage Nuclear Power Programme essentially links the fuel cycles of each stage in a manner that the availability of the nuclear fuel continues to multiply and the potential of nuclear energy generation several-hundred folds while graduating from one stage to the next.

Three Stage Nuclear Programme of India

In November 1954, Bhabha presented the three-stage plan for national development (Ramana MV) at the conference on "Development of Atomic Energy for Peaceful Purposes" which was also attended by India's first Prime Minister Jawaharlal Nehru. Four years later in 1958, the Indian government formally adopted the three-stage plan (Woddi, Paul et al, Page-7).

Stage I – Pressurized Heavy Water Reactor. In the first stage of the programme, natural uranium fuelled pressurized heavy water reactors (PHWR) produce electricity while generating plutonium-239 as a by-product. PHWR was a natural choice for implementing the first stage because it had the most efficient reactor design in terms of uranium utilization, and the existing Indian infrastructure in the 1960s allowed for quick adoption of the PHWR technology (http://en.wikipedia. org/wiki/India_three-stage_nuclear_power_programme#_cite_note-footnoteBucher20094-36). India correctly calculated that it would be easier to create heavy water production facilities (required for PHWRs) than uranium enrichment facilities (required for LWRs) (http://en.wikipedia. org/wiki/India_three-stage_nuclear_power_programme#cite_note-footnotegadekar2008-37). Natural uranium contains only 0.7 percent of the fissile isotope U^{235}. Most of the remaining 99.3 percent is U^{238} which is not fissile but can be converted in a reactor to the fissile isotope Pu^{239}. Heavy water (Deuterium Oxide: D_2O) is used as moderator and coolant (Ministry of External Affairs, Government of India). Indian uranium reserves are capable of generating a total power capacity of 420 GWe-years, but in order to ensure that existing plants get a lifetime supply of uranium, it becomes necessary to limit the number of PHWRs fueled exclusively by the indigenous uranium reserves. US analysts calculate this limit as being slightly over 13 GW in capacity (Tellis Ashley). Several other sources estimate that the known reserves of natural uranium in the country permit only about 10 GW of capacity to be built through indigenously fueled PHWRs (Manpreet Sethi), (Stephenson John et al), (Dewan Parag; Sarkar A), (Rai Ajai K). The three-stage programme explicitly incorporates this limit as the upper cut off of the first stage, beyond which PHWRs are not planned to be built (Anil Kakodakar). Almost the entire existing base of Indian nuclear power (4780 MW) is composed of first stage PHWRs, with the exception of the two Boiling Water Reactor (BWR) units at Tarapur (Banerjee Sri Kumar), (PTI Report). The installed capacity of Kaiga station is now 880 MW, making it the third largest after Tarapur (1400 MW) and Rawatbhata (1180 MW) (PTI Report). The remaining three power stations at Kakrapar (Business Standard Report), Kalpakkam (Subramanium Kandula) and Narora (Jayan, TV) have 2 units of 220 MW each, thus contributing 440 MW each to the grid. The 2 units of 700 MWe each, both PHWRs that are under construction at Kakrapar (Business standard Report), (Internet: http://en.wikipedia.org/wiki/India's_three-stage_nuclear_power_programme#CITEREFWorld_Nuclear_News2010) and Rawatbhata (World Nuclear News) respectively, and the one planned for Banswara (Deewan, Parag; Sarkar, A) would also come under the first stage of the programme, totaling a further addition of 4200 MW. These additions will bring the total power capacity from the first stage PHWRs to near the total planned capacity of 10 GW called for by the three-stage power programme (Anil Kakodkar), (Banerjee Sri Kumar). Capital costs of PHWRs is in the range of Rs. 6 to 7 crore ($1.2 to $1.4 million) per MW (Jain, SK, Page-9), coupled with a designed plant life of 40 years. Time required for construction has improved over a period of time and it is now about 5 years. Tariffs of the operating plants are in the range of Rs. 1.75 to 2.80 per unit, depending on the life of the reactor (Deewan, Parag; Sarkar, A,). In the year 2007–08 the average tariff was Rs.2.28. The tariffs of new plants to be set up, both indigenous and imported, are expected to be about Rs. 2.50 in the year 2015 (at 2007 prices) (Jain, SK, pp- 8).

Stage II – Fast Breeder Reactor. In the second stage, fast breeder reactors (FBRs) would use a mixed oxide (MOX) fuel made from Pu^{239}, recovered by reprocessing spent fuel from the first stage, and natural uranium. In FBRs, Pu^{239} undergoes fission to produce energy, while the U^{238} present in the mixed oxide fuel transmutes to additional Pu^{239}. Thus, the Stage II FBRs are designed to "breed" more fuel than they consume. It is estimated that for the same quantity of fuel in second stage, power generated would be six times that of stage one. (Ref: Discussion with Dr R Chidambaram, Principal Scientific Advisor to Government of India and the former Chairman of the AEC). Further once the inventory of Pu^{239} gets built up, thorium would be introduced as a blanket material in the reactor and transmuted to U^{233} for use in the third stage (Jain, SK, pp-3). The surplus plutonium bred in each of the fast reactors would then be used to set up more such reactors. This will lead to a growth of Indian civil nuclear power capacity to a point where the third stage reactors using thorium as fuel would be brought online. This point (graduation from second to third stage) is estimated to be approximately around 50 GW of nuclear power capacity. (Zee News), (Subramanyam TS), (Kamat, Nand Kumar). Theoretically, the natural uranium in the first stage using PHWRs is likely to yield around 29 EJ of energy. However same uranium once having gone through multiple fuel cycles in a fast breeder reactor (FBR) can be made to yield between 65 and 128 times more energy (Bucher, RG and Page-7). Studies with regard to the content of the Fast Breeder Test Reactor (FBTR) programme and the type of test reactor to be built were undertaken in the early 1960s. The construction of FBTR started in 1972 and completed in 1984 (Atomic Energy I India, Chapter XXIX, Published as Part Of Pursuit and Promotion of Science). It first reached criticality in October 1985, making India the sixth nation to have the technology to build and operate an FBTR after United States, UK, France, Japan and the former USSR[9] . The reactor was designed to produce 40 MW of thermal power and 13.2 MW of electrical power. Though the FBTR has rarely operated at its designed capacity however it has been possible to operate it up to a maximum power of 17.4 MW (Dr. Baldev Raj, Director, Indira Gandhi Centre for Atomic Research, "Fast Breeder Programme : An Inevitable Option For Energy Security" part of 2004-Technology Day Speech, AIR). It has also remained shut down between 1987 and 1989 due to technical problems. Critical components of a reactor; like main vessel, inner vessel and the roof slab of the reactor, rotating plugs, control rod drive mechanisms, sodium pumps, steam generators, remote fuel handling machines, turbo alternator, and instrumentation and control packages are being manufactured in India. Foreign input now constitutes only 20 per cent of the total cost (IBID), and it is mainly towards know how and the cost of the raw materials. An important achievement was the fabrication of mixed carbide fuel at BARC (IBID). This indigenously designed and developed fuel was unique, as the mixed carbide fuel core was being used as the driver for the first time anywhere in the world. The fuel burn up now has crossed 72,000 Mega Watt Days/Metric Ton of Heavy Metal (MWd/tHM). As a logical follow-up of FBTR, it was decided to build a prototype fast breeder reactor (PFBR) and the detailed design work was taken up at the Indira Gandhi Centre for Atomic Research (IGCAR). The financial sanction for the project was given by the Cabinet in September 2003. The total project cost sanctioned was Rs.3492 crore and the expected unit cost it was anticipated, would be about Rs.3.25 in the year 2010 when the plant was likely to be completed. The construction of PFBR began in 2004. The PFBR type of reactor is designed to operate with a mixture of Uranium Oxide and Plutonium Oxide (MOX) as fuel because of the extensive experience available in the world with this kind of fuel. Thereafter, Bharatiya Nabhikiya Vidyut Nigam Ltd (BHAVINI), a public sector company under the Department of Atomic Energy (DAE), was given the responsibility to build fast breeder reactors in India (Dewan and Sarkar, pp-88), (Zee News). The construction of the PFBR at Kalpakkam was scheduled to be completed by 2012, thereafter loading of the fuel was expected to be completed by early part of 2013, followed by one year of

---

9 In its present state as Legatee of USSR, Russia is also pursuing the fast breeder route for generating power. BN-600 reactor is operational since 1980, BN-800 reactor is scheduled to become operational in 2014 and the design for BN-1200 reactor is likely to be ready during the current year.

system testing after the reactor had achieved the criticality. Commercial generation of electricity was planned by 2015 (Zee News). *However latest indications are that it is unlikely to be ready by the date planned and may get further postponed to 2017. Thus there would have been an overall delay of over a decade by the time it gets completed, because the first date for completion which was given, was 2007. Therefore scientific community in India and R&D organizations, need to work harder due to appreciate criticality of this reactor for the future of the nuclear power generation plans of India.* It has also been experienced that the rate of breeding of plutonium using MOX is quite slow. On the contrary FBRs with metallic alloy of uranium, plutonium and zirconium are known to offer better and faster breeding. The type of mixed fuels and their details are as given in the Appendix C attached. India has further plans to undertake the construction of four more FBRs as part of the 12th Five Year Plan spanning 2012–17, thus targeting a total of 2500 MW from the five reactors (Jain, SK; pp-10), (Times of India, 2008). One of these five reactors is planned to be operated with metallic fuel instead of oxide fuel, as the design of the reactor has the flexibility to accept metallic fuel also, although the reference design of the reactor is for oxide fuel (Bucher, RG; pp-21). It has been reported by the DAE that the design on reactor using metallic fuel is likely to firm up only in next nine years and is likely to be introduced by 2020. If the future FBR is built with the provision of the use of metallic fuel instead of oxide fuel, the power production capacity due to availability of additional plutonium would increase to 15,500 MW by 2030 as against 11,500 MW which will be achieved with oxide fuel (Anshu Bharadwaj et al). Government of India has already allotted Rs.250 crore for pre-project activities for two more 500 MW units, although the locations of these reactors are yet to be finalized (Zee News).

Doubling time. Doubling time refers to the time required to extract double the amount of fissile fuel as an output, which was fed as an input into the breeder reactor (Tongia and Arunachalam). This concept is critical for understanding the time duration that is unavoidable while transitioning from the second stage to the third stage of Bhabha's plan, because building up a sufficiently large fissile stock is essential for the large deployment of the third stage. In Bhabha's 1958 papers on the role of thorium, he pictured a doubling time of 5–6 years for breeding U^{233} in the Th–U^{233} cycle. This estimate has now been revised to = or > 70 years due to technical difficulties that were unforeseen at the time conceptualization by Bhabha. There is another school of thought as evident from the latest publications of the

DAE that despite the delay which has already occurred, the doubling time of fissile material in the fast breeder reactors can be brought down to about 10 years by choosing appropriate technologies with short doubling time (Reuters Report dated 13 February 2010).

Table-4.2: Comparison between Breeder and Thorium Based Technologies to Compress Time

Type	U^{238} - Pu^{239} Cycle (Time in years)	Th - U^{233} Cycle (Time in years)
Oxide	17.8	108
Carbide-Lee	10	50
Metal	8.5	75.1
Carbide	10.2	70

Analysis: Above discussion and the Table-4.2; clearly brings out that it would take anywhere between a minimum of 10 and a maximum of 70 years to transit from Stage II to Stage III and such an indication gives the core area of immediate impending work, for the researchers in the R&D organizations to cut down the time to progress from Stage II where India is just about reaching and thereafter to graduate to Stage III when India will have enough fuel to start more reactors. Some of the hedging issues in this case will be; the progress on the design of the reactor that needs to be made in the absence of technical support from any other source, response of the NSG and finally the necessary funding. Also, India will have to be ready for the contingency when such a scenario does not materialize and therefore planning will have to be done for the energy management in such a situation. During the discussion with various conceptual level decision makers, like Dr R Chidambaram, Principle Scientific Advisor to government of India and the former Chairman AEC; Shri Shyam Saran, Chairman, Research and Information System for Developing Countries & the Chairman of NSAB and Shri BK Chaturvedi, Member (Energy), Planning Commission, it became clear, that though they all look forward to Stage III getting materialized as planned, but they all are planning to find alternative solutions during short to medium term wherein operationalization of the Stage III of India's Nuclear Programme, is not a part of the solution.

Stage III – Thorium Based Reactors. A Stage-III reactor or an Advanced nuclear power system involves a self-sustaining series of

Th^{232}-U^{233} fuelled reactors. This would be a thermal breeder reactor, which in principle can be refueled – after its initial fuel charge – using only naturally occurring thorium. According to the three-stage programme, Indian nuclear energy could grow to about 10 GW through PHWRs fueled by domestic uranium, and the growth above that will have to come from FBRs till about 50 GW (Majumdar, S). The third stage is to be deployed only after this capacity has been achieved (Subramaniam, TS). According to replies given during the Question Hour in the Indian Parliament on two separate occasions, 19 August 2010 and 21 March 2012, it was informed by the Government of India that a large scale deployment of the thorium based nuclear technology is likely only after the stabilization of the doubling time of nuclear fuel for at least three to four decades of the operations of the fast breeder reactors (Loksabha Q&A, 2010 and 2012). Therefore, Full exploitation of India's domestic thorium reserves is not likely to occur until after the year 2050 (Stephenson, John; Tynan).

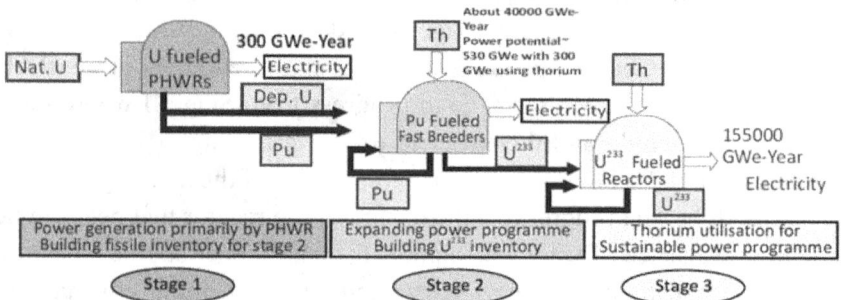

Source: Indian Member Committee's Report, published in Indian Energy Handbook2012, pp-43, published by World Energy Council, uploaded on www. wecimc.org/

Figure-4.2: of Three stage Nuclear Programme

Parallel Approaches

Since a long delay is anticipated in the direct thorium utilization in the three-stage programme, the country is now looking at reactor designs that allow more direct use of thorium in parallel with the sequential 'Three-Stage Programme' (Jain, SK, pp-4). There are three options, which are under consideration. These are; Accelerator Driven Systems (ADS) (Bibao y Leon, Sama), Advanced Heavy Water Reactor (AHWR) and

Compact High Temperature Reactor (CHTR). (Bucher, RG, page-14-20) (Diwan & Sarkar Page-89), (Subramaniam, TS). Another design of reactor namely; Molten Salt Reactor is also under consideration based on some recent reports (Banerjee, SK, pp-21), (World Nuclear Association, Mar 2012), (Subramaniam, TS), (Kalam, APJ Abdul).

Advanced Heavy Water Reactor (AHWR). Of the options mentioned above, the design for AHWR is ready for deployment. AHWR is a 300 MWe vertical pressure tube type, boiling light water cooled and heavy water moderated reactor, using U^{233}–thorium MOX and Pu ^{239}–thorium MOX (Krivit, Lehr & Kingery 2011, pp- 98). It is expected to generate 65 percent of its power from thorium and can also be configured to accept other types of fuels in the core. These are; enriched uranium and uranium–plutonium MOX (Banerjee 2010, pp- 16). There was another plan for constructing an AHWR with a plutonium–thorium core combination in 2007 (The Economic Times 2007), however the approved design is as mentioned above. This AHWR design was sent for an independent pre-licensing design safety review by the Atomic Energy Regulatory Board (AERB), the results of which were found to be satisfactory (Times of India, Chennai edition, 20 December 2008). Finally the AHWR design that will be taken up for construction is to be fueled with 20 percent low enriched uranium (LEU) and 80 percent thorium (One India News 2011), (Zee News 2009). The LEU for this AHWR design is readily available in the world market (Nuclear Energy Institute 2012). As of November 2011, construction was scheduled to have commenced after the site was to be identified by middle of 2012 (present status of construction is not known). After identification of the site, it will take another 18 months to get clearances on regulatory and environmental grounds. Construction is estimated to take six years. If everything goes according to plan, AHWR could be operational in India by the end of this decade (Rahman 2011), (Business Line 2012). However it needs to be noted that the design of the AHWR would offer very little growth for the fuel build up which is essential for wide deployment of the third stage, and therefore the impact of AHWR on the accumulated fissile material is likely to be negative (Tongia & Arunachalam 1997). Thus construction of AHWR may not contribute much to the growth of the Indian Three Stage Nuclear Plan. Significant part, however, is that this reactor will strengthen indigenization of the Indian nuclear programme, as it would be using thorium and as such will not reduce dependence on imported natural uranium.

Fuel Reserves and Research Capability of India

Indian energy resource base was estimated to be capable of yielding a total electric power output of the order shown in the Table-4.3 below (Tongia Rahul and Arunachalam), (Rethinaraj and TS Gopi), (Jain SK). Indian government recognized that thorium was a source that could provide power to the Indian people for a long time (Woddi, Paul et al PP-8), (Maitra, 2009, pp-59).

Table-4.3: Power Potential of Indian Resources

Energy resource type	Amount (tons)	Power potential (TWe-year)
Coal	54 billion	11
Hydrocarbons	12 billion	6
Uranium (in PHWR)	61,000	0.3–0.42
Uranium (in FBR)	61,000	16–54
Thorium	~300,000	155–168 or 358

Source: As above

Uranium Reserves. According to a report issued by the IAEA, India has limited uranium reserves, consisting of approximately 54,636 tons of "reasonably assured resources", 25,245 tons of "estimated additional resources", 15,488 tons of "undiscovered conventional resources, and 17,000 tons of "speculative resources". According to NPCIL, these reserves are sufficient to generate only about 10 GWe for about 40 years (Iyengar PK et al). In July 2011, it was reported that a four-year-long mining survey done at Tummalapalle mine in Kadapa district of Andhra Pradesh had yielded confirmed reserve figure of 49,000 tons with a possibility that it could rise to 150,000 tons (Bedi Rahul). These are promised to be one of the top 20 of the world's reserves. Mr SK Banerjee, the then Chairman of AEC, said on a visit to a nuclear plant in the Western State of Rajasthan that if what is assumed to be a possibility; comes true, it will become the largest uranium mine in the world (IBID). But Department of Atomic Energy officials warned that the mineral, which is refined into nuclear fuel to produce energy and power, is not "high but low-grade uranium" (IBID). The Atomic Minerals Directorate for Exploration and Research (AMD) of India, which explores uranium in the country, has so far discovered

44,000 tons of natural uranium ($U3O8$[10]) in just 15 kilometres (9.3 miles) of the 160 kilometers (99 miles) long belt (TS Subramanium). This was an increase from an earlier estimate of 15,000 tons for that area (Dharur Suresh).

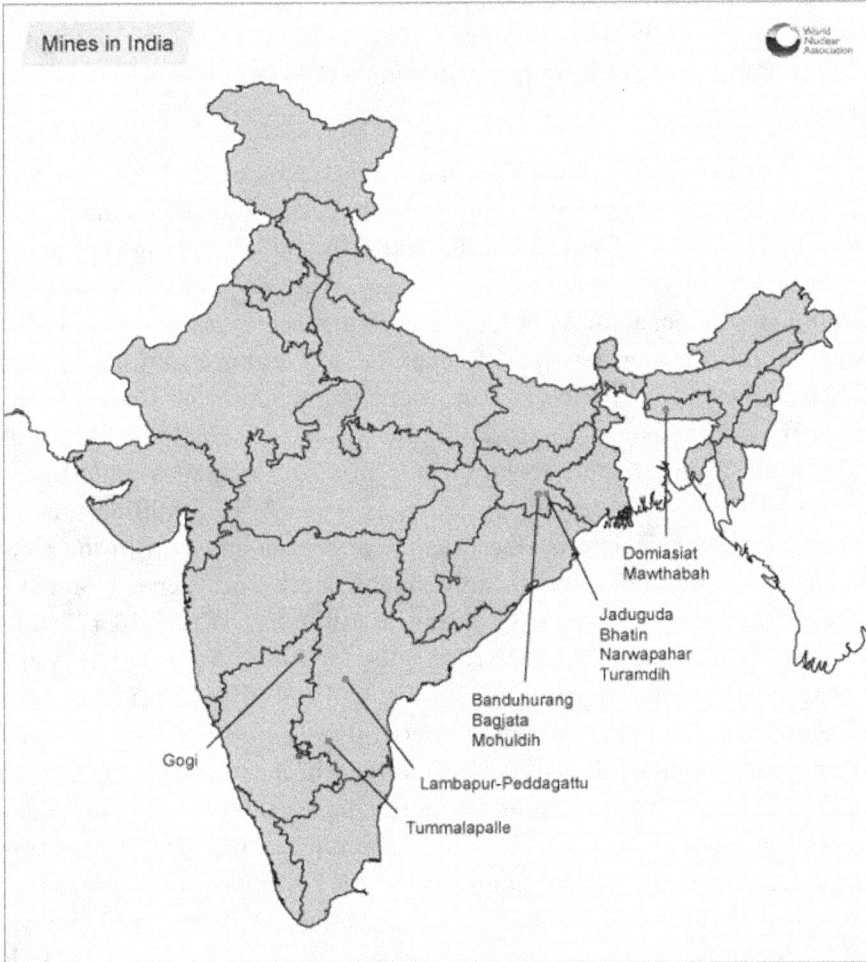

Figure-4.3: Uranium Mines in India

Source: Nuclear Power Plants, published by World Nuclear Association, up dated upto 10 April 2013 uploaded on http://www.world-nuclear.org/info/Country-Profiles/Countries-G-N/India/#.Ud1o4fmmjdA

Uranium Exploration. Exploration is carried out by the Atomic

---

10 U308 Corporation is a Canadian uranium exploration company, focused on rapidly growing resources to meet the rising demand for clean nuclear power.

Minerals Directorate for Exploration and Research (AMD). Mining and processing of uranium is carried out by Uranium Corporation of India Ltd (UCIL), a subsidiary of the Department of Atomic Energy (DAE), in Jharkhand near Calcutta. All mines shown in Figure-4.3 are underground except Banduhurang. Common mills are near Jaduguda (2500 tons/ day) and Turamdih (3000 tons/ day, expanding to 4500 tons/ day). Jaduguda ore is reported to be of low grade, containing only 0.05-0.06 percent of the uranium.

Thorium. India has only around 1–2 percent of the global Uranium reserves. On the other hand, thorium reserves are bigger; around 12–33 percent of global reserves, according to IAEA and US Geological Survey (McHugh, Liam), (Fin, AL), (Patel, Sonal), (Bromby Robin). Several in-depth independent studies put Indian thorium reserves at 30 percent of the total world's thorium reserves (Bucher, RG), (Gordon Sandy), (Jayaram KMV), (Ferguson Charles D). As per official estimates shared in the country's Parliament in August 2011, the country can obtain 846,477 tons of thorium from 9,63,000 tons of ThO_2, in association with other heavy metals. This ThO_2 is readily available as part of 10.7 million tons of monazite sand available on the beaches of Kerala and also in the river sands of Kerala. Indian monazite contains about 9–10 percent of ThO_2 (Press Information Bureau, Government of India). The 8,46,477 tons figure compares with the earlier estimates for India, made by IAEA and US Geological Survey of 3,19,000 tons and 2,90,000 to 6,50,000 tons respectively. The 8,00,000 tons figure is given by other sources as well (Krivit, Steven et al). It was further clarified in the country's Parliament on 21 March 2012 that, "Out of nearly 100 deposits of the heavy minerals, at present only 17 deposits containing about 4 million tons of monazite have been identified as exploitable. Mineable reserves are ~70 percent of identified exploitable resources. Therefore, about 2,25,000 tons of thorium metal is available for nuclear power programme (Department of Atomic Energy, Government of India). India is generally considered as the leader of thorium based research in the world (Press Trust of India), (Rehman Maseeh). It is also, by far the most committed nation as far as the use of thorium fuel is concerned, and no other country has done as much neutron physics work on thorium as India has done (Maitra, pp-61). The country has published about twice the number of papers on thorium as its nearest competitors, during each of the years from 2002 to 2006 (Banerjee Sri Kumar). BARC had the highest number of publications in the thorium area, across all research institutions in the world during the period 1982-2004. During the same period, India ranks an overall second behind the United States in the research output on thorium (Kademani). Analysis shows that majority of the authors involved in thorium research publications appear to be from India (Internet, Wikipedia). According to Siegfried Hecker, a former director (1986–1997) of the Los Alamos National Laboratory in the USA,

> *"India has the most technically ambitious and innovative nuclear energy program in the world. The extent and functionality of its nuclear experimental facilities are matched only by those in Russia and are far ahead of what is left in the US"* (Kademani, BS).

In recent times lots of beach sand, rich in monazite is being exported from Kerala at times illegally (Ajay K Das, Mining Weekly.com, 12 October 2012) *(Author: It is indeed a serious national security issue and it needs to be declared a national asset and a total ban on its export be imposed.)*

Depleted Uranium. Uranium enrichment produces many tons of depleted uranium (DU) which consists of U^{238} with most of the easily fissile U^{235} isotope removed. U^{238} is a tough metal with several commercial uses, for example; aircraft production, radiation shielding, and armor, as it has a higher density than lead. Depleted uranium is also controversially used in munitions; DU penetrators (bullets or APFSDS tips) which are also referred as "self sharpened", due to uranium's tendency to fracture along shear bands (David Hambling) and (JB Stevens and RC Batra).

Indigenous Resources for Nuclear Energy Conversion: An Analysis.

The domestic reserve of 80,000 to 1,12,000 tons of uranium (approx 1 percent of global uranium reserves) is large enough to supply all of India's commercial and military reactors as well as supply all the needs of India's nuclear weapons arsenal. Currently, India's nuclear power reactors consume, at the most, 478 tons of uranium per year (Ashley J Tellis). *Even if India were to enhance its nuclear power output by four times (along with the reactor base) to 20 GW by 2020, nuclear power generation would only consume 2000 tons of uranium per annum. Based on India's known commercially viable reserves of 80,000 to 1,12,000 tons of uranium, this represents a 40–50 years uranium supply for India's nuclear power reactors.*

As per the provisions of the Indo-US Civil nuclear Agreement, uranium from indigenous sources which is being used to generate plutonium for the indigenous weapons' programme has been separated from the uranium which is meant for power generation programme. It, however will, in no way, affect either of the essential activities. It may further be noted that with reprocessing and breeder reactor technology becoming a reality in near future (First PFBR is already in advanced stage of construction), this supply is likely to get stretched out over a long period of time. Furthermore, the uranium requirement of India's Nuclear Arsenal are only a fifteenth (1/15) of what is required for power generation (approximately 32 tons), meaning that India's domestic fissile material supply is more than enough to meet all needs for its strategic nuclear arsenal. Therefore, India has sufficient uranium resources to meet its strategic (for military use) and power requirements in the foreseeable future.

Present Status of Nuclear Power Generation in India

Growth of Nuclear Technology in India. India's first research nuclear reactor and its first nuclear power plant were built with the assistance from Canada (David Martin), (Fuhrmann, Mathew). Based on a contract signed in 1956, a 40 MW research reactor, named as CIRUS, went critical in 1960. One of the assurances given by India while signing that contract was that it would not be used for military purposes. However no effective safeguards against such an use were formally spelt out as part of the contract (David Martin), (Fuhrmann, Mathew). The agreement for India's first nuclear power plant at Rajasthan, Rajasthan Atomic Power Plant-1(RAPP-1), was signed in 1963. It was followed by signing of contract for the RAPP-2 in 1966. The technical and design information for these reactors was given free of charge by the Atomic Energy Canada Limited (AECL) to India. The 200 MWe RAPP-1 Reactor was based on the technology used in Canada Deuterium Uranium (CANDU) reactor at Douglas Point and it began operation in 1972. It had only 45 percent indigenous content. Due to some technical problems, the reactor had to be down rated from 200 MW to 100 MW. These reactors contained rigid safeguards to ensure that neither they, nor their bye-products (plutonium) could be used for a military programme. The United States and Canada terminated their assistance after the detonation of India's first Peaceful Nuclear Explosion (PNE) in 1974. First casualty of the termination of assistance was completion of the RAPP-2, which was, at that point in time, was under construction. Due to sanctions, the RAPP-2 could not be completed in time and was completed much later through indigenous efforts in 1981.

Nuclear Power as a Source of Electricity. It is the fifth-largest source of electricity in India after; thermal, crude oil, natural gas and hydro electricity (12th Plan Document). As of 2012, India had 20 nuclear reactors in operation in six nuclear power plants (NPP), generating a total of 4,780 MW (2.9 percent of total installed base) (PTI in Hindustan Times, 27 November 2010), Information has been upgraded and has been disseminated by NPCIL, uploaded on www.npcil.nic.in during January 2011 (The Times of India, dated 19 January 2011). 21st reactor, Kudankulam-1 of 1000 MW capacity has since attained criticality and limited power supply from this plant, with effect from 22 October 2013, has started and is being fed into the power grid. Another six reactors are under construction and when completed, are expected to add an additional 5,300 MW (Verma, Nidhi) to the nuclear power kitty. Current status of operational/ under construction/ planned, NPPs is as tabulated below:-

Table-4.4: Nuclear Power Reactors in India: Present, Under Construction and Planned for Future

Unit	Type	Capacity (MWe)	Since
Operational Reactors			
Tarapur Power Plant			
• TAPS-1 (Tarapur, Maharashtra)	BWR	160	28 October 1969
• TAPS-2 (Tarapur, Maharashtra)	BWR	160	28 October 1969
• TAPS-3 (Tarapur, Maharashtra)	PHWR	540	18 August 2006
• TAPS-4 (Tarapur, Maharashtra)	PHWR	540	15 September 2005
Rajasthan Power Plant (Rawat Bhata)			
• RAPS-1 (Rawatbhata, Rajasthan)	PHWR	100	16 December 1973
• RAPS-2 (Rawatbhata, Rajasthan)	PHWR	200	1 April 1981
• RAPS-3 (Rawatbhata, Rajasthan)	PHWR	220	1 June 2000
• RAPS-4 (Rawatbhata, Rajasthan)	PHWR	220	23 December 2000

Unit	Type	Capacity (MWe)	Since
• RAPS-5 (Rawatbhata, Rajasthan)	PHWR	220	4 February 2010
• RAPS-6 (Rawatbhata, Rajasthan)	PHWR	220	31 March 2010
Kalpakkam Power Plant (Tamil Nadu)			
• MAPS-1 (Kalpakkam, Tamil Nadu)	PHWR	220	27 January 1984
• MAPS-1 (Kalpakkam, Tamil Nadu)	PHWR	220	21 March 1986
Narora Power Plant			
• NAPS-1 (Narora, Uttar Pradesh)	PHWR	220	1 January 1991
• NAPS-2 (Narora, Uttar Pradesh)	PHWR	220	1 July 1992
Kakarpar Power Plant			
• KAPS-1 (Kakrapar, Gujarat)	PHWR	220	
• KAPS-2 (Kakrapar, Gujarat)	PHWR	220	
Kaiga Power Plant			
• KGS-1 (Kaiga, Karnataka)	PHWR	220	6 November 2000
• KGS-2 (Kaiga, Karnataka)	PHWR	220	6 May 2000
• KGS-3 (Kaiga, Karnataka)	PHWR	220	6 May 2007
• KGS-4 (Kaiga, Karnataka)	PHWR	220	27 November 2010
Kudankulam Power Station			
• KNPP-1 (Kudankulam, Tamil Nadu)	VVER −1000	1000	10 August 2012@
Total Capacity		**5780**	
Under Construction			
Units Under Construction	**Type**	**Capacity (MWe)**	**Expected Date**
• KNPP-2 (Kudankulam, Tamil Nadu)	VVER −1000	1000	Mar-2014
• KAPS-3 (Kakrapar, Gujarat)	PHWR	700	Jun-2015
• KAPS-4 (Kakrapar, Gujarat)	PHWR	700	Dec-2015

Unit	Type	Capacity (MWe)	Since
• RAPS-7 (Rawatbhata, Rajasthan)	PHWR	700	Jun-2016
• RAPS-8 (Rawatbhata, Rajasthan)	PHWR	700	Dec-2016
• PFBR (Kalappakam, Tamil Nadu)$	PFBR	500	2004#
Total Capacity		**4300**	

Proposed*			
Unit proposed	**Type**	**Capacity (MWe)**	**Expected Date**
Jaitapur Nuclear Power Project	European Pressurized Reactor	9900	2017
Kudankulam, Tamil Nadu percent	VVER	2 x 1200 = 2400	
Total Capacity		**12300**	

Source:

- NPCIL website: www.npcil.nic.in
- $-BHAVINI website: www.bhavini.nic.in
- percent- Nuclear Power Plants in India: www.mapsofindia.com › Maps

Note:

@ Attained criticality on 13-14 July 2013 and limited power production has commenced since 22 October 2013. Initially it was 400 MWe and gradually will be stepped up to rated 100 MWe in a graduated manner. Delay has been on account of public protest against nuclear energy due to perceived safety issues.

*   In addition to above 16 X PHWRs of 700 MWe capacity are being taken up progressively for construction at five different inland sites which have already been identified. India is also planning to set up a number of

PWRs of indigenous design in next one decade (PTI Report, published in The Economic Times, dated 29 June 2013).

Progress as on May 2013 is 95 percent. All the major equipment has been erected and the loading of dummy fuel bundles at peripheral locations is in progress. Indigenously developed mixed oxide type fuel pins for the first core of the PFBR are under manufacture (IBID).

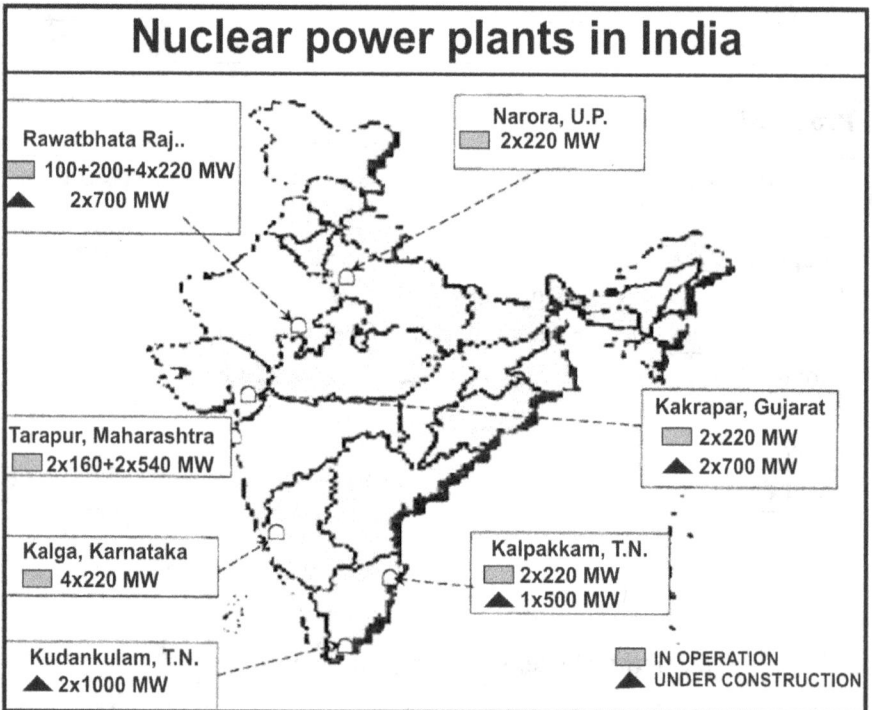

Nuclear power plants in India

Rawatbhata Raj..
100+200+4x220 MW
▲ 2x700 MW

Narora, U.P.
2x220 MW

Tarapur, Maharashtra
2x160+2x540 MW

Kakrapar, Gujarat
2x220 MW
▲ 2x700 MW

Kalga, Karnataka
4x220 MW

Kalpakkam, T.N.
2x220 MW
▲ 1x500 MW

Kudankulam, T.N.
▲ 2x1000 MW

IN OPERATION
▲ UNDER CONSTRUCTION

Figure-4.4: Location of Operational/ Under Construction Nuclear Plants

Source: Nuclear Power Plants, published by World Nuclear Association, up dated upto 10 April 2013 uploaded on http://www.world-nuclear.org/info/Country-Profiles/Countries-G-N/India/#.Ud1o4fmmjdA

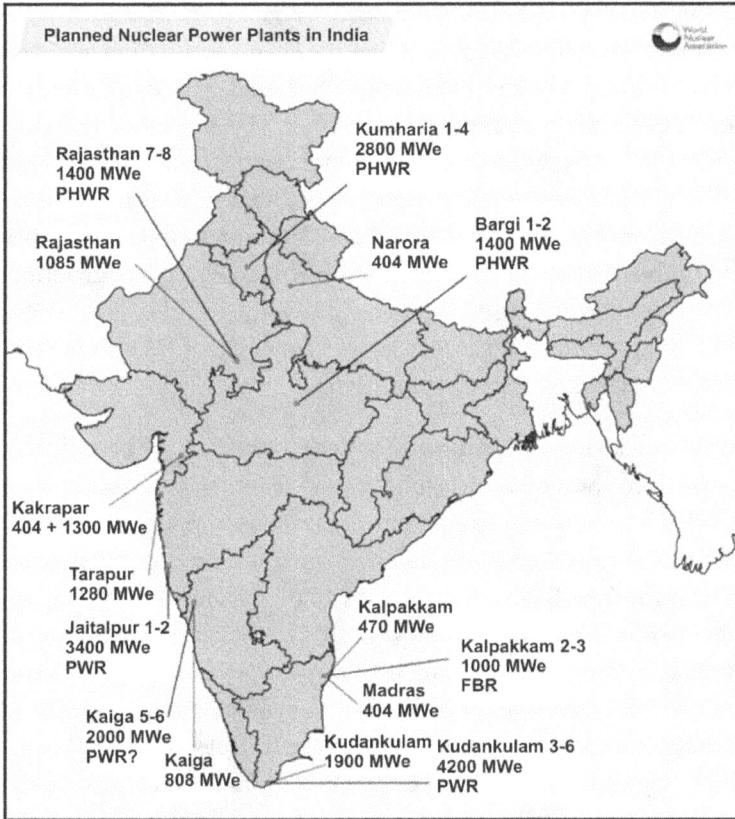

Figure-4.5 : Locations of Proposed Nuclear power Plants

Source: Nuclear Power Plants, published by World Nuclear Association, up dated upto 10 April 2013 uploaded on http://www.world-nuclear.org/info/Country-Profiles/Countries-G-N/India/#.Ud1o4fmmjdA

Note: Aim of the ongoing nuclear power programme of India is to build a capacity of 14,600 MW of nuclear energy by 2020 and by 2050 the total contribution from the nuclear energy will be 25 percent in India (IBID).

Future Plans. India now envisages increasing the contribution of nuclear power to overall electricity generation capacity from 2.8 percent to 9 percent within next 25 years (Business Standard, dated 21 January 2009). By 2020, India's installed nuclear power generation capacity is being planned to increase to 20,000 MW (2.0×10^{10} Watts, which is 20 GW) (Business Standard, retrieved 26 August 2010) or by an estimation by the World Nuclear Association in April 2013, it has been revised to 14,600 MW. *(author:This figure estimated by the World nuclear Association appears to be more realistic based on the ground realities).* Indigenous atomic reactors include TAPS-3, and 4, both of which are 540 MW reactors (NPCIL website. Retrieved on 21 August 2011). India's US $ 717 million fast breeder reactor project is expected to be operational by 2012-13 [11] (The Hindu dated 16 June 2009). Indian President A.P.J.Abdul Kalam, stated while he was in office, that "Energy independence is India's first and highest priority. India has to go for nuclear power generation in a big way using thorium-based reactors." In October 2010, India drew up an ambitious plan to reach a nuclear power capacity of 63,000 MW in 2032 (The Economic Times, 11 October 2010).

Safety Status of Indian Nuclear Plants.   According to the United Nations Scientific Committee on Effects of Atomic Radiation (UNSCEAR), regular nuclear power plant operation including the nuclear fuel cycle causes radioisotope releases into the environment amounting to 0.0002 mSv (milli-Sievert)[12] per year of public exposure as a global average (UNSCEAR Report (2008). (It is small compared to variation in natural background radiation, which averages 2.4 mSv/a globally but frequently varies between 1 mSv/a and 13 mSv/a depending on a person's location as determined by UNSCEAR) (IBID). As of a 2008 report, the remaining legacy of the worst nuclear power plant accident (Chernobyl) is 0.002 mSv/a in the form of global average exposure (a figure which was 0.04 mSv per person averaged over the entire populace of the Northern Hemisphere in the year of the accident in 1986, although it was far higher among the most affected local populations and recovery workers) (IBID). India's safety record as compared to other nuclear power user nations has been impeccable. IAEA in their review during 2013 had following to say (Dr R Chidambaram):-

- Indian nuclear power reactors are safe against extreme natural events like earthquake, tsunami, floods etc and have margins and features in design to withstand them.

- The assessment of seismic margins indicates the plant (RAPS-3 and 4) can withstand several times the design peak ground acceleration values. It may be noted that RAPP reactors are

---

11 It has already been revised to 2015 and is likely to slip further to 2017.

12 Sievert (Sv) is a unit of equivalent radiation dose, effective dose and committed dose in SI unit.

considered as some of the safest in the world (Pallav Bagla).

- Assessment of maximum flood level from tsunami, tide, wave run up indicate margins exist for coastal as well as inland sites.

- Recommendations were made to take the safety to much higher level- most recommendations have been implemented.

Public Protests. In recent times, particularly post Fukushima incident in Japan in March 2011, there has been a spurt in the protests by the local populations around proposed Indian NPP sites. Populations around proposed Indian NPP sites have launched protests that are now finding resonance around the country, raising questions about atomic energy as a clean and safe alternative to fossil fuels (Sidharth Srivastava). There have been mass protests against the French-backed 9900 MW Jaitapur Nuclear Power Project in Maharashtra and the 2000 MW Kudankulam Nuclear Power Plant in Tamil Nadu. Getting swayed by the public mood, the Government of West Bengal has refused permission to a proposed 6000 MW facility near the town of Haripur, where six Russian reactors of 1000 MW each were planned to come up (Sidharth Srivastava), (Fiona Harvey). A Public Interest Litigation (PIL) has also been filed against the government's civil nuclear programme at the Supreme Court (Sidharth Srivastava), (Ranjit Devraj). While, apprehensions about the likely nuclear disaster of the agitating public and leaders who are steering the protest, may not be based on facts as India has one of the best safety record in the world, but perceptions are not always based on facts or logic and many of them may be motivated by considerations other than genuine apprehensions.

Capacity Factor. Despite public protests, the capacity factor of Indian reactors was at 79 percent in the year 2011-12 compared to 71 percent in 2010-11. Nine out of twenty Indian reactors recorded an unprecedented 97 percent capacity utilization factor during 2011-12. With the imported uranium from France, the 2 X 220 MW PHWR reactors at Kakrapar have recorded a capacity utilization factor of 99 percent, during 2011-12. The overall availability factor for the year 2011-12 was at 89 percent.

Progress on Technology

As of 2013, attaining a net energy gain from sustained nuclear fusion reactions, excluding natural fusion power sources such as the Sun, remains an ongoing area of international physics and engineering research.

However, despite more than 60 years of relentless pursuits all over the world, to find ways and means to harness fusion energy by the research fraternity, commercial fusion power production remains unlikely before 2050 (Web Archive: "Beyond ITER").

India has been making advances in the field of thorium exploitation cycle, by working on the design and the development of a prototype atomic energy reactor at Kalpakkam, Tamil Nadu. This reactor presently christened as Prototype Fast Breeder Reactor (PFBR) will be using thorium and low-enriched uranium, a key part of 'India's three stage nuclear power programme' (Pham, Lisa).[13] In this connection 40 MW Fast Breeder Test Reactor (FBTR) made by India using mixed carbide fuel core (fabricated at BARC) as the driver for the first time anywhere in the world, is operational since 1985. Though maximum power generated by this reactor has been only 17.4 MWe but indigenous manufacture of critical components of the reactors with foreign input constituting only 20 percent of the total cost, mainly towards the knowhow and the cost of the raw materials (Dr Baldev raj, 2004) gave India tremendous confidence in operating a fast breeder reactor, besides breeding Pu^{239} and U^{233} for further use. It also gave a much needed experience to Indian nuclear establishment in the handling of mixed fuel and use of closed cycle.

Kalpakkam Mini Reactor (KAMINI Reactor). India has been attempting for some time to simultaneously work on the design of a reactor which can be used for the third stage of the India's nuclear programme. This reactor is a manifestation of that effort. It is a research reactor located at IGCAR, Kalpakkam. Jointly designed by IGCAR and BARC, it is fueled with U^{233} metal (fuel is in the form of an alloy of uranium and aluminum) produced by irradiation of thorium in another reactor. It is cooled and moderated by de-mineralized light water and reflected by beryllium oxide. Its capacity is 30 kW of thermal power at full power and it attained criticality on 29 Oct 1996. It was the first reactor in the world, designated specially to use U^{233} as the fuel. It is in line with India's vision to use thorium to produce nuclear energy on large scale in third stage of her three stage nuclear programme. This technology demonstrator

---

13 It will be a 500 MWe fast breeder reactor, which has been designed by Indira Gandhi Centre for Atomic Research (IGCAR), using a MOX (Uranium Oxide+ Plutonium Oxide) as fuel. Project was sanctioned at a cost of 3492 Crores and BHAVINI was designated as the construction agency. The reactor is coming up at Kalpakkam with the original PDC as 2010 which has now been extended to 2015. Present progress is 95.2 percent.

is meant to be a precursor of that endeavour.

Compact High Temperature Reactor (CHTR). It is a 100 kW thermal reactor which uses U^{233} + thorium (TRISO coated particle) as fuel, lead-bismuth as coolant and beryllium oxide as the moderator. It will operate at a very high temperature (1000°C). Feasibility of this reactor is complete and the experimental set up is under development.

Participation in ITER. The country has also recently re-initiated its involvement in the LENR research activities (B Sivakumar in Times of India), in addition to supporting work done in the fusion power area through the ITER initiative (ITER-India uploaded on internet).

Indian Experience of Waste Management and Reprocessing

Waste Management- India is operating waste management facilities for entire nuclear fuel cycle for over three decades. It has been experienced that the decontamination factor ranging from 10 to 1000 is achieved depending upon the process employed and the characteristic of the waste. India is self reliant in management of all type of radioactive waste arising during operation of nuclear facilities (S Kumar et al). Some of the methods employed are as follows:-

- For low and intermediate level (LIL) waste generated in a NPP chemical treatment process is employed and the residue is retained as sludge.

- At RAPS site, waste is concentrated by solar evaporation.

- At Trombay, a plant is being setup for treatment based on reverse osmosis process.

- The intermediate level alkaline waste is being treated using indigenously developed resorcinol formaldehyde resin.

- Solid waste is concentrated by compacting, baling and incineration depending upon the nature of the waste. Cement matrix is used for immobilizing of the process concentrate as chemical sludge and ash for incineration.

- The solid waste, depending upon the content is disposed off in underground engineer trenches which are created near the surface disposal facility.

- The gaseous waste is treated *in-situ*. High efficiency particulate air (HEPA) filters and impregnated activated carbon is employed to restrict the release of airborne activity to the environment.

Reprocessing- Indian reprocessing journey started way back in 1964 with the commissioning of a reprocessing plant at Trombay, serving to demonstrate the indigenous capability and expertise in this vital area of technological importance. Currently, India has three operating reprocessing plants based on PUREX[14] technology; one each at Trombay, Tarapur & Kalpakkam. While the Trombay facility reprocesses spent fuel from research reactors, the plants at Tarapur and Kalpakkam process the oxide fuels from PHWRs. Operating experiences over the years have contributed to the mastering of the PUREX technology, leading to higher recoveries, lower exposures and reduced environmental discharges. Standardization of the designs has been achieved. Additional reprocessing facilities are being setup with the active participation of Indian industry to accelerate the programme. Reprocessing of irradiated thorium has been carried out by employing the THOREX[15] process. The challenges in reprocessing of mixed oxide fuel with uranium, plutonium and thorium are being addressed. The first Plutonium Plant at Trombay reprocesses research reactor spent fuel with a capacity of 60 tons per year. Second and third plant located at Tarapur and Kalpakkum have reprocessing capacity of 100 tons each per year. Reprocessing capacities are being augmented in a phased manner to match the plutonium requirement. The planning of reprocessing capacity has to match with the requirement of Plutonium and U^{233} by FBRs and AHWRs (Chapter 6-Indian Programme on Reprocessing-BARC). Result of a cost benefit analysis suggests that the

---

14 PUREX is a chemical method used to purify fuel for nuclear reactors or nuclear weapons. It is an acronym standing for Plutonium Uranium Extraction. PUREX is the de facto standard aqueous nuclear reprocessing method for the recovery of uranium and plutonium from used "spent" or "depleted" nuclear fuel. It is based on liquid–liquid extraction ion-exchange. PUREX process was invented as part of the Manhattan Project.

15 U^{233} can be recovered and purified from neutron-irradiated thorium reactor fuels through the thorium extraction, or THOREX, process, which employs tri-butyl phosphate extraction chemistry. Irradiated fuel, containing either thorium metal or oxide, is dissolved in nitric acid containing a small amount of fluoride ion. U^{233} and thorium are co-extracted into a tri-butyl phosphate solution, which is then contacted with an aluminum nitrate solution to remove traces of accompanying fission products. Dilute nitric acid is used to preferentially remove thorium from the scrubbed organic phase. U^{233} remaining in the tri-butyl phosphate solvent is stripped into acidified water; the resulting strip solution is passed through an ion-exchange resin bed in order to concentrate and purify the U^{233}.

cost of reprocessing each kilogram of spent fuel would be approximately Rs. 26,000 (approx. $600) with assumptions favourable to reprocessing, and close to Rs. 30,000 (approx. $675) under other assumptions. These costs are lower than the corresponding figures for reprocessing plants in Europe, the USA, and Japan. No wonder most of the Western countries go for waste disposal rather than reprocessing and are following uranium route instead of thorium route because in their case adequate quantity of uranium is available and as such they prefer using uranium as a fuel and generally do not need reprocessing of waste. This methodology, in overall terms, works out economically more viable (MV Ramana and JY Suchitra).

Vulnerability to Strength through International Cooperation

As has been explained earlier, India's domestic uranium reserves are small and due to dwindling domestic uranium reserves (Seema Singh), electricity generation from nuclear power in India, had declined during the period 2006-08 by 12.83 percent (Ministry of Power). This kind of vulnerability has made India increasingly dependent on uranium imports to fuel its nuclear power industry. However the imports, which, as it is, had reduced to driblets post PNE of 1974, got totally dried up, post 1998 nuclear test (Operation Shakti), when UN Security Council passed Resolution 1172 condemning the tests and US imposed economic sanctions under their Anti Proliferation Law of 1994. It was followed by Japan and some other countries close to USA like Australia. To make matters worse, India's refusal to sign NPT & CTBT hardened the attitude of the Nuclear Suppliers Group (NSG) and as such imports became even more difficult. To enhance India's degree of difficulty the breeder technology (second stage of the nuclear programme) could not got commercialized as per plans.

It was realized by the Government of the day that the only way out of the sticky situation was to go in for international cooperation, whatever might be the cost (*against the wishes of the Indian Nuclear Establishment, which is of the opinion that India should continue to go self reliance route to retain its independence of action and access to indigenous resources unhindered*). The most important step in this direction was taken when India and USA signed the historic; Indo US Civil Nuclear Deal in 2008. This accord helped India to come out of an international isolation which was forced on India by world community since 1998, post nuclear tests by India in May 1998 (The tests consisted of five detonations, of which the first was a fusion bomb and the remaining four were fission bombs). New vistas of cooperation opened up not only with the USA but with other members of the NSG after Indo US Civil Nuclear Deal was signed. Following a waiver from the NSG[16] in September 2008 which allowed India to commence international nuclear trade (uploaded on news.outlookindia.com retrieved 22 Aug 2010), India has signed bilateral deals on civilian nuclear energy technology cooperation with several other countries, including France (up loaded on www.rediff.com/news/2008/jan/25france.htm), the USA (Reuters Report published in livemint.com. 09 October 2008), the UK (Avril Ormsby) , Canada (Montreal Gazette. 29 November 2009) and South Korea (The Times Of India. 25 July 2011). India has also uranium supply agreement with Russia (Anil Sasi), (BBC News 11 February 2010). In fact, since early 1990s, Russia has been a major supplier of nuclear fuel to India (A PTI Report uploaded on expressindia.com dated 02 Apr 2006). In addition to above, agreements have also been signed with Mongolia (Financial Express, 15 September 2009), Kazakhstan (Sanjay Dutta), Argentina (The Hindu, 24 September 2010), and Namibia (Republikeir, 02 September 2010). Besides government to government deals, an Indian private company (Dharni Sampada) has also won a uranium exploration contract in Niger (Internet upload: www.taurianresources.co.in). Relevant details of important agreements and the issues entailed are as follows:-

- **USA-** The nuclear agreement with USA led to India issuing a 'Letter of Intent' (LOI) for purchasing plants with capacity of 10,000 MW from the USA. One of the advantages which US accrued was likely reduction in the carbon signature of India due to her switching over to nuclear energy (however limited extent to which, it may have been) from thermal power (Victor, David G.," the India Nuclear Deal Implications for Global climate Change," Testimony before the US Senate Committee on Energy

---

16 Nuclear Suppliers Group (NSG) is a multinational body concerned with reducing nuclear proliferation by controlling the export and re-transfer of materials that may be applicable to nuclear weapon development and by improving safeguards and protection on existing materials. It was founded in 1974 in response to the Indian nuclear test earlier in that year. A series of meetings from 1975 to 1978 resulted in agreements on the guidelines for export, these were published as INFCIRC/ 254 by the IAEA. Only Listed items could be exported to non-nuclear states if certain International Atomic Energy Agency safeguards were agreed to, or if exceptional circumstances relating to safety existed. Initially the NSG had seven members which has now become (as on 2009) 47 members. India, despite stated support from the USA, UK and France, is still not a member of this organization.

and National Resources, 18 July 2006) (However the road ahead, post Indo US deal has not been exactly smooth. Liability concerns and a few other issues are preventing further progress on the subject. This law (The Civil Liability for Nuclear Damage Act, 2010 or Nuclear Liability Act) gives accident victims the right to seek damages from plant suppliers in the event of a mishap. It has "deterred foreign players like General Electric and Westinghouse Electric, a US-based unit of Toshiba, with companies asking for further clarifications on compensation liability for private operators" (Power Engineering Magazine. 27 February 2012).

• **Russia** - Russia has an ongoing agreement of 1988 vintage with India regarding establishing of two *vver* (water-cooled water-moderated light water power reactors) 1000 MW reactors at Kudankulam in Tamil Nadu (George Nirmala). A 2008 agreement caters for provision of additional four third generation VVER-1200 reactors of capacity 1170 MW each (Sasi Anil). Russia has assisted in India's efforts to design a nuclear plant for its nuclear submarine (NTI Report dated 14 August 2009). In 2009, Russia clarified that she would not agree to impose curbs on the export of sensitive technology to India. A new accord was signed in Dec 2009 with Russia gives India freedom to proceed with the closed fuel cycle, which includes mining, preparation of the fuel for use in reactors, and also reprocessing of spent fuel (PTI Report of 07 Dec200), (Bagchi Indrani).

• **France** - After the NSG agreed to allow nuclear exports to India, France was the first country to sign a civilian nuclear agreement with India, on 30 September 2008 (Samanta Pranab Dhal). During the December 2010 visit of the French President Nicholas Sarkozy to India, framework agreements were signed for the setting up of two third-generation EPR reactors of 1650 MW each at Jaitapur, Maharashtra by the French company AREVA. The deal caters for the first set of two of six planned reactors and the supply of nuclear fuel for 25 years (Yep, Eric & Jagota). The contract and pricing is yet to be finalized. Construction is unlikely to commence any time before 2014 because of regulatory issues and difficulty in sourcing major components from Japan due to India not being a signatory to the Nuclear Non-Proliferation Treaty (Makrand Gadgil).

- **Mongolia** - India and Mongolia signed a crucial civil nuclear agreement on 15 June 2009 for supply of uranium to India, during Prime Minister Manmohan Singh's visit to Mongolia, making it the fifth nation in the world to seal a civil nuclear pact with India. The MoU on "development of cooperation in the field of peaceful uses of radioactive minerals and nuclear energy" was signed by senior officials in the department of atomic energy of the two countries (Financial Express, 15 September 2009).

- **Namibia** - On 02 September 2009, India and Namibia signed agreement, on civil nuclear energy, which allows for the supply of uranium from Namibia to India. It also allows for setting up of nuclear reactors by India in Namibia ('Republikein online' dated 02 September 2009). It is an important agreement as Namibia is the fifth largest producer of uranium in the world.

- **Argentina** - On 14 October 2009, India and Argentina signed an agreement in New Delhi on civil nuclear cooperation among other pacts. As per this accord, both India and Argentina have agreed to encourage and support scientific, technical and commercial cooperation for mutual benefit in this field (Chatterjee Amit Kumar), ('One India' (online) dated 14 October 2009).

- **Canada** - The Prime Ministers of India and Canada signed a civil nuclear cooperation agreement in Toronto on 28 June 2010 which, when fully implemented, will provide access for Canada's nuclear industry to India's expanding nuclear market and also fuel for India's reactors. Canada is one of the world's largest exporters of uranium (Sinha Mohnish) and Canada's heavy water nuclear technology is marketed abroad with CANDU-type units operating in India, Pakistan, Argentina, South Korea, Romania and China. On 6 November 2012, India and Canada finalized their 2010 nuclear export agreement, opening the way for Canada to begin uranium exports to India (BBC Archives 06 November 2012).

- **Kazakhstan** - On 16 April 2011 during Indian PM; Dr Manamohan Singh's visit to Astana, India and Kazakhstan signed an inter-governmental agreement for Cooperation in Peaceful Uses of Atomic Energy, that envisages a legal framework for the supply of fuel, construction and operation of atomic power plants, exploration and joint mining of uranium, exchange of scientific and research information, reactor safety mechanisms and use of radiation technologies for health care. After the talks, the Kazakh President, Nursultan A Nazarbaev announced that his country would supply India with 2100 tonnes of uranium and was ready to supply more, if India asks for it. India and Kazakhstan already have a mechanism for civil nuclear cooperation in place since January 2009, when Nuclear Power Corporation of India Limited (NPCIL) and Kazakh nuclear company KazAtomProm signed an MoU during the visit of president Nazarbaev to Delhi. Under the contract, KazAtomProm supplies uranium which is used by Indian reactors (Times of India 17 April 2011), (Indian Express 16 April 2009).

- **Republic of Korea (South Korea)-** South Korea became the latest country to sign a nuclear agreement with India after it got the waiver from the NSG in 2008. On 25 July 2011 the agreement was signed, which will allow South Korea with a legal foundation to participate in India's nuclear expansion programme, and to bid for constructing nuclear power plants in India (Srinivas Laxman).

- **European Union -** India and EU have decided to co-operate in civil nuclear research and development and enhance exchanges in the field of fusion energy research (PTI Sep 29, 2008).

Impact Indo US Civil Nuclear Pact: An Analysis. This agreement has been able to bring India back from the list of nuclear pariah states to mainstream. It is expected that the nuclear power production will expand substantially in years to come due to this agreement. This agreement will allow India to carry out trade of nuclear fuel and technologies with other countries and significantly enhance its power generation capacity. When all related issues are resolved and the agreement becomes fully operative, India is expected to generate an additional 25,000 MW of nuclear power by 2020, bringing total estimated nuclear power generation to 45,000 MW (Bibhudatta Pradhan and Archana Chaudhary / Bloomberg). It may be noted that India has already been using imported enriched uranium for LWRs that are currently under IAEA safeguards, but it has developed other aspects of the nuclear fuel cycle to support its reactors. Development of select technologies was seriously getting affected due to limited imports for all these years. Use of heavy water reactors has been particularly a compulsion for India for last few years as this technology with all its elements has fully been Indigenized and however limited the stocks of U^{235} might have been, but they are there and was being put to use. But limited availability of indigenous uranium has been affecting the growth of nuclear power industry. Although Indian R&D community is making effort to expedite development of commercially viable thorium based power generation system but still a lot of ground is required to be covered and hence the immediate need to boost up the supply of uranium and related technology for the growth of nuclear energy based power generation. *(India has also done a great amount of work in the development of a thorium centered fuel cycle. The fact that thorium can theoretically be utilized in heavy water reactors has tied the development of the two. A prototype reactor that would burn Uranium-Plutonium fuel while irradiating a thorium blanket is under construction at the Chennai/ Kalpakkam Atomic Power Station.)* However it may be premature to consider that this agreement is a panacea of energy problems of India. In this connection, few aspects merit consideration, which are as follows:-

- US Hyde act when in conflict with the Indian act will be overriding the latter. Thus Indian programme will now be a captive of US rules and therefore it would be pertinent to raise a question- *Is US trying to impose NPT and CTBT on India in an indirect manner?*

- While act has been in place for last five years but not much of progress is happening on ground. India's Liability Act is perceived by some of the NSG members as stringent and often quoted as a reason for the slow progress of the implementation of the Indo-US Accord- *Does that mean US and other supplier countries and their vendors lobby is trying to arm twist India to dilute her law?*

- Technology which is being provided is BWR/ LWR/ VVER. Much of these technologies are in sync with Indian plan to use plutonium generated in stage-I as the feed stock for stage-II. *How much of the plutonium will be generated and will India be able to make use of it for energizing Stage-II without host country's permission?* As against these technologies PHWR technology which India has totally indigenized is far more effective for overall growth of Indian nuclear programme. Therefore *will it not be a good idea to get only fuel ex import and use PHWRs for the generation of power?*

- A major vulnerability; which India is said to be suffering from is the shortage of indigenous natural uranium. Firstly, it has already been established through a staff check of the resources that India can sustain a power generation programme of 20,000 MW for 40 years instead of 10,000 MW which is the accepted figure. Secondly, recently discovered Tummalapalle mines in Andhra Pradesh (Kadapa district) are said to be having sufficient natural uranium available to further progress Stage-I of the Indian nuclear programme to a far greater extent of satisfaction. Therefore; *is it not the time to review the Indo-US Civil Nuclear programme?*

- A detailed appraisal of Indo US agreement is given at Appendix E.

Participation of Indian Industry in Nuclear Power Generation Programme

Present Status. The erection of NPP is governed by Atomic Energy Act 1962. As per this law, the construction of new plants is to be undertaken only by the PSUs (Reference: Section 3 (a) of The Atomic Energy Act, 1962 (inserted vide amendment act of 1987)). The two designated PSUs by the DAE are; NPCIL and BHAVINI. Other PSUs may join them, if required/ desired. Private Sector companies may join them only as a junior equity partner or provide equipment/ work services support. It needs to be noted that in June 2008 Moody's estimated that the cost of installing new nuclear capacity in the U.S. might possibly exceed \$7,000/ kWe in final cost (David Sclissel and Bruce Biewald). As far as India is concerned this cost will be much more than that. Firstly; because of the cost escalation due to inflation since 2008 is to be taken into account and secondly; due to cost difference between the two countries. The 12th Plan proposals have since been finalized. These proposals envisage start of work on 11 reactors based on indigenously developed technologies with further distribution of eight 700 MW PHWRs, two 500 MW FBRs and one 300 MW AHWR and eight LWRs of 1000 MW or higher capacity with foreign technical cooperation. These nuclear power reactors are expected to be completed progressively in the 13th and 14th Plans. The 16 PHWRS and LWRs are expected to cost \$40 billion (Nuclear Power in India updated up to 10 April 2013). Therefore it is essential that Indian industry be involved in support of the nuclear programme with a view to reduce burden on the national exchequer and also reduce the time delay. Dependence, only on two PSUs (NPCIL and BHAVINI), which with their limited capacities, contribute substantially to this time delay . It also needs to be appreciated that the capacity building of the Indian industry will further add to the CNP of India.

Existing system of Private Participation. Due to a forced isolation of over 30 years of the Indian nuclear establishment on account of Indian PNE in 1974, a number of Indian industries have developed capabilities to produce equipment and parts of equipment relevant for NPP. L&T and BHEL are to name two most important contributors. L&T has been producing heavy components for 17 of India's PHWRs and has also secured contracts for 80 percent of the components for the fast breeder reactor at Kalpakkam. L&T also manufactures reactor vessels for PHWRs and FBRs, critical equipment & systems for heavy water plants, fuel re-processing plants and plasma reactors. L&T also offers onsite integration and installation of massive structure of reactor main vessel, reactor safety vessel, end shield, calandria, coolant channels assembly and reactivity devices for new and operating plants. Further it is providing solutions for Life extension services for existing PHWRs include in service inspection and coolant channel replacement for operating nuclear power plants. Now a days L&T is actively involved in the prestigious International Thermonuclear Experimental Reactor (ITER) project. There work has been internationally recognized in the sense that they have been certified by the American Society of Mechanical Engineers (ASME) to fabricate nuclear-grade pressure vessels and core support structures, achieving this internationally recognized quality standard in 2007, and further ASME accreditation in 2010. Presently it is one of about ten major nuclear-qualified heavy engineering enterprises worldwide (IBID). BHEL has also built its capacity in nuclear sector over the years. For this, they have a close cooperation with NPCIL. As part of their energy & capacity addition programme they have been manufacturing 81 percent of major equipment required for nuclear projects on primary side and on secondary side integration of system up to a capacity of 540 MWe. Out of 17 Reactors, which presently are in operation in the country, BHEL has supplied conventional island, TG sets for 12 reactors; including Tarapur Units 3&4 (540 MWe each). They have also built first-ever four steam generators for new reactors of rating 700 MWe. They have recently signed an MoU with the GE Hitachi for cooperation in Nuclear Island and formed a JV with NPCIL for Conventional island of NPP. They have already started identification of technology partner for higher size Nuclear TG sets (PK Agarwal).

Need for Enhanced Private Participation. To raise the contribution of the nuclear energy in the energy basket of India from its present meager contribution of 4780 (or 5780 with the contribution of Kudankulam- I taken into account) MWe to 20,000/ 1,46,000 MWe by 2020, the effort of Two PSUs of the DAE, namely; NPCIL and BHAVINI will have to be boosted by an involvement of the private sector and the other PSUs. A number of companies including Anil Ambani Group firm Reliance Energy, Tata Power, GMR, GVK and aluminum manufacturer NALCO are keen to enter nuclear power business and have approached the DAE for setting up of NPPs. However; the current Indian law; Atomic energy Act of 1962, does not allow participation of the private sector companies in nuclear power generation. The Atomic Energy Act-1962 may need an amendment, in case involvement of the private sector is to graduate from providing equipment support to participation in the total construction of the NPP. In this Connection replies to two of the parliament questions (first question was by Shri Pradeep Majhi on 24 February 2010 and the second was by Shri S Semmalai on 13 march 2013) are significant because they clarify the current government policy. The gist of the replies to the two questions is that no change is envisaged necessary to the existing policy with respect to construction of the NPPs by the two PSUs of the DAE. The Law already has two provisions which are relevant in this regard. These are, firstly; that the private companies can provide equity as junior partners and secondly; the private players as well as other PSUs can undertake component/ equipment supply and work services. It was further clarified that this policy would continue as hither to fore and a status quo ante to be maintained as far as amendment to existing law; Atomic Energy Act 1962, is concerned (Shri Prathvi Raj Chauhan, Minister of State for Science and Technology, Earth sciences (Independent Charge) and PMO in reply to the question No 413 of Shri Pradeep Majhi on 24 February 2010 in Loksabha and by Shri V Narayan Swami, Minister of State in PMO in reply to a question No 238 of Shri S Semmalai on 13 march 2013 in Loksabha).

Industrial organizations like the Associated Chamber of Commerce and Industry of India (ASSOCHAM) and Federation of Indian Chamber of Commerce and Industry (FICCI) feel that an amendment to the law is necessary to help India in generating some 20,000 MW of nuclear power by 2020, notwithstanding the nuclear deal with the US and the subsequent international cooperation. Such an approach will give a lot of strength to India while dealing with members of the NSG. A large number of Indian private sector companies like Reliance Energy, Tata Power, GMR Energy Private Limited, GVK Power and Infrastructure Limited and ALSTOM Projects (who is already active in a number of nuclear projects within the framework of existing law: manufacture of reactors, rotors and turbines); are keen to get into NPP construction on their own/ in collaboration with other foreign firms. Reliance Energy is already planning an investment of Rs 12,000 cores to establish a capacity of 2000 MW (A PTI Report, Published in Hindu dated 16 Apr 2010) and Tata Power is Planning to invest US $ three billion to establish a capacity of 2200-3400 MW in collaboration with the GE of USA (IANS Report published in Hindustan Times, 15 August 2008). *However it is an interesting piece of information that in all the countries of the world all operating nuclear power plants were developed by state-owned or regulated utility monopolies to date* (Ed Crooks, Financial times, 12 September 2010). Therefore the stand of the Indian Government is not very different from rest of the world. One possible reason could be that these are highly capital intensive projects having long gestation period and therefore many of the risks associated with the construction costs, operating performance, fuel price, and other factors are borne by the consumers, tough indirectly, rather than suppliers in case the erection is taken up by a government agency. In case private sector undertakes the construction, the liability for the delay will be that of the private builder as such private builders are generally reluctant to undertake these projects. *("It is felt that it is not such a major issue and can be addressed by following a suitable business model"- Author.)*

JVs with other PSUs. There are two PSUs namely Indian Oil Corporation (IOC) and National Thermal Power Corporation (NTPC) which are trying to have JV with NPCIL (A PTI Report, Published in Hindu dated 16 Apr 2010). The JV with NTPC has already coalesced into a joint venture company by name, "Anushakti Vidhyut Nigam", which has already been incorporated for developing atomic power projects in the country. NPCIL holds 51 percent of the equity share capital and NTPC holds the balance 49 percent of the equity share capital. The preliminary work of the first project of this company is in progress in Hisar district of Haryana (The Hindu Business line , 22 Aug 2012). The IOC is willing to invest Rs. 8,000-10,000 crore over next 6-7 years and the oil refiner may take equity anywhere between 26-49 percent. The Atomic Energy Act presently allows NPCIL to form a JV with a public sector company only. It has also come to light that the Indian Railways has also approached the

NPCIL for setting up a 700 MW captive power plant and discussions are already in progress to work out the details.

Foreign Investment in India's Nuclear Sector

- Post Indo US Civil Nuclear Accord and the NSG's special waiver, Indian Government is now encouraging foreign investment. It intends to set up 'nuclear parks' supplied by foreign companies and operated, for the time being, by the NPCIL. Each of these 'parks' are planned to be having an installed generation capacity between 8,000 to10,000 MW at a single site. It is felt that the establishment of these nuclear parks will turn out to be a quantum leap towards capacity buildup, as the current maximum installed capacity at one site is only 1,400 MW (Tarapur Atomic Power Station in Maharashtra, with four reactors),.

- Russian company *Atomstroyexport*,[17] a government subsidiary, has reached a deal with NPCIL to build sixteen nuclear reactors in India. One of these units of 1000 MW, has already attained criticality at Kudankulam in Tamil Nadu and second is in advanced stage of completion at the same place (Kudankulam). However decision about Unit-3 and Unit-4 at Kudankulam is stuck because of dispute between India and Russia due to issues which have come up due to India's liability act. This aspect is likely to come up during the 14th Indo-Russian Annual Summit Talks scheduled to be held during Prime Minister Dr Manmohan Sigh's visit to Russia from 20-22 October 2013 (Vinay Shukla, Russia & India Report, 15 October 2013).

- French company AREVA NP (a joint venture between AREVA and Siemens) have agreed to construct six 1650 MW reactors in Jaitapur, Maharashtra. These will be of European pressurized reactor, a variant of PWR. The NPS will have a collective capacity of 9900 MW, making the Jaitapur NPS; the largest in the world. However it is understood that this is an un-tested reactor. There is a strong movement against establishment of this plant and also the liability issues plaque it. Recent reports, however, suggest that the

17 Atomstroyexport (Russian: Атомстройэкспорт) is the Russian Federation's nuclear power equipment and service export monopoly. It belongs to Atomenergoprom holding with 49.8 percent of shares owned by Gazprombank. The activities of Atomstroyexport are financially supported by the Russian government

issue has substantially been resolved and the construction is likely to commence shortly.

• Private US companies namely; GE-Hitachi Nuclear Energy and Westinghouse Electric; have been given sites at Kovvada in Sri Kakulam District of Andhra Pradesh and Mithi virdi in Bhavnagar District of Gujarat, respectively. A total of 12 reactors are scheduled to be coming up through Indo US Collaboration. There will be six Advanced Boiling Water Reactors (ABWR) of a capacity of 1350 MWe each would be coming up at Kovvada. Thus finally a NPS of a total capacity of 9564 MWe would be coming up at Kovvada (Times of India-India Times, 11 July 2013). At Mithi virdi, a NPS having six PWRs (AP-1000 series) of 1100 MWe each would be coming up in collaboration with GE Hitachi Nuclear Energy (Pranab Dhal Samanta, 10 June 2012). Unfortunately both the proposed NPSs are presently affected by public protests and also due to a lack of resolution of liability issues which have emerged on account of newly formulated India's Nuclear Liability Act.

Impact of NSG Waiver on the Nuclear Trade. It was a historic moment for India when 45-member NSG decided to resume civil nuclear commerce with India (Internet upload, "Indian companies likely to benefit from nuclear deal" http://www.stockinvest.in/posts/Indian_companies_likely_to_benefit_from_nuclear_deal). India gained unique status as the only country having nuclear weapons, who has been allowed to do global nuclear commerce without signing either the NPT or CTBT, which had been a pre-condition till now for entering the elite nuclear club. The deal will not only give India access to nuclear fissile material and technology to progress a credible nuclear energy programme, but it will also open up certain key high-tech industries such as Pharmaceutical, IT, space and defence. Experts say with the NSG deal, India needs to look at allowing private sector participation for realizing its plans of adding 63,000 MW of nuclear power. This will require an investment of over Rs 6,00,000 crores, since each MW of nuclear power costs about Rs 10 crore. NPCIL officials revealed that they have already done exploratory meetings and technical discussions with the three major reactor suppliers – AREVA of France, General Electric and Westinghouse Electric Corporation of the US for supply of reactors for these projects. They are also on the look out for the Indian companies which can have a tie up with these major players. Other relevant aspects are as follows:-

- As many as 400 Indian and foreign firms are seen as the beneficiaries of the far-reaching NSG verdict. India will/ can now attract over $40 billion in foreign investment over the next 10-15 years as the result of private sector entry into India's nuclear power generation programme.

- As per the appreciation of the NPCIL; there are at least a dozen technologically-competent private players in the power sector in India, who can rope in strategic alliances and joint ventures with reactor manufacturers. Eventually, these players will have the potential to become reactor manufacturers themselves.

- Already R-Power, NPCIL, JSW, BHEL and L&T have lined up plans worth over Rs 1,00,000 crore for foraying into this sector. Larsen & Toubro is planning to form a Rs 2,000-crore ($463 million) joint venture with the NPCIL.

- FICCI expects another 200 medium and small firms to get into the act as ancillary producers to the big companies, thereby giving a new direction to efficient and cheaper power production in the country.

Economics of Nuclear Power

Trends in Indian Power sector. Total commercial energy consumption is likely to increase by 7.5 times (at a growth rate of 6.9 percent) over next 30 years (2001-02 to 2031-32) in a BAU scenario. Consumption by 2020 is likely to reach 1200 TWh (A KPMG Report). An extrapolation indicates that the power requirement by 2030 is likely to reach 950,000 MW (The Economic Times 06 July 2006). On demand side India's per capita demand in 2032 is likely to reach 2429 kWh at an anticipated GDP growth rate of 8-9 percent. Though this figure is still quite low as compared to developed countries like USA (it will only be 19 percent of the demand of the USA) but still a near fivefold rise on the present figure. On the supply side; to meet the forecasted electrical consumption based on projected growth rate of GDP of 8-9 percent, the Planning Commission projects a need of 306-337 GW of total generation capacity by 2016-17 and 778-960 GW by 2031-32 (John Stepenson and Peter Tynan).

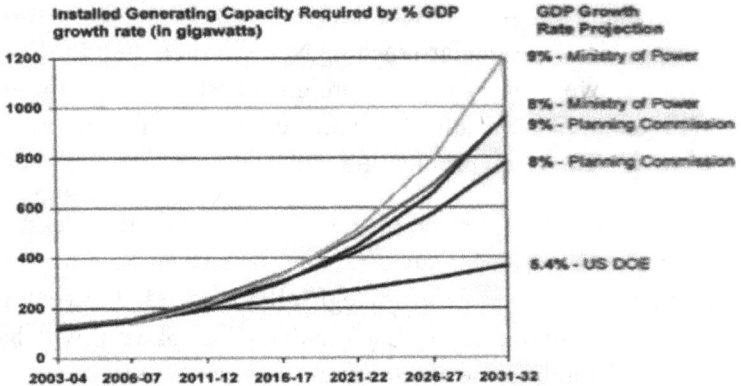

Sources: U.S. Department of Energy. *International Energy Outlook, 2006,* E Administration, Office of Integrated Analysis and Forecasting. Washington Government of India, Planning Comission. *Integrated Energy Policy: Re;* Committee, New Delhi, August 2006.

Figure-4.6: Installed Generating Capacity versus GDP Growth

Table-4.5: Production of Power

Year	Power in MW
2010	90,000 @
2020	241,000

Source: RNCOS Report, "Power Consumption to Double up to 2020" dated 29 June 2010.

Note: @- Total Installed capacity during the Year 2010 was 147,402.81 MW (CMIE Report).

   As is evident from the above figures read in conjunction with Table 4.5, that there is a gap between the demand and the supply of the power, which is widening and is unlikely to reduce any time in foreseeable future. Thus there is a need to find ways and means to bridge this gap. One of the major limiting factors for evolving a mitigating strategy is a requirement for massive amount of funds to build up energy infrastructure. According to "Indian Power Sector Analysis", a RNCOS market research report, India is estimated to be requiring investments worth US $ 1250 billion in energy infrastructure, till 2030. 76 percent of these investments will be going to power generation, transmission and distribution (RNCOS Report dated 29 June 2010). Therefore to bridge this broadening power demand-supply gap, one of the important solutions would be to inject private investment to support the government funding. Government policies, to encourage such a model, are the need of the hour. In case the nuclear energy sector is considered sensitive then economic model could be such that funding from private players be enhanced to such an extent that desired government funds are available for the nuclear sector.

Cost of Nuclear Power. In principle, nuclear energy has the potential to be of relatively low cost. It ranges from 3.8 to 6.7 cents per kWh. However in the case of India the cost is 2-3 times more than these figures. Some of the important reasons are as follows:-

- Total availability of the natural uranium itself is quite low (to support a programme of 10000 GW for a period of 40 years (PK Iyengar et al). *(In view of the analysis done earlier in this chapter, this conclusion can be considered at best debatable- Author!)*

- The ore having uranium is of low grade (having as low as 0.1 percent uranium as compared to the ore from other sources which have natural uranium in the range of 12-14 percent (Planning commission, Integrated Energy policy).

- Capital cost of building NPP with long gestation period (five to six years) for its completion adds to the cost. Besides; ideal gestation period for completion with an the unintended delay in completion, adds to the cost.

- Absence of private funding adds to the cost as establishment charges and the opportunity cost increases.

- Waste management/reprocessing of waste is expensive. Cost of reprocessing each kilogram of the spent fuel would be approximately Rs 26,000 with assumptions favourable to reprocessing and Rs 30,000 if assumptions are not favourable to reprocessing (MV Ramana).

- Insurance liability against accidents- Earlier in the absence of any Indian law dealing with the liability of the supplier/ manufacturer, it was assumed that in the case of an accident it will be the government of India who will be responsible for the mitigation and thus it was in the form of a subsidy. However; post enactment of the civil liability for nuclear damage act, 2010 this issue stands addressed. *(Author: this act may need a review in the light of an extremely determined opposition by the manufacturers' lobby. Their opposition is based on their argument that the Indian law is not in consonance with the Vienna convention on the subject.)*

India's nuclear programme would require an overall investment of about Rs 35,000-40,000 Crores per annum for next twenty years or so and the cumulative sum would be in the range of about US $160 billion. Not to forget; that to build and thereafter operate/ maintain all the plants planned, a minimum of over a lakh of trained/ skilled personnel along with necessary infrastructure would be needed (Anshu Bharadwaj et al).

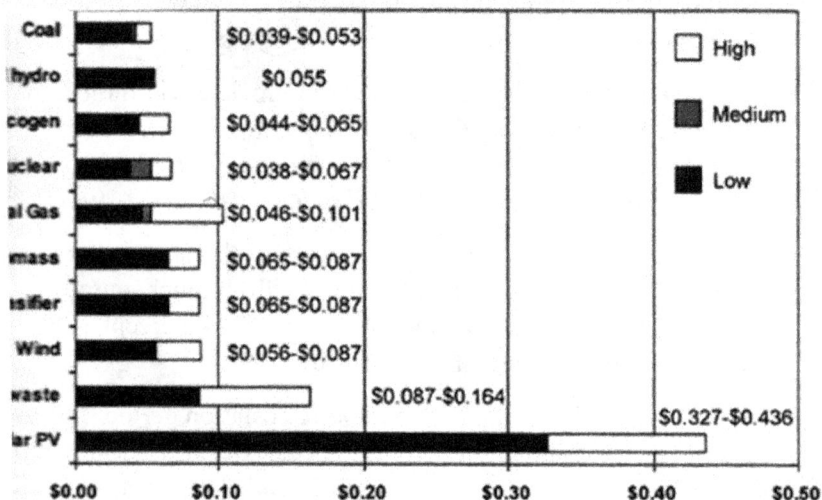

Figure-4.7: Cost Comparisons per kWh (US $)

Sources:

- EIA,"Annual Energy Outlook, 2006". DOE/EIA-0383 (2006), Washington DC, February 2006.

- Government of India Planning Commission," Integrated energy policy: Report of the Expert Committee, New Delhi, dated August 2006.

- Victor, David G.," the India Nuclear Deal Implications for Global climate Change," Testimony before the US Senate Committee on Energy and National Resources, 18 July 2006, available at: www. cfr.org/publication/11123/india_nuclear_deal.html

Notes:

- One of the important assumptions, while working out the comparative cost of power between a NPP and a Coal based thermal plant, is about the transportation cost of the coal, which is added to the calculations. In this assumption; the distance of the power plant from pith head is assumed to be only 1200 kilometers, which may need a review, as this figure would be far from being true in many cases. (MV Ramana, pp-48).

• Another aspect which needs to be included in the costing of the nuclear power is the cost of de-commissioning of plant as and when it happens. That will give a more realistic assessment.

• An examination of the recently built LWR and FBR show that the capital cost of the NPP will range from Rs 9-13 Crores (least expensive will be PHWR[18] and the most expensive will be FBR) per MW and with that the cost per unit of the electricity would work out to be in the range of Rs 3.18 to 4.32.

• In Indian context, taking all aspects into account, the levelized cost of electricity through nuclear route compares well with the electricity from other sources. It is illustrated with following bar chart:-

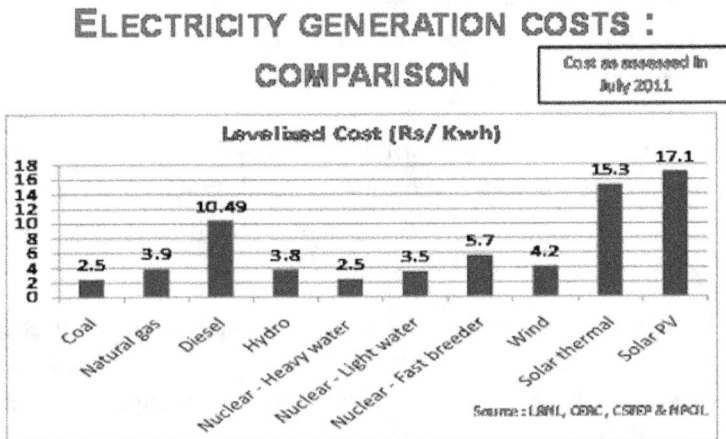

ELECTRICITY GENERATION COSTS : COMPARISON

Cost as assessed in July 2011

Levelised Cost (Rs/ Kwh)

Coal 2.5 | Natural gas 3.9 | Diesel 10.49 | Hydro 3.8 | Nuclear - Heavy water 2.5 | Nuclear - Light water 3.5 | Nuclear - Fast breeder 5.7 | Wind 4.2 | Solar thermal 15.3 | Solar PV 17.1

Source : LBNL, CERC, CSTEP & NPCIL

Additional Aspects which need to be considered while examining comparative costs
• Distance from pit head
• Opportunity cost
• Medical cost
• Waste disposal
• Discounts and cost of preparation of fuel for FBR Vs PHWR

Figure-4.8: Electricity Generation Costs: Comparison

---

18 PHWR has been totally indigenized and as such its cost turns out to be the lowest.

An appraisal of India's Nuclear Programme

Growth of nuclear energy programme of India is unique in more than one way. Firstly India was probably one of the first countries to have realized the importance of nuclear energy for power generation and started to acquire capability to exploit it as early as early 1950ies. Secondly in conception and so also in implementation the Indian nuclear programme is by and large indigenous (India has been able to master the entire nuclear cycle including reprocessing of used fuel. Its three stage plan is highly imaginative and plans to exploit indigenous resources optimally. The uniqueness of this programme is that it has withstood the test of time and even after sixty years it is still relevant in Indian context. India's track record on safety issues has been highly commendable.[19] Over the years India has been able to build a good infrastructure for the R&D. The acquisition of capability to plan, design, construct and operate NPP of PHWR origin is the second mile stone in India's journey on growth path. Next point of significance, in this trajectory of growth has been the development of the capacity to design, plan and construct; FBR and AHWR. Finally; the plant load factor of Indian plants has been comparable with the reactors of the advanced countries (USA now dominates the top 25 positions, followed by South Korea and Russia followed by Japan, Taiwan and India. The average PLF for the USA is 87 percent and for India; it is over 80 percent (World Nuclear Association, April 2012)). India so far is the only country which has a country specific Nuclear Accord, despite not being a signatory to either NPT or CTBT and has a waiver from the NSG to do trade in nuclear related equipment/ technologies/ material.

This is where the good part ends. India is also unique in the sense that most of the projections have historically been slipping. Projections made in 1960ies and subsequently have consistently been slipping and some of the glaring slippages have been as tabulated below:-

---

19 After Chernobyl accident an international scale to classify nuclear accidents/ incident was developed by the IAEA in collaboration with OECD Nuclear Agency in 1992. It is named as International Nuclear and Radiological Event Scale (INES). As per this scale levels 1-3 are termed as incidents and events 4-7 are termed as accidents. Any event without safety significance is classified as "Below Scale/Level 0". Presently 60 IAEA members use this scale. On this scale Chernobyl and Fukushima were at 7 and Three Mile Island was placed at 5. In India according to Significance Event Report (SER) compiled by AERB; during the five year period; 2003-2008, there was only one incident at Level 2 with all other incidents being at Level- 1/ 0; mostly Level- 0. (G Balachandran)

Table-4.6: Slippages in Targets

Issue	Year	Target Projected	Target Achieved
Power Projection	1980	8000 MW	600 MW
Power Production	1987	20-25,000 MW	950 MW
Power Production	2000	43,500 MW	2,700 MW
FBTR	1972		1985 [20]
PFBR	2005	2010	Not yet ready
Operationalization of imported LWR/ VVER/PWR	2002	2007	• Criticality at Kudankulam-1 was achieved in July 2013. Power generation is likely to commence only by end August 2013 [21] Total delay of six years. • Other projects of Russian, French and US origin are also slipping due to one or the other reason.

Source: MV Ramana, pp-44

Planning Commission is forecasting that due to finite nature of the indigenous coal, with a mere five per cent per annum increase in the consumption, it is likely to run out in 45 years or so, as far as economically extractable coal is concerned (Anshu Bhardwaj et al,pp-01)). Though highly unlikely, yet planning will have to be done for the worst case scenario. To hedge against such an eventuality, a strategy needs to be worked out wherein a boost to energy conversion, through nuclear energy

---

20 Slippage has been in terms of capacity. Instead of 40 MWt and 13.2 MWe, at best it has achieved a maximum 17.4 MWt and an average of 10.5 MW. (G Srinivasan et al)

21 Limited power generation has now commenced with effect from 22 October 2013 and the same is being fed into the grid.

route in conjunction with the renewable energy route, assumes a great importance for India's energy security in long term context (beyond 2030 and more realistically beyond 2050).

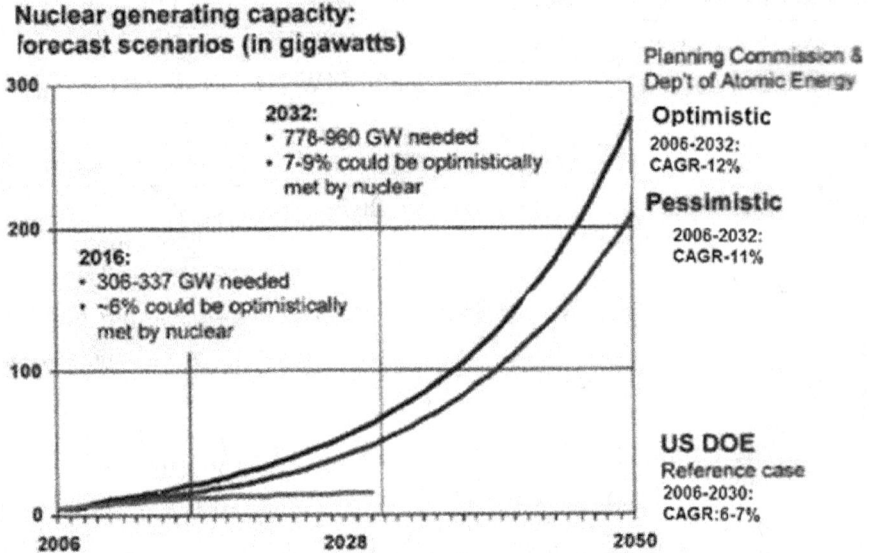

Nuclear generating capacity: forecast scenarios (in gigawatts)

Planning Commission & Dep't of Atomic Energy

2032:
- 778-960 GW needed
- 7-9% could be optimistically met by nuclear

Optimistic
2006-2032:
CAGR-12%

Pessimistic
2006-2032:
CAGR-11%

2016:
- 306-337 GW needed
- ~6% could be optimistically met by nuclear

US DOE
Reference case
2006-2030:
CAGR:6-7%

300 — 200 — 100 — 0

2006   2028   2050

Figure-4.9 Forecast: Nuclear Generating Capacity (in GW)

Source:

- EIA, "Annual Energy Outlook, 2006, DOE/EIA-0383 (2006), Washington DC February 2006.

- Planning Commission of GOI," Integrated Energy Policy: Report of the Expert Committee, New Delhi, August 2006.

Note: Assumptions for the growth trajectory is based on following:-

- GDP growth to be 8-9 percent.

- **Optimistic Scenario-**

  o FBR Technology gets successfully validated.

  o Newly discovered uranium mines like Tummalapalle in Andhra Pradesh are exploited without any hitch so that PHWR planned to be erected are successfully operationalized without any time delay which has been happening in past due to paucity of indigenous uranium.

o India Succeeds in acquiring LWRs of capacity of 8000 MW through import, notwithstanding the delays which are happening presently due to issues emerged post enactment of India's liability act.

o India is able to assimilate the LWR technology through import which has the capacity to fill a substantial part of the energy void in the interim period (short and medium term).

o India successfully operationalizes AHWR by 2022 to exploit vast indigenous thorium resources.

• **Pessimistic Scenario-** All above less acquisition of LWRs ex import

Table 4.7 gives two scenarios which are based on assumptions by the planning commission as mentioned above.

Table-4.7: Nuclear Power Projection

Year	Power Projection (in MW)	
	Optimistic	Pessimistic
2010	11,000	9,000
2020	29,000	21,000
2030	63,000	48,000
2040	131000	104,000
2050	275,000	208,000

Source: Anshu Bhardawaj et al, pp-1

Analysis. An analysis based on the Figure-4.9 and the Table-4.7 flags few issues which are as follows:-

• Current projections appear to be based on assumptions of certain technological breakthroughs becoming a reality in the time frame envisaged, however firstly the growth experience so far does not add credibility to this assumption and also the increasing degree of difficulty in desired advanced technological breakthroughs is going to add to uncertainty. Cases in point, to name a few, are;

breeder technology, indigenization of LWR, AHWR becoming operational and mixed carbide fuel becoming a reality.

- Another assumption about the growth of nuclear energy assuming an important role in the energy supply is based on fast breeder technology becoming fully commercial. DAE has committed to the nation that FBR will contribute a major share to energy supply side by adding 200 GWe in 2050. To achieve this; a roadmap has been prepared. As per that; by 2020 four more oxide fueled FBRs of 500 MWe will be constructed. During this period carbide fueled FBR will be developed and one of these four reactors will be operated with metallic fuel. Beyond 2020, a series of 1000 MWe metallic fueled reactors will be constructed. Reactor physics aspects for 500 MWe and 1000 MWe FBR designs have been such that the doubling time, a pre-requisite for initiating Stage-III of the Indian Nuclear Programme of 8-10 years, will be achievable. (Dr Baldev Raj, July 2006). Against these assumptions the reality is that the PFBR is scheduled to achieve criticality only by 2015, which itself is becoming debatable and even if that happens, the doubling time will take a period of at least 8-10 years after PFBR becomes operational and thus even in the most optimistic scenario it will go up to 2023- 25 and as such, energy conversion from thorium route will not be feasible before 2025. Such a time line will adversely affect India's plans for achieving energy security by 2030.

- If public protest, post Fukushima against Kudankulam is any indicator, the road to establishment of new NPPs is unlikely to be smooth.

- The rate of growth of accretion of the nuclear power from 1950 to 1980 was six per cent and from 1980 to 2000 it was eight percent expecting it to meet the target of 11-12 percent, as planned, appears to be highly ambitious, more so because despite Indo-US accord and NSG waiver, nothing much is happening on the infusion of technology and other related developments. In this connection growth rate predicted by DOE of USA; six-seven percent appears to be realistic. However in this kind of a very depressive situation, there is a silver lining. Recently, a 540 MW PHWR at Tarapur attained criticality eight months ahead of schedule. This shows that the Indian prowess for the construction/ erection of the NPPs has come of age and in future a more compressed time frame for new NPPs can be expected. This definitely is a ray of hope for a sustained development of the nuclear power generation programme of India. The slippages are more on account of default by those countries, who had earlier agreed to provide support. One stated reason by, many of them, is the stringent nature of the Indian Nuclear Liabilities Law. However behind that veneer of righteousness, are the geopolitical pressures/ strings attached with the support pledged and China's attempt to influence decisions of the NSG. In this connection, some of the recent developments, within India, have been highly positive. Two of those are as follows:-

o   A better understanding on the part of political decision makers not to get swayed by the public protests- such an approach has helped the Central Government as well as the Tamil Nadu State government to deal with the public protests with due resolve and Kudankulam attained criticality. This criticality will go a long way in clarifying many a doubts about the safety of nuclear plants.

o   Even public perceptions, post Kudankulam-1 attaining criticality, appear to be changing. This gives the hope that growth rate after all may not stagnate at six-seven percent.

•   It needs to be realized that, even if the highly optimistic targets planned are realized, the nuclear power will be able to add to power inventory only about six percent by 2016, seven-nine percent by 2032 and 20 percent only by 2052 because, hopefully by then, cost effective thorium based power generation technology would have operationalized.

•   To achieve the targets set, a system's analysis suggests that a very major effort would be needed at the highest decision making level to enhance capabilities of quicker and integrated decision making, capacity to ink technical collaboration with foreign players based on mutual interdependence, building up of the technical/ administrative threshold with a larger base of technical and managerial manpower, across the entire spectrum of activities and finally; ability to organize funds through policy review. Specific areas which need immediate attention are as follows:-

o   Uranium Mining- removing hurdles of land acquisition issues, public perception management, safety issues and related logistic issues.

o   Fuel Fabrication- especially development of mixed carbide fuel instead of MOX which presently is being used and has limitation in producing enough fissile material.

o   Reprocessing of spent fuel and waste management.

o   Careful site selection with a view to avoid situations like Haripur in west Bengal and Jaitapur in Maharashtra- a well planned awareness campaign is required to be launched.

o   Funds Management- funds required to achieve the set targets are substantial and from government funding in view of the prevailing geo-economic scenario and CAD of the country a more imaginative policy will have to be thought off.

o   International Cooperation- strategy to exploit geopolitical situation by strengthening linkages based on interdependence especially with USA, Japan Russia and France to increase nuclear power generation capacity.

o   Capacity Building- A very large scientific manpower for research & development, technical manpower to build and run the plants/ infrastructure and managerial manpower to manage growth in an integrated manner within the nuclear establishment and with other forms of generation, transmission and end use will be needed.

A SWOT Analysis of India's nuclear programme is given at Appendix E attached.

Some Relevant Acts and Enabling Legislations

Atomic Energy Act- 1962. It was promulgated on 15 September 1962 and since been amended twice; first time on 23 December 1986 and second time on 08 September 1987. This act repeals Atomic Energy Act 1948. This act describes organization necessary for the growth of nuclear energy in India, stipulates and lays down rules of business meant to provide for the development, control and use of atomic energy for the welfare of the people of India and for other peaceful purposes and for matters connected there with. The details of the act are given at Appendix F. The details of the amendments are given at Annexes III and IV to Appendix F.

US- India Civil Nuclear Agreement. Popularly known as the "123 Agreement", signed between the United States of America and the Republic of India. The background for this agreement was a joint statement by Indian Prime Minister Dr. Manmohan Singh and then U.S. President George W. Bush on July 18, 2005. One of the important highlight of this Joint Statement was; that India had agreed to separate its civil and military nuclear facilities and to place all its civil nuclear facilities under IAEA safeguards. In exchange, the United States had agreed to work toward full civil nuclear cooperation with India (Office of the Press Secretary, White House," Joint Statement Between President George W. Bush and Prime Minister Manmohan Singh" dated 18 June 2005). This Joint statement also gives the frame work for the act. The detailed appraisal of the agreement is given at Appendix G and the text of the Accord signed is given at the Annexure-V to Appendix G. Some of the important features of the agreement are as follows:-

- This U.S.-India deal took more than three years to come to fruition as it had to go through several complex stages, including amendment of the U.S. domestic law, specially the Atomic Energy Act of 1954, a civil-military nuclear Separation Plan in India, an India-IAEA safeguards (inspections) agreement and the grant of an exemption for India by the Nuclear Suppliers Group, an export-control cartel that had been formed mainly in response to India's first nuclear test in 1974.

- In its final shape, the deal places under permanent safeguards, those nuclear facilities that India has identified as "civil" and permits broad civil nuclear cooperation, while excluding the transfer of "sensitive" equipment and technologies, including civil enrichment and reprocessing items even under IAEA safeguards.

- On August 18, 2008 the IAEA Board of Governors approved (Staff Report, "IAEA Board Approves India-Safeguards Agreement" Published in IAEA, News Letter dated 01 August 2008) and on February 2, 2009, India signed an India-specific safeguards agreement with the IAEA (Staff Report," India Safeguards Agreement Signed" published in IAEA News Letter dated 02 February 2009). Once India brought this agreement into force, inspections began in a phased manner on the 35 civilian nuclear installations India has identified in its Separation Plan.

- The deal is seen as a watershed in U.S.-India relations and introduces a new aspect to international nonproliferation efforts.

- **Approval of the Safe Guard Agreement by the IAEA.** On August 1, 2008, the IAEA approved the safeguards agreement with India, after which the United States approached the Nuclear Suppliers Group (NSG) to grant a waiver to India to commence civilian nuclear trade (outlookindia.com dated 02 October 2009). The 45-nation NSG granted the waiver to India on September 6, 2008 allowing it to access civilian nuclear technology and fuel from other countries (Siddharth Vardarajan," Thirty Words that saved the Day", Published in The Hindu dated 09 September 2008). The implementation of this waiver made India the only known country with nuclear weapons which is not a party to the Non Proliferation Treaty (NPT) but is still allowed to carry out nuclear commerce with the rest of the world.

- **Approval by the US House of Representatives.** The US House of Representatives passed the bill to approve the Indo-US nuclear deal on September 28, 2008 (Diwakar & Chidanand Rajghatta, 29 September 2008), Two days later, India and France inked a similar nuclear pact making France the first country to have such an agreement with India (Pranab Dhal Samanta, 30 September 2008). On October 1, 2008 the US Senate also approved the civilian nuclear agreement allowing India to purchase nuclear fuel and technology from the United States. U.S. President, George W. Bush, signed the legislation on the Indo-US nuclear deal, approved by the U.S. Congress, into law, now called the United States-India Nuclear Cooperation Approval and Non-proliferation Enhancement Act, on October 8, 2008. Finally, the agreement was signed by the then Indian External Affairs Minister Shri Pranab Mukherjee and his counterpart the then Secretary of State Ms Condoleezza Rice, on 10 October 2008.

- **US Interest: A Driver for the Agreement.** The law indicates a shift in US foreign policy towards a stronger strategic partnership through civil nuclear cooperation with India put forth few economic, strategic and resource arguments. These are as follows:-

  o Growth of nuclear energy in the energy basket of India will aid her in reducing its reliance on oil and gas (Leonard Weiss) in longer run.

  o The USA appreciates that the accretion of nuclear energy in India's energy inventory will contribute to the mitigation efforts of the USA, on global warming because India is likely to emerge as major consumer of energy in future and nuclear energy being relatively a clean energy would go a long way in contributing towards international efforts on mitigation of the global warming.

- This agreement will also help the USA, to generate more jobs in its domestic market, by encouraging export of nuclear energy related technologies and material.

- Finally USA is hoping that with her recent diplomatic efforts she will be able to form an axis led by her with countries with common geopolitical interest and that common interest is to counter China's growing stature in the Asia pacific region on account of her economic muscle. The countries which USA hopes will form this axis are India, South Korea, Australia, Malaysia, Philippines and Vietnam initially and will be joined by Indonesia in a little delayed time frame.

- **Indian Interests: Some Unanswered Questions-** While India, post Indo US Civil nuclear accord, was of the view that this accord will help her to overcome her energy woes in long run but, from the initial joint statement of President Bush and Prime Minister Dr Manmohan Singh of 18 July 2005 the final accord has changed substantially. The accord is subservient to US laws. Therefore how does it affect India's non military component to go for nuclear test. In such an eventuality US will not only abrogate the deal but will also demand all the material provided as a part of the accord. Does it not mean entry of NPT and CTBT from back door? US is not willing to be governed by India Liability act which would amount to liability getting transferred to India which would mean higher cost of the power and in case of any mishap vendor is not held accountable at all. Finally PWR technology or its variants are likely to affect the growth of indigenous PHWR technology and also the FBR technology, both of which are critical for India's nuclear energy growth. Such an approach will definitely affect the India's capacity to act independent on its nuclear policy and will make India vulnerable to blackmail by nuclear haves. Indian decision makers will have to take all these issues into account to formulate a measured response strategy.

India's Civil Liability for Nuclear Damage Act-2010. It aims to provide a civil liability for nuclear damage and prompt compensation to the victims of a nuclear incident through a no fault liability to the operator, appointment of Claims Commissioner, establishment of Nuclear Damage Claims Commission and for matters connected therewith on incidental thereto. The details of the act as specified in the Government of India Gazette notification are as given in the Appendix H. As a consequence to this act most of the foreign vendors and countries including USA who were earlier very enthusiastic about the nuclear collaboration with India are now not showing as much interest. No wonder, work on no new reactor, other than Kudankulam-I and II has as yet commenced. During the U.S. Secretary of State John Kerry's India visit earlier this year, the American side barely hid its disappointment over the slow pace of progress in reaping the benefits of the India-U.S. civil nuclear energy deal. One of the most important reasons for the slow progress has been the provisions of the Liability act which they consider tough, although Indian Parliament while passing the bill had felt that to deal with the contingency of a nuclear accident, liability has to be that of the supplier. The recent leakages in the media suggest that attempts are being made to dilute these provisions under U.S. pressure. It is important that the supplier countries have to factor into India's domestic compulsions, the joint declaration just said that over the past year, negotiations leading to the construction of nuclear power plants in Gujarat (Mithivirdi) and Andhra Pradesh (Kovvada) have continued with notable progress being made in land acquisition. The U.S. Nuclear Regulatory Commission would assist India's Atomic Energy Regulatory Board (AERB) to certify and license the operations in India of U.S.-origin nuclear power plants. Early establishment of new nuclear power stations is critical for India as it is estimated that India where power shortage for 2013-14 is estimated at 6.7 percent but the stiff public resistance to new power plants in India and the outlook of the parliament members make it quite tough to go against the provisions of the Law. Dick Stratford, Director, Office of Nuclear Energy, Safety & Security at the U.S. Department of State articulates views of the US government that the Issues need to be resolved at the earliest. The French too have problems with the Act, as do the Russians as it pushes up the price of construction. The latter, however, say that existing agreements with India insulate them from liability. US is engaging India in a dialogue on the subject, Stratford, who is a key figure in the U.S. nuclear think tank, added. Other US officials are blunter in their opposition to the Act for several reasons. They feel that the delay in getting the issue resolved will push up the cost of power; the suppliers, including Indian, will be made liable to pay millions of rupees for a long period for faulty equipment that cost just a few hundreds of rupees. (*Author: a debatable issue and also a question of principle. The USA and other countries who are questioning the necessity of the stringent provisions of this law need to note that if for India these reactors are critical for the enhancement of the power generation, they are equally critical for these vendors and supplier countries for their business interests. Indian decision makers also need to remember that post Bhopal gas tragedy, even after 30 years of the incident and a full generation having been affected by the ill effects of the gas leak, the perpetrator of the gas leak; The, Union Carbide is still free from any punitive action*) Their final argument is little more reasonable because the liability fixed is well above the guidelines laid down in the Vienna convention[22]. Indian Law differs from International Conventions only as far as fixing of upper limit is concerned (Balachandran); however their argument that the plant operator and not the supplier should be made liable, to say the least, is not reasonable (*nageshkumar.s@thehindu.co.in*)

---

22 Vienna Convention on Civil Liability for Nuclear Damage is a1963 Treaty, that governs issues of liability in case of nuclear accident. It was concluded in Vienna on 21 May 1963 and entered into force on 12 November 1977. The Convention has been amended by a 1997 protocol. The depository is the International Atomic Energy Agency. As of May 2013, 39 countries have ratified it and 80 countries have adopted it. Protocol sets the possible limit of the operator's liability roughly equivalent to $400 million. The convention defines additional amounts to be provided on the basis of installed capacity and UN rate of assessment. As per this liability of the operator is absolute and time limit for completion is 10 years from the time of accident. (IAEA publication). India is not a signatory to this Convention. There is another Convention called Paris Convention of 1960 amended from time to time (last amendment 2004) which sets the upper limit of the Third Party Nuclear Liability.

5

Energy Management

Policy Issues

Administrations come and go, politicians' stars rise and fall, but the work of the government goes on. It is carried forward by professionals of bureaucracy, technocrats and other professionals of the concerned field, under the political leadership of the day. It is this well synergized, collective and coordinated effort, which has bearing on nation's energy security. Therefore the government policy should be formed by studying the trends based on institutional memory buttressed with experience of the involved staff and thereafter extrapolating the conclusions after subjecting them to due checks for future scenario, to cater for future needs, in response to environmental; geostrategic/ technological breakthroughs/ economic developments envisaged. In doing so trends need to be studied in the technological environment of the day and the extrapolation for future needs to be based on the likely future scenario which takes into account the growth trajectory of the technology. Thus to a substantial degree there is a need to have a continuity and consistency in the formulation of rules and the statutes that emerge from legislative committees, technical discussions, media awareness and judicial activism. It also reflects the thought process & vision of the decision maker and also the capability of the concerned staff to prepare the case scientifically. In the process of formulation a perspective of minimum one or may be two to three decades and the contours of environment down the line have to be envisaged through techniques like scenario writing. Thereafter based on the net assessment of the emerging scenario the strategy and the policies are formulated. However certain defining moments, which were not forming the part of the extrapolated trajectory to the future, need to be factored into the policy formulation. For example discovery of atomic energy in 1940ies, 1973 oil and petroleum crisis, in recent times advent of Shale gas and the climate changes are some of those game changers which have impacted the energy policy formulation. Periodic occurrences of such game changers (including looking for those game changers) call for building in a review system in the main menu. It is felt that the next big things in the field of energy are likely to be; commercial exploitation of the gas hydrates, thorium cycle becoming commercially and technologically viable, development of fusion energy through successful completion of the ITER experiment, fuel cells to economically and technologically exploit Hydrogen, use of algae, enhancement of efficiency of PV systems, OTEC and tidal energy attaining commercial viability and cost effective & technologically feasible waste to energy conversion in a sustained manner.

There are two schools of thought as far as role of decision maker is concerned. First is; 'hands off' approach and the second is, 'active involvement'. Both the approaches have their merits and demerits. While in the case of first; technical people have free hand within the vision enunciated by the decision maker but such an approach has problems of direction of progress, coordination problems with agencies not directly under technical head and also there is no time control. In the case of second, active involvement results into better coordination, better review procedures resulting into timely mid course corrections and the value addition which active involvement results into. Such a system will help in the evolution of a more flexible policy catering for all contingencies. However; such a system will invariably be slower. It has invariably been noticed that finally, the approach to be adopted will also be a function of the personality of the decision maker.

Another important aspect of the policy is; its propensity for enforcement. Therefore, while formulating the policy this aspect be borne in mind. There is a related issue about the effectiveness of the enforcement/regulatory mechanism. It should be highly effective and reviewed from time to time to ensure its continued effectiveness against the latest challenges emerging. Policy framework should also have provisions to deal with capacity building of industry, as well as that of HR (Including skilled manpower across the entire spectrum of activities), R&D, and infrastructural build up. Besides guidelines these policies should also have provisions for the enforcement monitoring and review inbuilt into them. One of the most important guiding principles is that the policies should be formulated in such a way that they continue to remain sensitive to the 'felt need of the environment'.

The US Experience in Evolution of Energy Management Mechanism

Multiplicity in the approach to energy management is not typical to India. Even the only superpower of the world; USA had its share of problems in reaching a state where they felt that there was a need to follow an integrated strategy to manage energy issues across the entire spectrum of research, supply & demand and capacity buildup simultaneously. During 1960ies the energy responsibility was dispersed among numerous specialized agencies who kept coming up with growth strategies with respect to technologies/ energy domain, which they were handling independently and in the absence of a centralized agency for coordination and control, each one of them exercised the prerogatives of their respective bureaucratic fiefdoms. One lesson that emerged was that there was a need to have an agency which looks at Energy as one monolithic resource and tries to manage all the facets related to supply and demand side management in a manner that even future requirements and technological growth of new emerging technologies are factored in formulating strategies. In all such policy frameworks emphasis on R&D has to be laid along with guidelines for conservation so that demand is kept under check and the supply continues to remain sustained.

USA realized after a few iterations that the way ahead would be a consolidation of energy functions into a new department of energy and natural resources except Atomic Energy Commission (AEC), which was to remain an independent agency (Vito A. Stagliano). It was established through an executive order of the President (Richard Milhous Nixon, 37th President of the USA from 1969 to 1974) in 1973. Among other things it created a counsellor to the President for natural resources, an assistant secretary of Interior for Energy and Minerals and the first Federal Office of Energy Conservation. As part of the order a new White House Energy Policy Office was established. In addition, the Congress was requested to create a cabinet level department for energy and natural resources and added a proposal to establish a separate Energy Research and Development Administration (ERDA). The order also directed the Department of Commerce to work with Environmental Protection Agency (EPA) on a program of voluntary energy efficiency labels for major home appliances, established a new division of Energy and Science in the office of Management of Budget and brought the Oil Policy Committee, which coordinated oil import policy, under the Treasury Department (Vito A.

Stagliano). This model is a good model; which has withstood the test of time.

India can consider examining this kind of model which can be considered for application with certain modifications to meet typical Indian conditions to make energy management in India far more comprehensive.

Energy Management in India

Energy has too many parameters related to different resources which need to be addressed in a coordinated manner to address core issues for optimization of energy supply and right sizing of demand in near term, short & medium term and long term. Also hedging issues which have a bearing on supply/demand, like; impact of global warming, logistics management, environmental issues, public perception management and many other issues need to be simultaneously tackled. Finally; management should also cater for a *Force Majeure* like natural/ manmade calamities, international events like Gulf War so that sustained supply of energy is not interrupted. Some of the important elements of a good energy management system in Indian context should be following:-

- Establishment of a Central Agency/ Department Headed by a Cabinet Minister- to ensure, formulate and review policies related to integrated use of energy and monitoring of its follow up. One of the responsibilities of this ministry will be to evolve a system of coordination between Ministries of finance, commerce, external affairs, environment and all the energy and energy resources related ministries with respect to all issues related to sustained enhancement of the availability of energy in all forms and simultaneously reduce the demand by demand side management. Presently this function is being addressed by Planning Commission, NSAB and PMO for all forms of energy except nuclear energy. For nuclear energy, this function is being performed by the AEC. Function of inter ministerial coordination is being done by the Cabinet Committee on Security (CCS). Growth of a particular resource or an enabling infrastructure is being addressed by the concerned ministry. Thus; issues are dealt by Ministry of Coal, Mo P&NG, MNRE, Ministry of Rural development, Ministry of Science and Technology, Ministry of Earth Sciences Ministry of Water Resources, Ministry of Urban development, Ministry of Power, Ministry of Agriculture, AEC and other supporting ministries. Certain subjects pertaining to energy are not on concurrent list and as such are dealt by the respective States. Besides coordination this agency should have capability for following:-

o   Forecasting of demand and supply by a scientific method.

o   System of technology appreciation through a system's approach.

o   Identify areas for further action and then monitor progress with strict time lines of the drawn plan through a scientific system wherein human biases and slip ups are obviated.

o   System of regular feedback to evolve course correction from time to time.

•   **Research and Development-**   continuous R&D, making budget provisions for the same and systems & procedures to integrate new technologies into the supply chain at appropriate time and level. Presently India spends less than three percent of its budget on R&D. Establishment of a National Energy Budget to fund the research and development activities in consultation with academic institutions and the industry will go a long way in addressing the issues well in time and in an holistic manner. Recommended thrust areas are following:-

o   Clean coal technologies to exploit local coal optimally.

o   Emphasis on exploration of sedimentary basins of the county; on shore and in EEZ for both natural gas and crude oil.

o   Enhance efficiency of systems related to exploitation of renewable sources of energy as this along with nuclear energy is going to be the main stay of energy matrix in long term.

o   Accelerating research in exploitation of thorium, carbide fuel for FBRs and other aspects of Nuclear energy exploitation with or without support from foreign agencies.

o   Widen the net of R&D for exploitation of pet coke, gas hydrates, CBM, shale gas, waste to energy systems, biomass and geo thermal energy.

o Research also needs to be done in materials.   .

- **Supply side Management-**

    o Use diplomatic leverage to enhance supply of LNG in near and medium term. It will not only improve the availability of energy but will enhance interdependence which will help to usher in peace and prosperity in the region.

    o Acquisition of oil/ gas/ coal equities wherever feasible through international cooperation or through commercial negotiations. Creation of a sovereign fund to do acquisition of energy bearing properties abroad be progressed.

    o Guarding against the non traditional threats to energy supply and checkmating the efforts of China to deny energy resources should be tackled through a well coordinated politico military and diplomatic strategy.

    o Use international cooperation in the field of nuclear energy to ensure sustained and improved supply of uranium & supply of LWR/ PWRs.

    o Laying emphasis on renewable energy exploitation.

    o Enhancing efficiency of PV systems and wind generators should be a challenge for the R&D and they should be encouraged to go for it

    o Exploitation of hydro energy through small hydro plants to ensure that environmental degradation is minimized without compromising the potential of hydro energy. Cooperation with neighbouring countries like Bhutan and Nepal for hydro energy be further strengthened to enhance interdependence and create win-win situation for everyone.

    o An imaginative policy imperative should be aimed to ensure cooperation with Tajikistan, Sri Lanka and China in the field of Hydro energy. Leveraging technology and diplomacy should be part of a well thought strategy.

o   Quickly improve grid system and off grid utilization of local resources for local uses.

o   and start building up relationships for resources and technology for nuclear, Shale gas and gas Hydrates.

o   Speed up the establishment of a Strategic reserve to cater for unforeseen contingencies. Quantum of reserve in terms of number of days needs to be worked out. This reserve needs to be built up in a graduated manner. Recommended final figure is 60 days reserve.

o   Policy revision be considered for involving private sectors in energy generation including nuclear energy. After all with certain checks and balances many other countries are also doing the same. Private sector which is driven by their profit motives are likely to usher in more professionalism.

- **Demand Side Management-**

o   Reduce consumption of gasoline products either by blending or through the usage of alternate fuels. While planning the blending the entire supply chain management needs to be addressed with necessary technological innovations and the infrastructural build-up which such a strategy may call for. In addition, before going on this approach, further environmental impact of blended fuel and impact of changing the crop pattern on food security needs to be studied in detail.

o   Enhance efficiency of equipment through standardization, enforcement of these norms through legislation/ policy formulation and system of punitive measures in case of default.

o   Enforcing green building norms- This is where industry also will have to be taken on board to ensure that building materials, electrical fittings, air conditioning equipment which lend themselves to reduction in energy demand are introduced in the market.

o   Afforestation, both; voluntary as well as compensatory to reduce ambient temperature with a view to reduce power demand and Rain Water Harvesting with a view to recharge aquifer so that energy spent on pumping is reduced. Though laws on the subject exist and environmental courts have also been setup consequent to 186th Report of the Law Commission, but a better enforcement mechanism be put in place with a view to ensure more effective enforcement.

o Time Zoning instead of single Indian Standard Time (IST) be examined with a view to optimize the use of sun light hours and ensure reduced power demand. In this connection Professor Dilip Ahuja Committee of Ministry of Power has already done a lot of work in 2010-11. It may be revived.

o More and more cities should be covered with mass rapid transportation system. In addition; within large complexes battery driven vehicles should be made available at affordable cost so that precious resources of petroleum products could be minimized. Enforcement of BHARAT norm should be strictly enforced to enhance vehicular efficiency with attended benefit of addressing climate change and pollution issue.

o Enhancing the efficiency of motor vehicles upward of 50 percent will help to save up to 86 million tons of oil by 2031-32. Similarly if more than 50 percent of the existing freight transportation by road is shifted to railways, saving of another 36 million tons can be achieved (Integrated Energy Policy of the Government of India -2006)

• **Financial Management**- to achieve energy security in next two decades an exorbitant investments worth US $ 1250 billion in energy infrastructure, with 76 percent of the investment going to power generation, transmission and distribution (RNCOS Report dated 29 June 2010), would be required. As far as India's nuclear programme is concerned; an overall investments of about Rs 35,000-40,000 Crores per annum for about twenty years with cumulative sum in the range of about $160 billion would be needed. It will be quite a task to manage this kind of fund through government sources and therefore it is essential that involvement of the Indian industry be facilitated through necessary amendments to law, if required, particularly in the case of nuclear energy domain. It needs to be done at the earliest. Pricing and tariff issues have recently been addressed both in case of Coal (Higher tariff for thermal plants in coastal area has been recommended by Planning commission) as well as gas as per Rangarajan committee's recommendation (besides raising the price the committee has also recommended that the market should determine the price). However tariff issues continuously need to be dealt in a imaginative manner so that all stake holders have equal degree of difficulty/ comfort, lest the country lands in situation where KG D-6 suddenly gets dry or thermal power plants located in coastal areas and having imported coal as the feed have cost differential to contend with. Therefore there is a need to improve the business environment with better decision making.

• **Capacity Building-** In the entire energy management domain consisting of; technical, financial, operations, infrastructural buildup, strategic/ logistics management, research and many other related fields, plenty of professionals from conceptual level to skilled worker's level man power, would be needed. In consultation with academic institutions and the state labour departments this manpower will have to be prepared in perpetuity; with a view to cater for the needs of expanding energy management field. Another capacity building which is needed is in the field of industrial buildup for which a coordinated effort needs to be made in consultation with ASSOCHAM, FICCI and CII.

• **Use of IT for an Effective Energy management.** The numbers of parameters that need to be monitored/ managed are so enormous that an IT based solution needs to be developed which is suitable for Indian conditions. A programme by name Long Range Energy Alternatives Planning System (LEAP) developed by Stockholm Environment Institute as part of their Community for Energy environment and Development programme appears to be a good tool which can be used after suitable India specific modifications to study the efficacy of the IT based solutions and thereafter develop an India specific programme for forecasting, planning and monitoring for exercising energy management through a Wide Area Network. The summary of the important features of the LEAP programme are given at Appendix J.

Need for a Long Term View on R&D

Shale gas has turned out to be a game changer in recent times in US Energy Matrix on supply side. The USA had started working on its exploitation as early as 1940ies. The present state of its role in the energy matrix of the us is a result of almost six decades of the hard work. Similarly in USA Krug SYNFUEL programme in 1952 demonstrated that it was possible to liquefy coal and produce oil from shale. At that point in time, cost was the inhibiting factor. Research continued and it may be noted that now this technology is becoming commercially viable and even US is likely to have oil from this route by 2015 (Internet and John M Broder and Clifford Krauss). In addition to the USA, even South Africa is commercially exploiting it. Another example of long gestation period of development is wind energy. First known modern windmill to generate electricity was installed in Scotland in 1887 and thus it has taken more than a century for the technology to mature. This clearly brings out the long gestation period which entails a R&D project (Vito A. Stagliano).

R&D is an expensive proposition with no confirmed probability of success. Nixon sanctioned a sum of $ 10 billion in 1973 to be spent in next five years and also ordered launch of a national conservation drive to reduce consumption of energy for personal effect by five percent over next 12 months. These instructions though did not meet their objective fully but put USA on a path which helped USA forty years down the line to become energy exporting country (Executive Energy Message)

The first Prototype Fast Breeder Reactor (PFBR) at Kalpakkam in Tamil Nadu is under construction. The project has reached advanced stage of construction and is getting poised for commissioning. The project has achieved the physical progress of 94.85 percent till April 2013 (Official web site of the BHAVINI). It is a mid course validation of a thought which was conceptualized in 1950ies when Bhabha presented his 'Three Stage Nuclear Programme' for India. In this connection it needs to be remembered that although so far India has barely reached stage two and third stage is still far off, yet; as has been deliberated in earlier parts, success of Three stage nuclear programme is essential for the energy security of India in long term and early operationalization of Stage-II is absolutely critical for the growth of the programme. Therefore decision makers need to remember that instead of getting into a panic mode and abandoning the self reliance route and going for import route may cause more harm than any good in long term.

6

Conclusion

It has been established through the discussion in this book that the nuclear energy indeed will increasingly assume a more significant role in building of the energy security of India in years ahead. The analysis of all possible energy bearing resources available indigenously or those to which India has access, it clearly emerges that beyond 2032, it will be an important element in the energy basket of India. Some of the important reasons for such an optimism are; likelihood of breeder technology assuming maturity, international cooperation on nuclear issue becoming more institutionalized after having got most of the nitty-gritties related to implementation of the mutual/ collective agreements for the international cooperation for civil nuclear energy based power generation resolved amicably and finally; availability of additional quantities of uranium ore from mines like Tumnapalle and other such mines, which are presently affected by public protest, start getting produced to reduce dependence on foreign supply of the uranium. In this connection, some of the important arguments made by the 'Nay Sayers' are based on either insufficient understanding of the big picture or in some cases with vested interests. One of the important issues which presently is being debated for its efficacy is; FBR technology which India is doggedly trying to make a commercially viable and technologically sustainable break through. It may be noted that not many countries are following this technology for nuclear power generation, as such evolution and testing of this technology will be practically an indigenous endeavour. Further it needs to be appreciated that the success of India's 'Three Stages Nuclear Plan' would largely depend on successful operationalization of the breeder technology. This highlights the criticality of breeder technology for the growth of nuclear energy exploitation in India, particularly as finally India will have to adopt thorium route due to abundant availability of thorium in India. The Nay Sayers are basing their argument on the premise that it is an untested technology. They are factually wrong (Besides Russia even in India,

FBTR is operational since 1985 and the thorium based, KAMINI Reactor is operational since 1996. This argument has already been examined in the earlier parts of the book and it has been brought out beyond any doubt that this technology is neither untested nor in terminal decline. Most important part, as explained earlier, is that India has an indigenous resource; thorium, which through leveraging of technology can be exploited and leaving that and going for a technology which is based on a resource; uranium, which is in short supply, cannot be considered logical). Their line of argument clearly brings out that they are extremely myopic in their approach and are failing to see the big picture. Their third argument is based on safety aspects of nuclear energy. Once again their argument is devoid of sound logic and it is based on an unknown fear. It needs to be considered that it is a myth that nuclear energy is less safe as compared to coal. This issue has been analyzed in detail in Chapter-III and Chapter-IV. India's safety record on the use of nuclear energy is a testimony to the fact that nuclear energy is safe in Indian context. It can therefore be concluded that nuclear energy is as safe as any other form of energy.

Rationale for India to opt for FBR route is two fold. First reason; of course is the potential for the availability of thorium in India which is believed to be in the range of 25 percent of the total holding of the world and the second and the historical reason is; India's commitment to disarmament. It may be noted that thorium cannot be weaponized. This indeed is major difference with uranium which has the capacity for destructive applications. In fact not going for breeder technology (it should be safe and finally cost effective, which should be the objective of the R&D community of India) is not in India's national interests because that will render a country like India who is short of uranium, vulnerable to international coercion by countries having large quantities of uranium with them. Thus any approach other than following FBR route amounts to India willingly going for a permanent handicap which she can ill afford. Therefore, though the breeding technology is still not fully developed and use of thorium breeders are still just out of conceptual stage, (KAMINI reactor based on this technology is operational) yet India needs to continue to push on with this approach for its own good, because India who has one of the largest reserves of thorium and being amongst the nations which will see the highest surge in power demand with its growth. Thus onus is now on Indian R&D community to make, firstly; FBR technology operational at the earliest and simultaneously put a lot of effort to develop a commercially viable thorium reactor earliest. In this connection India's plan to operationalize AHWR is significant. This reactor which uses thorium as the fuel, once operationalized will breed its own fuel (in a way it is a jump to Stage-III directly). It will also provide valuable inputs for the use of thorium in power generation cycle. Various technologies for Thorium-based plants, which have a promising future, are already being developed and deployed to test their technical and commercial feasibility in a number of countries including India. They are at various stages of testing. One of the technologies entails   breeding of fissile U^{233} isotope in the conventional reactors or through Molten Salt Reactors (MSR) which uses salts to trap the fissile material and do not react with air or burn in air or water. In this technology, the operational pressure is near the ordinary atmospheric pressure, and hence the cost of construction is low and there is no risk of a pressure explosion (APJ Abdul Kalam). Safety argument in any case is to say the least is based on JIC (just in case) syndrome. There had been only three major accidents in the world in last sixty years and in India not even one. Therefore saying that nuclear energy is less safe than thermal energy is a case of being too cautious.

It needs to be remembered that for a safe future of mankind clean sources of energy are absolutely inescapable and nuclear energy which is one of the cleanest form of energy has a great role to play in India's future energy security plans. It needs to be seen that due to poor quality of coal and inadequate reserves of petroleum products / natural gas the import bill will keep rising and also intangible impact on health and environment due to excessive release of Carbon and CO_2 in the atmosphere; will be some of the challenges, which will have to be tackled. In this connection it needs to be factored in, that present consumption of energy per capita is quite low but as industrialization increases and the GDP improves, the energy consumption per capita will increase at least to the level of the World average which will call for more stringent energy management and more cleaner forms of energy. Thus there is a need to diversify into sources like renewable and nuclear (particularly thorium route) for future energy needs. Systemic efficiency and imaginative measures to reduce the demand is the order of the day and all out efforts in these areas need to be made.

India is a diverse country and all possible forms of energy need to be added to the kitty with conversion technologies for all these sources becoming extremely efficient and cost effective, because every kW will count, energy management will have to be done in an integrated manner in such a way that local sources help to meet the local needs and surplus/ deficiency to demand be catered through an efficient grid system. Planning will have to be for at least till 2050 and these plans should be so flexible that emerging geopolitical developments and breakthroughs in the domain of technology are fully exploited. Finally, energy management will have to be IT leveraged with a view to ensure that large numbers of parameters which impact it, are factored into the decision matrix for their individual influence and also for their collective effect. Such a strategy will also help to avoid subjectivity of any kind.

Mechanics of Nuclear Fission Reactions

The chemical element isotopes that can sustain a fission chain reaction are called nuclear fuels and are said to be fissile. The most common nuclear fuels are U^{235} (the isotope of uranium with an atomic mass of 235 and of use in nuclear reactors) and Pu^{239} (the isotope of plutonium with an atomic mass of 239). These fuels break apart into a bimodal range of chemical elements with atomic masses centering near 95 and 135 (fission products).

Most nuclear fuels undergo spontaneous fission only very slowly, decaying instead mainly via an alpha/beta particle decay chain over periods of millennia to eons. In a nuclear reactor or nuclear weapon, the overwhelming majority of fission events are induced by bombardment with another particle, a neutron, which is itself produced by prior fission events. Nuclear fissions in fissile fuels are the result of the nuclear excitation energy produced when a fissile nucleus captures a neutron. This energy, resulting from the neutron capture, is a result of the attractive nuclear force acting between the neutron and nucleus. It is enough to deform the nucleus into a double-lobed "drop," to the point that nuclear fragments exceed the distances at which the nuclear force can hold two groups of charged nucleons together, and when this happens, the two fragments complete their separation and then are driven further apart by their mutually repulsive charges, in a process which becomes irreversible with greater and greater distance. A similar process occurs in fissionable isotopes (such as U^{238}), but in order to cause fission in such an isotope (U^{238}), additional energy is required which can be provided by fast neutrons (such as those produced by nuclear fusion in thermonuclear weapons).

In nature there are only three isotopes, namely; U^{235}, U^{238} and Th^{232} which can be used as nuclear fuel:-

- U^{235} as such.

- U^{238} after getting transmuted to Pu^{239} after undergoing a fission reaction.

- Th^{232} after transmuting into U^{233}

  Naturally occurring uranium consists of 99.3 percent of U^{238} and only 0.7 percent of U^{235},

i.e. for 1 nucleus of U^{235} there are 140 nuclei of U^{238} in the sample.

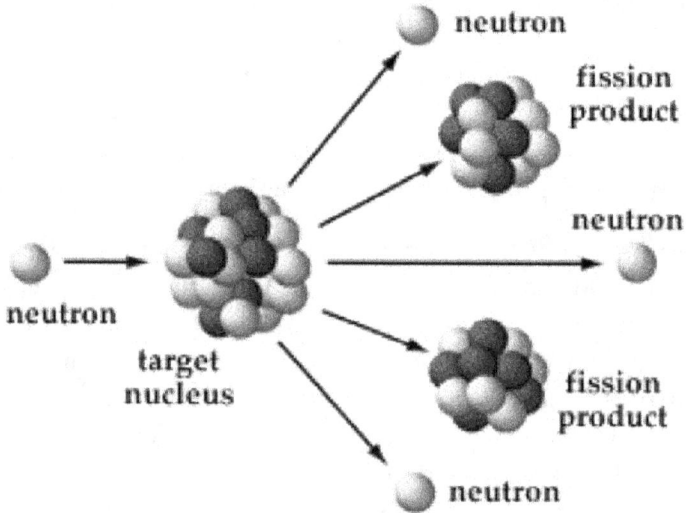

Figure- A.1: Basic Nuclear Fission Principle

Note: The two nuclei produced during the fission are most often of comparable size, typically with a mass ratio around 3:2 for common fissile isotopes.

Case of U²³⁵

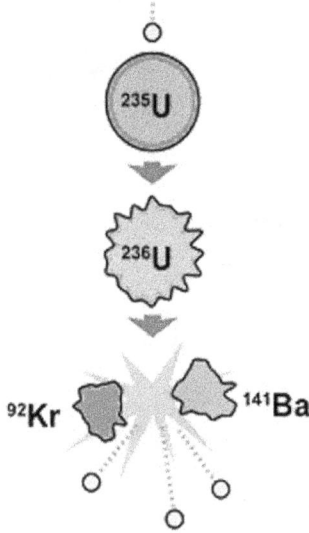

Figure- A.2: Breakdown of a Nucleus

Fission of heavy elements is an exothermic reaction which can release a large amount of energy (~1 MeV per nucleon) both as electromagnetic radiation and as kinetic energy of the fragments (heating the bulk material where fission takes place). In order that fission produces energy, the total binding energy of the resulting elements must be larger than that of the starting element. Fission is a form of nuclear transmutation because the resulting fragments are not the same elements as the original one. Typical fission events release about two hundred million eV (200 MeV) of energy for each fission event; e.g. for U^{235}: ~235 MeV. By contrast, most chemical oxidation reactions (such as burning coal) release at most a few eV per event. Therefore nuclear fuel contains at least ten million times more usable energy per unit mass than chemical fuel. E.g.: 1 gram of U^{235} is equivalent to 1 ton of coal (=> 3.5 ton of CO_2). In more measureable terms one gram of U^{235} can produce one MW of energy per day.

Fission Reaction

Neutron
Nucleus

Compound Nucleus in an excited state of high internal energy

Fission Fragments
~200 MeV of Energy

Fast-n

Radiation

$$_{92}U^{235} + _0n^1 \longrightarrow _{36}Kr^{92} + _{56}Ba^{141} + 3(_0n^1) + Energy$$

$$_{92}U^{235} + _0n^1 \longrightarrow _{42}Mo^{95} + _{57}La^{139} + 7(_{-1}e^0) + 2(_0n^1) + Energy$$

Mass 'm1'= 236.0526 g

Mass 'm2'= 235.8332 g

Difference in mass $\Delta m = 0.2194$ gm

$E = \Delta m \times c^2$

c, velocity of light = 3×10^8 m/s

Fission of 1 gm of U-235 per day generates ~1 MW Power

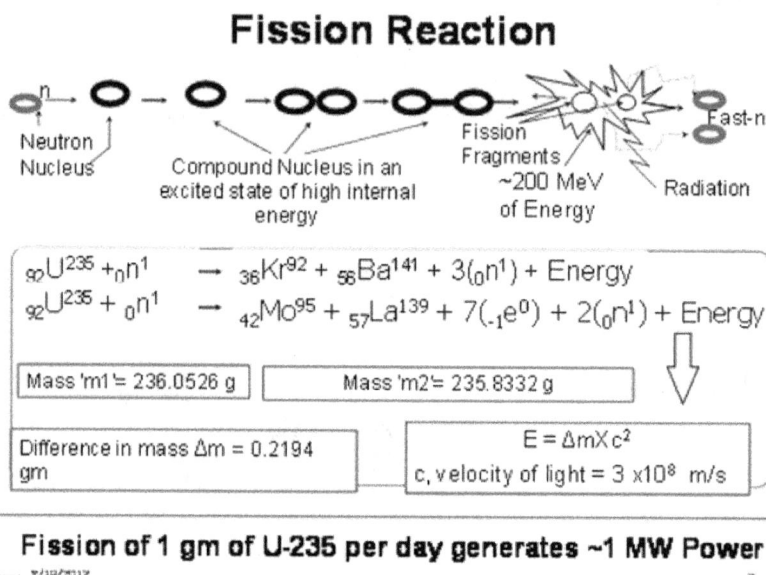

Figure- A.3: Fission Reaction

Conversion of fertile material to fissile material

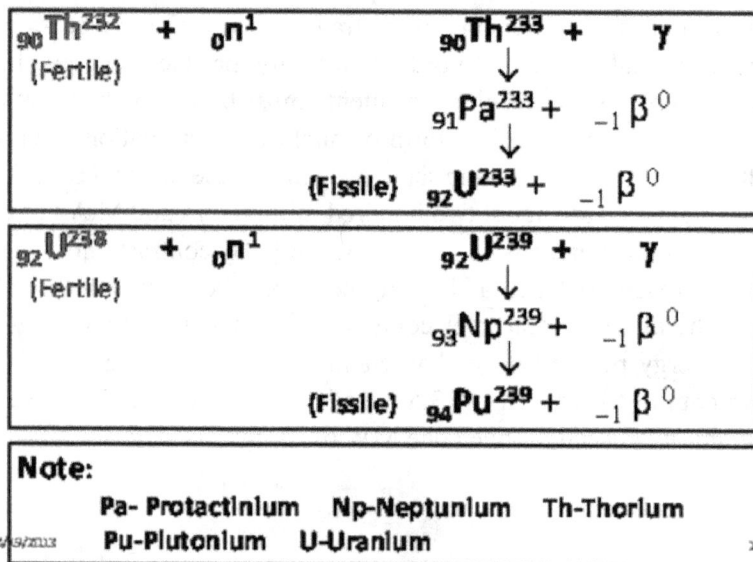

$_{90}Th^{232}$ + $_0n^1$ (Fertile)	$_{90}Th^{233}$ + γ
	$\downarrow$
	$_{91}Pa^{233}$ + $_{-1}\beta^0$
	$\downarrow$
	{Fissile} $_{92}U^{233}$ + $_{-1}\beta^0$

$_{92}U^{238}$ + $_0n^1$ (Fertile)	$_{92}U^{239}$ + γ
	$\downarrow$
	$_{93}Np^{239}$ + $_{-1}\beta^0$
	$\downarrow$
	{Fissile} $_{94}Pu^{239}$ + $_{-1}\beta^0$

Note:

Pa- Protactinium   Np-Neptunium   Th-Thorium
Pu-Plutonium   U-Uranium

Figure- A.4: Fertile to Fissile

Chain Reaction.

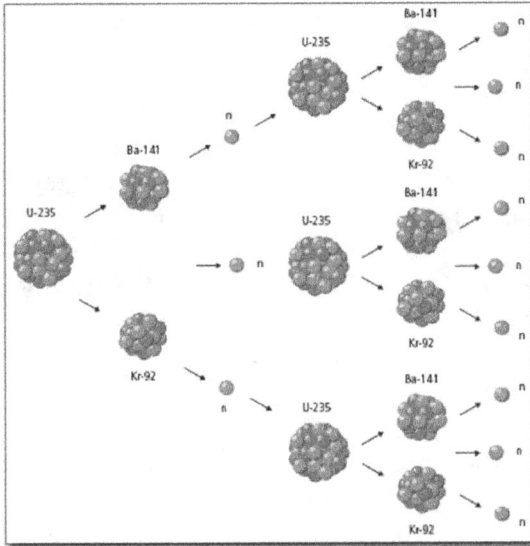

Figure-A.5: Chain Reaction

Fission chain reactions can be used in nuclear power plants as well as nuclear weapons. Nuclear power plants operate by precisely controlling the rate at which nuclear reactions occur, and that control is maintained through the use of several redundant layers of safety measures. Moreover, the materials in a nuclear reactor core and the uranium enrichment level make a nuclear explosion impossible, even if all safety measures failed. Nuclear weapons are specifically engineered to produce a reaction that is so fast and intense that it cannot be controlled after it has started. When properly designed, this uncontrolled reaction can lead to an explosive energy release.

Moderators. To control such a nuclear chain reaction, neutron poisons and neutron moderators can change the portion of neutrons that will go on to cause more fission. Nuclear reactors generally have automatic and manual systems to shut down the fission reaction, if monitoring detects unsafe conditions. Commonly-used moderators include regular (light) water (in 74.8 percent of the world's reactors), solid graphite (20 percent of reactors) and heavy water (5 percent of reactors). Some experimental types of reactors have used beryllium as moderator. Hydrocarbons have been suggested as another possibility.

Mitigation of Heat Generated

The reactor core generates heat in a number of ways:

- The kinetic energy of fission products is converted to thermal energy when these nuclei collide with nearby atoms.

- The reactor absorbs some of the gamma rays produced during fission and converts their energy into heat.

- Heat is produced by the radioactive decay of fission products and materials that have been activated by neutron absorption. This decay heat-source will remain for some time even after the reactor is shut down.

A kilogram of U^{235} converted via nuclear processes releases approximately three million times more energy than a kilogram of coal burned conventionally (7.2×1013 joules per kilogram of U^{235} versus 2.4×107 joules per kilogram of coal).

Cooling. A nuclear reactor coolant is usually water but sometimes a gas or a liquid metal (like liquid sodium) or molten salt is circulated past the reactor core to absorb the heat that it generates. The heat is carried away from the reactor and is then used to generate steam. Most reactor systems employ a cooling system that is physically separated from the water that will be boiled to produce pressurized steam for the turbines, like the pressurized water reactor. But in some reactors the water for the steam turbines is boiled directly by the reactor core, for example the boiling water reactor.

Schematic layout of Power Generation.

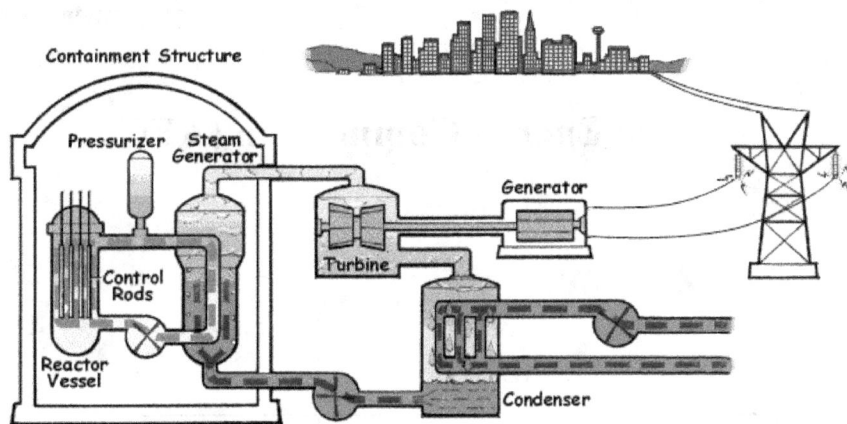

Figure- A.6: Power generation through a Fission Reaction

Source: SS 2011: Introduction to Nuclear and Particle Physics, Part-2, "Nuclear reactions, Nuclear Energetics by Goethe Universitat, Frankfurt AM Main, pp-28

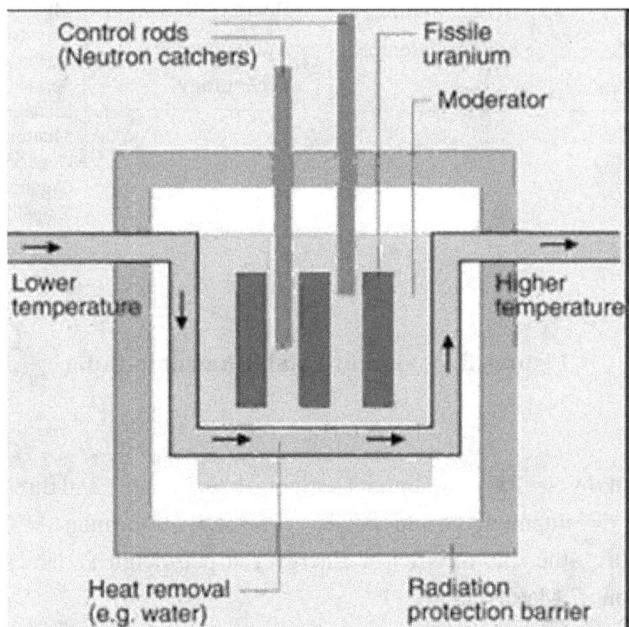

Figure- A.7: Blow up of Arrangement inside a Reactor

Source: Same as above.

Appendix B

Atomic Energy Commission (AEC)

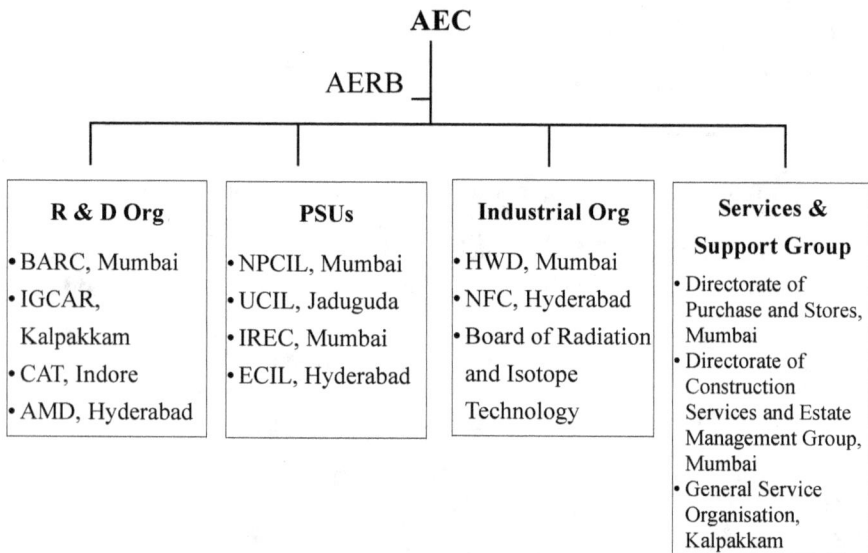

AEC

AERB

R & D Org	PSUs	Industrial Org	Services & Support Group
• BARC, Mumbai • IGCAR, Kalpakkam • CAT, Indore • AMD, Hyderabad	• NPCIL, Mumbai • UCIL, Jaduguda • IREC, Mumbai • ECIL, Hyderabad	• HWD, Mumbai • NFC, Hyderabad • Board of Radiation and Isotope Technology	• Directorate of Purchase and Stores, Mumbai • Directorate of Construction Services and Estate Management Group, Mumbai • General Service Organisation, Kalpakkam

Figure- B.1: Nuclear Establishment in India

Source: A talk by Sri Ratan K Sinha, Distinguished Scientist and director Reactor design and development Group BARC (Presently Chairman AEC), India's Energy Security-the role of Nuclear Energy", at petroleum Federation of India, New Delhi on 27 May 2005.

Bhabha Atomic Research Centre (BARC)

• **Groups-** BARC has been divided into a total of 19 groups. Details of these groups are as follows:-

o Administrative.

o Automation and Manufacturing.

o Beam Technology Development.

o Bio-Science.

o Chemical Engineering and Technology.

o Chemistry.

o Electronics and Instrumentation.

o Engineering Services.

o Health Safety and Environment.

o Knowledge management.

o Material.

o Medical.

o Nuclear Fuel.

o Nuclear Recycle.

o Physics.

o Radio Chemistry and Isotopes.

o Reactor.

- o   Reactor Design and Development.

- o   Reactor Projects.

- •   **Divisions** - These groups are further sub divided into 71 divisions.

- •   **Strength-**

- o   Scientists and Engineers-   4130.

- o   Staff-   14,900.

Source: A talk by Sri Ratan K Sinha, Distinguished Scientist and director Reactor design and development Group BARC (Presently Chairman AEC), India's Energy Security-the role of Nuclear Energy", at petroleum Federation of India, New Delhi on 27 May 2005.

Goals of R&D Activities in BARC

• To develop indigenous nuclear Technologies for following purposes:-

o For generating energy.

o For non power applications.

• To undertake 'Research, Development, Demonstration and Deployment' (RD3) in current as well as futuristic technologies, material and equipment.

• To share results of the research with the industrial undertakings of the DAE which are as follows:-

o Nuclear Power Corporation of India Limited (NPCIL).

o Nuclear Fuel Complex (NFC).

o Heavy Water Board (HWB).

o Indian Rare Earth Limited (IREL).

o Uranium Corporation of India Limited (UCIL).

o Electronics Corporation of India Limited (ECIL).

• Strive for excellence in all areas of nuclear science and technology. Some of the identified areas are as follows:-

o Utilization of the research reactors.

o Taking front and backend of the nuclear cycle to the logical conclusion.

o Production of radio isotopes and development of the radiation technology.

Source: A talk by Sri Ratan K Sinha, Distinguished Scientist and director Reactor design and development Group BARC (Presently Chairman AEC), India's Energy Security-the role of Nuclear Energy", at petroleum Federation of India, New Delhi on 27 May 2005.

Reactor Classification

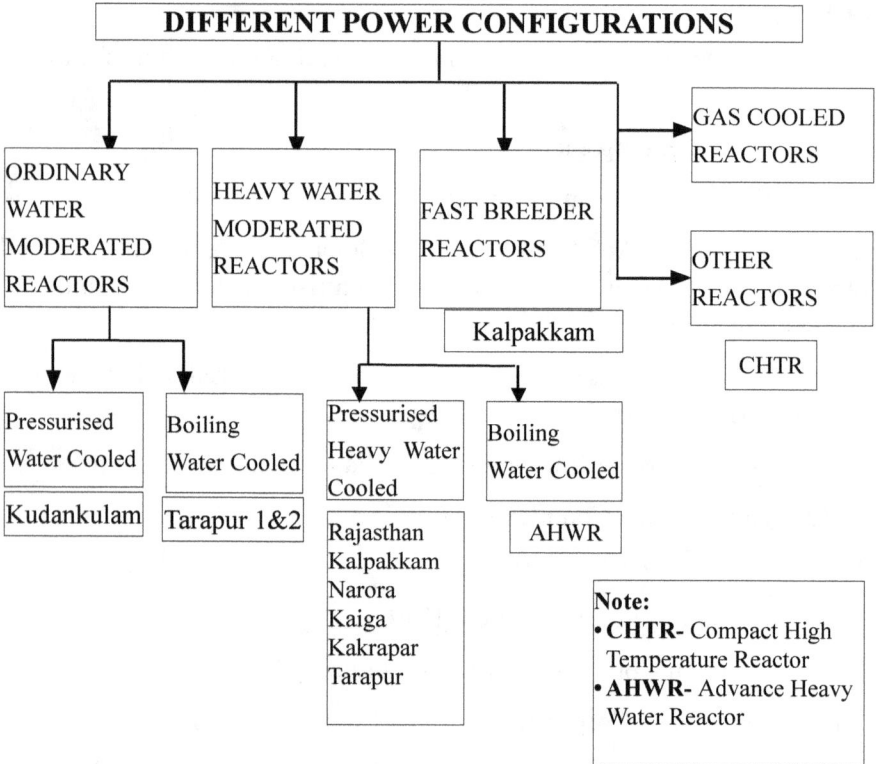

DIFFERENT POWER CONFIGURATIONS

ORDINARY WATER MODERATED REACTORS

HEAVY WATER MODERATED REACTORS

FAST BREEDER REACTORS

GAS COOLED REACTORS

OTHER REACTORS

Kalpakkam

CHTR

Pressurised Water Cooled

Boiling Water Cooled

Pressurised Heavy Water Cooled

Boiling Water Cooled

Kudankulam

Tarapur 1&2

Rajasthan Kalpakkam Narora Kaiga Kakrapar Tarapur

AHWR

Note:
• **CHTR-** Compact High Temperature Reactor
• **AHWR-** Advance Heavy Water Reactor

Figure- C.1: Classification of Reactors

Nuclear Fuels

Nuclear fuel is a material that can be 'burnt' by nuclear fission or fusion to derive nuclear energy. Nuclear fuel can be referred to the fuel itself, or to physical objects (for example bundles composed of fuel rods) composed of the fuel material, mixed with structural, neutron moderating, or neutron reflecting materials.

Most nuclear fuels contain heavy fissile elements that are capable of nuclear fission. When nucleus of these elements are struck by neutrons, they are in turn emit neutrons resulting into a self-sustaining chain reaction with release of energy at controlled rate in a power generation programme and at a uncontrolled rate in a nuclear weapon.

The most common fissile nuclear materials are U^{235} and Pu^{239}. The nuclear fuel cycle is the process which entails; mining, refining, purifying, using, and ultimately disposing of nuclear fuel in a sequential manner.

Formation of an Oxide Fuel Pellet. For fission reactors, the fuel (typically based on uranium) is usually based on the metal oxide; the oxides are used rather than the metals themselves because the oxide melting point is much higher than that of the metal and because it cannot burn, being already in the oxidized state. Uranium dioxide (UO_2) is a black semiconducting solid. It can be made by reacting uranyl nitrate with a base (ammonia) to form a solid (ammonium uranate). It is heated (calcined) to form U_3O_8 that can then be converted by heating in an argon / hydrogen mixture (700 °C) to form UO_2. The UO_2 is then mixed with an organic binder and pressed into pellets, these pellets are then fired at a much higher temperature (in Hydrogen/Argon) to sinter the solid. The aim is to form a dense solid which has few pores. The thermal conductivity of uranium dioxide is very low compared with that of zirconium metal, and it goes down as the temperature goes up.

Mixed oxide, or MOX fuel, is a blend of plutonium and natural or depleted uranium which behaves similarly (though not identically) to the enriched uranium feed for which most nuclear reactors were designed. MOX fuel is an alternative to low enriched uranium (LEU) fuel used in the LWRs which predominate nuclear power generation. Some concern has been expressed that used MOX cores will pose fresh challenges for disposal of waste material. In this connection it is relevant to note that MOX itself is a means to dispose of surplus plutonium by transmutation. Currently (March, 2005) reprocessing of commercial nuclear fuel to make MOX is done in England and France, and to a lesser extent in Russia, India and Japan. People's Republic of China has also started work on fabrication of MOX, however her programme on the subject is at planning stage presently.

Metal fuels have the advantage of much higher heat conductivity than oxide fuels but cannot survive high temperatures as oxide fuel can do. Metal fuels have a long history of use; stretching from the Clementine reactor in 1946 to many test and research reactors. Metal fuels have the potential for the highest fissile atom density. Metal fuels are normally alloyed, but some metal fuels have been made with pure uranium metal. Uranium alloys that have been used are as follows:-

- Uranium-aluminum.

- Uranium-zirconium.

- Uranium-silicon.

- Uranium-molybdenum.

- Uranium-zirconium hydride.

Any of the aforementioned fuels can be made with plutonium and other actinides as part of a closed nuclear fuel cycle. Metal fuels have been used in water reactors and liquid metal fast breeder reactors, such as Experimental Breeder Reactor-II (EBR-II)[1]. The TRIGA[2] (Training,

---

1 Experimental Breeder Reactor-II (EBR-II) is a reactor designed, built and operated by Argonne National Laboratory in Idaho. It was shut down in 1994. Its fuel consisted of uranium enriched to 67 percent. The fuel rods also contained 10 percent zirconium. It was a sodium cooled reactor with a thermal power rating of 62.5 MW. It had a steam plant that produces 19 MW of electrical power through a conventional turbine generator.

2 TRIGA is a pool type reactor that can be installed without a containment building, and is designed for use by scientific institutions and universities for purposes such as undergraduate and graduate education, private commercial research, non-destructive

Research, Isotopes, General Atomics) reactor uses uranium-zirconium-hydride (UZrH) fuel, which has a prompt negative temperature coefficient, meaning that; as the temperature of the core increases, the reactivity decreases—so it is highly unlikely for a meltdown to occur and as such, a reactor is safe against accidents like Fukushima. Most cores that use this fuel are "high leakage" cores where the excess leaked neutrons can be utilized for research. TRIGA fuel was originally designed to use highly enriched uranium; however in 1978 the U.S. Department of Energy launched its Reduced Enrichment for Research Test Reactors program, which promoted reactor conversion to low-enriched uranium fuel. In a fast neutron reactor, the minor actinides produced by neutron capture of uranium and plutonium can be used as fuel. Metal actinide fuel is typically an alloy of zirconium, uranium, plutonium and the minor actinides. It can be made inherently safe as thermal expansion of the metal alloy will increase neutron leakage.

Ceramic fuels; other than oxides have the advantage of high heat conductivities and melting points, but they are more prone to swelling than oxide fuels and are not fully understood as well. This is often the fuel of choice for reactor designs that NASA produces. One advantage of these fuels is that; the Uranium Nitride has a better thermal conductivity as compared to UO_2. Second advantage is that the uranium nitride has a very high melting point. It is an expensive fuel.

Uranium carbide is in the form of pin-type fuel elements for liquid metal fast breeder reactors during their intense study during the 'Sixties' and 'Seventies'. However, recently there has been a revived interest in uranium carbide in the form of plate fuel and most notably, micro fuel particles (such as TRISO [3] particles). The high thermal conductivity and high melting point makes uranium carbide an attractive fuel. In addition, because of the absence of oxygen in this fuel (during the course of irradiation, excess gas pressure can build from the formation of Oxygen or other gases) as well as the ability to complement a ceramic coating (a ceramic-ceramic interface has structural and chemical advantages), uranium carbide could be the ideal fuel candidate for certain Generation

---

testing and isotope production. It uses Uranium-Zirconium hydride as fuel.

3 Tri-structural isotropic particles (TRISO particle)are spherically layered composite of a kernel of UO2, surrounded by a porous graphite buffer layer which is surrounded by a dense pyrolytic carbon layer. This type of fuel is useful for liquid metal fast breeder reactor.

IV reactors such as the gas-cooled fast reactor.

Liquid fuels are liquids containing dissolved nuclear fuel and have been shown to offer numerous operational advantages compared to traditional solid fuel approaches. Liquid-fuel reactors offer significant safety advantages due to their inherently stable "self-adjusting" reactor dynamics. This provides two major benefits: - virtually eliminating the possibility of a run-away reactor meltdown, - providing an automatic load-following capability which is well suited to electricity generation and high temperature industrial heat applications. Another major advantage of the liquid core is its ability to be drained rapidly into a passively safe dump-tank. Another huge advantage of the liquid core is its ability to release xenon gas which normally acts as a neutron absorber and causes structural occlusions in solid fuel elements (leading to early replacement of solid fuel rods with over 98 percent of the nuclear fuel unburned, including many long lived actinides). In contrast Molten Salt Reactors (MSR) are capable of retaining the fuel mixture for significantly extended periods, which not only increases fuel efficiency dramatically, but also incinerates the vast majority of its own waste as part of the normal operational characteristics.

Molten salt fuels have nuclear fuel dissolved directly in the molten salt coolant. Molten salt-fueled reactors, such as the liquid fluoride thorium reactor (LFTR), are different than molten salt-cooled reactors that do not dissolve nuclear fuel in the coolant. Molten salt fuels were used in the LFTR known as the 'Molten Salt Reactor Experiment', as well as other liquid core reactor experiments. The liquid fuel for the molten salt reactor was a mixture of lithium, beryllium, thorium and uranium fluorides: LiF-BeF2-ThF4-UF4 (72-16-12-0.4 mol percent). It had a peak operating temperature of 705°C in the experiment, but could have operated at much higher temperatures, since the boiling point of the molten salt was in excess of 1400°C.

Fusion fuels include tritium (H_3) and deuterium (H_2) as well as helium-3 (He_3). Many other elements can be fused together, but the larger electrical charge of their nuclei means that much higher temperatures would be required for fusion to happen and as such presently only the fusion of the lightest elements is being seriously considered as a future energy source. Although some fusion reactions have sustained for a few minutes but utilizing fusion fuel as a net energy source remains only a theoretical possibility.

Engineering of Nuclear Fuel

- **Uranium dioxide** (UO_2) powder is compacted to cylindrical pellets and sintered at high temperatures to produce ceramic nuclear fuel pellets with a high density and well defined physical properties and chemical composition. Such fuel pellets are then stacked and filled into the metallic tubes. The metal used for the tubes depends on the design of the reactor. Most reactors now use a zirconium alloy which, in addition to being highly corrosion-resistant, has low neutron absorption. The tubes containing the fuel pellets are sealed: these tubes are called fuel rods. The finished fuel rods are grouped into fuel assemblies that are used to build up the core of a power reactor.

- **Cladding** is the outer layer of the fuel rods, standing between the coolant and the nuclear fuel. It is made of a corrosion-resistant material with low absorption cross section for thermal neutrons, usually Zircaloy or steel in modern constructions. Cladding prevents radioactive fission fragments from escaping the fuel into the coolant and contaminating it. As an aftermath of the Fukushima Daiichi NPP disaster, a new method of covering active nuclear fuel pellets with ceramic silicon carbide (SiC) is being developed at Massachusetts Institute of Technology. SiC, as compared to zirconium alloy used in most water cooled plants, produces up to thousand times less hydrogen when reacting with hot steam.

PWR fuel consists of cylindrical rods put into bundles. The Zircaloy tubes and the fuel cladding gap is filled with helium gas to improve the conduction of heat from the fuel to the cladding. The fuel bundles usually are enriched several percent in U^{235}. The uranium oxide is dried before inserting into the tubes to try to eliminate moisture in the ceramic fuel that can lead to corrosion and hydrogen embrittlement. The Zircaloy tubes are pressurized with helium to try to minimize pellet-cladding interaction. However this arrangement has a possibility that the fuel rod failure may occur over long periods.

In BWR, the fuel is similar to PWR fuel except that the bundles are "canned". This is primarily done to prevent local density variations from affecting neutronics and thermal hydraulics of the reactor core.

CANDU fuel bundles consist of sintered (UO_2) pellets in zirconium alloy tubes, welded to zirconium alloy end plates. Current CANDU designs do not need enriched uranium to achieve criticality (due to their more efficient heavy water moderator), however, some newer concepts call for low enrichment to help reduce the size of the reactors.

Sodium bonded fuel consists of fuel that has liquid sodium in the gap between the fuel slug/ pellet and the cladding. This fuel type is often used for sodium cooled liquid metal fast reactors. The fuel slug may be metallic or ceramic. The sodium bonding is used to reduce the temperature of the fuel.

Fusion fuels include tritium (H_3) and deuterium (H_2) as well as helium-3 (He_3). Many other elements can be fused together, but the larger electrical charge of their nuclei means that much higher temperatures would be required for fusion to happen and as such presently only the fusion of the lightest elements is being seriously considered as a future energy source. Although some fusion reactions have sustained for a few minutes but utilizing fusion fuel as a net energy source remains only a theoretical possibility. (Science Daily, 25 July 2013)

India's Nuclear Energy Programme: A SWOT Analysis

Strengths

It is a mission oriented programme, where emphasis, right from the beginning, had been laid, to optimize the indigenous resources and has evolved as a tailor made programme to meet the power needs of India in long, medium and short terms.

By and large, it is an indigenously developed programme which has been strengthened due to international restrictive regimes and has got evolved, may be at times slowly, but surely quite steadily and today India has been able to master the entire nuclear energy conversion cycle both uranium based as well as thorium based (stage-II).

It is a highly imaginative three stage development plan where bye products of each stage are feed stock for the next stage and also the issues of waste management are addressed adequately. Second aspect of the programme is to make use of indigenous resources. Another important aspect of the programme is the development of technologies which are beneficial for areas other than energy production like; medical; agriculture etc.

Evolution of a good infrastructure for the development of technologies for various aspects related to nuclear cycle and related fields of waste management, research, design & development of reactors, fuels & collateral fields and capacity building to create human resources & industrial capacity to undertake typical construction & fabrication of equipment jobs.

Weaknesses

Tradition of slippages. Since the entire programme has grown against tremendous amount of international pressure, coercion and restrictive regimes. These challenges, besides upsetting the time plan for energy availability, had a very heavy financial impact also, because a programme which started with a budget outlay of certain amount has invariably not been able to finish in the allocated amount and as such has resulted into financial drain due to inflation and opportunity costs getting added to it.

System of forecasting, at best, has been quite mediocre because the programme has rarely, if ever, has been able to stick to projections. There are two important reasons for the same, firstly; a tendency to base forecasting on very optimistic assumptions, secondly; not having a system to timely anticipate likely inhibitors. Important Cases in point are power production predictions and development of breeder technology.

Fragmented decision making frame work of India, which has been extremely slow and not focused. Case in point is decision of the Ministry of Commerce, Government of India to decide to export Monazite Sand without taking into account the future needs of India's own nuclear programme.

Lack of consensus on the role of nuclear energy, in future energy supply matrix and also on the strategy for exploitation of indigenous resources.

Opportunities

Indo-US Civil Nuclear Agreement has opened new vistas and India, which post Operation SHAKTI (Nuclear Tests)- 1998, had become an international pariah has joined the main stream and not only the USA but other countries, having natural and equipment based resources related to nuclear energy, are also coming forward to do trade with India on nuclear technologies and supply of material required.

India has a NSG waiver and India specific safeguard agreement with the IAEA without affecting its nuclear weponization programme.

Growth of the Indian Industrial Sector in the field of technology and technological innovations. Such a growth can be leveraged to support the growth of nuclear power industry.

Capacity of the nation to support indigenous nuclear energy programme, which has grown over the years despite international restrictive regimes. Years of living in a hostile geopolitical environment which is not supportive of Indian endeavours to achieve energy independence has made India more determined and confident to tackle the state of technological deprivation and the international blackmail.

Consistent GDP growth of last few years (notwithstanding the recent volatility and uncertainties) has given a robust economic muscle to India to finance its energy related projects in general and nuclear energy related projects in particular. India's own economic strength has a contributory factor in not such a healthy state of economy of Europe, Japan and the US (notwithstanding the recent revival in the US economy) has helped India to attract attention of the international nuclear energy suppliers who are desperately looking for new markets.

Threats

Public Protests, based on perceived and genuine fears about safety and fear of losing land, have become quite frequent. In fact, mining of uranium in Meghalaya and Andhra Pradesh, where major deposits have been found, has not progressed due to public protests. Kudankulam was almost sabotaged and proposed plants at Haripur in West Bengal and Jaitapur have got stuck due to protests by the locals. Sometimes it is genuine fears on account of lack of information which can be corrected by launching awareness campaign, but at times it is instigated by interested lobbies which range from anti national campaign engineered by foreign powers to rival business lobbies.

Lack of faith of the decision makers in the future of nuclear energy is a reality and probably based on their perception that alternatives can provide better options. Such a state leads to indecision and indifference which slows down the progress with major financial setbacks along with cascading effects which a delayed programme results into.

Programme based on many technologies which at best are in conceptual state presently. Case in point is thorium reactor which India is having only a pilot plant (KAMINI) presently. Similar is the case with carbide and other metallic fuels which need to be developed simultaneously lest India gets stranded after PFBR becoming critical.

Limited international cooperation despite NSG waiver, is a reality. But for some supply of Uranium no plant has come up in last four years since the signing of the accord. Probably India's liability act is deterring other countries to come forward or certain geopolitical lobbies like China are putting impediments in the smooth progress of the technology and equipment import.

Infusion of technology ex import, which is essentially based on use of enriched uranium for power generation, has a potential to derail India's plans to generate additional power by exploiting indigenous thorium resources.

THE ATOMIC ENERGY ACT, 1962

NO. 33 OF 1962

[15th September, 1962]

An Act to provide for the development, control and use of atomic energy for the welfare of the people of India and for other peaceful purposes and for matters connected therewith. Be it enacted by Parliament in the Thirteenth Year of the Republic of India as follows:-

1.   **Short Title, Extent and Commencement**

(1) This Act may be called the Atomic Energy Act, 1962.

(2) It extends to the whole of India.

(3) It shall come into force on such date as the Central Government may, by

Notification in the Official Gazette, appoint.

2.   **Definition and Interpretation**

(1) In this Act, unless the context otherwise requires -

(a) "Atomic energy" means energy released from atomic nuclei as a result of any process, including the fission and fusion processes;

(b) "Fissile material" means uranium-233, uranium-235, plutonium or any material containing these substances or any other material that may be declared as such by notification by the Central Government; ++(bb) "Government Company" means a company in which not less than fifty one percent of the paid up share capital is held by the Central Government;

(c) "Minerals" include all substances obtained or obtainable from the soil (including alluvium or rocks) by underground or surface working;

(d) "Notification" means notification published in the Official Gazette;

(e) "Plant" includes machinery, equipment or appliance whether affixed to land or not; ++ This has been inserted vide the Atomic Energy (Amendment) Act 1987 (N0. 29 of 1987)

(f) "Prescribed equipment" means any property which the Central Government may by notification, prescribe, being a property which in its opinion is specially designed or adapted or which is used or intended to be used for the production or utilization of any prescribed substance, or for the production or utilization of atomic energy, radioactive substances, or radiation, but does not include mining, milling, laboratory and other equipment not so specially designed or adapted and not incorporated in equipment used or intended to be used for any of the purposes aforesaid;

(g) "Prescribed substance" means any substance including any mineral which the Central Government may, by notification, prescribe, being a substance which in its opinion is or may be used for the production or use of atomic energy or research into matters connected therewith and includes uranium, plutonium, thorium, beryllium, deuterium or any of their respective derivatives or compounds or any other materials containing any of the aforesaid substances;

(h) "Radiation" means gamma rays, X-rays, and rays consisting of alpha particles, beta particles, neutrons, protons and other nuclear and sub-atomic particles, but not sound or radio waves, or visible, infrared or ultraviolet light;

(i) "Radioactive substance" or "radioactive material" means any substance or material which spontaneously emits radiation in excess of the levels prescribed by notification by the Central Government.

(2) Any reference in this Act to the working of minerals shall be construed as including a reference to the mining, getting, carrying

away, transporting, sorting, extracting or otherwise treating of minerals.

(3) Any reference in this Act to the production or use of atomic energy shall be construed as including a reference to the carrying out of any process, preparatory or ancillary to such production or use.

3.   **General Powers of the Central Government.** Subject to the provisions of this Act, Central Government shall have power -

(a) [1] To produce, develop, use and dispose of atomic energy either by itself or through any authority or Corporation established by it or a Government company and carry out research into any matters connected therewith;

(b)[2]   To manufacture or otherwise produce any prescribed or radioactive substance and any articles which in its opinion are, or are likely to be, required for, or in connection with, the production, development or use of atomic energy or such research as aforesaid and to dispose of such described or radioactive substance or any articles manufactured or otherwise produced.

(bb) (i) To buy or otherwise acquire, store and transport any prescribed or radioactive substance and any articles which in its opinion are, or are likely to be, required for, or in connection with, the production, development or use of atomic energy; and

(ii) To dispose of such prescribed or radioactive substance or any articles bought or otherwise acquired by it either by itself or through any authority or corporation established by it, or by a Government company;

(c) To declare as "restricted information" any information not so far published or otherwise made public relating to -

(i) The location, quality and quantity of prescribed substances and transactions for their acquisition, whether by purchase or otherwise, or disposal, whether by sale or otherwise;

(ii) The processing of prescribed substances and the extraction or

---

1 Inserted vide the Atomic Energy (Amendment) Act 1987 (No. 29 of 1987).

2 Substituted vide Atomic Energy (Amendment) Act 1987 (No. 29 of 1987).

production of fissile materials from them;

(iii) The theory, design, construction and operation of plants for the treatment and production of any of the prescribed substances and for the separation of isotopes;

(iv) The theory, design, construction and operation of nuclear reactors.

(v) Research and technological work on materials and processes involved in or derived from items (i) to (iv);

(d) To declare as "prohibited area" any area or premises where work including research, design or development is carried on in respect of the production, treatment, use, application or disposal of atomic energy or of any prescribed substance;

(e) To provide for control over radioactive substances or radiation generating plant in order to —

(i) Prevent radiation hazards;

(ii) Secure public safety and safety of persons handling radioactive substances or radiation generating plant; and

(iii) Ensure safe disposal of radioactive wastes;

(f)[3] To provide for the production and supply of electricity from atomic energy and for taking measures conducive to such production and supply and for all matters incidental thereto either by itself or through any authority or corporation established by it or a Government Company;

(g) To do all such things (including the erection of buildings and execution of works and the working of minerals) as the Central Government considers necessary or expedient for the exercise of the foregoing powers.

4.   **Notification of discovery of uranium or thorium.**

(1) Every person who, whether before or after the commencement of this Act, has discovered or discovers that uranium or thorium

---

3 IBID 37

occurs at any place in India shall, within three months after the date of commencement of this Act or after the discovery, whichever is later, report the discovery in writing to the Central Government or to any person or authority authorized by the Central Government in this behalf.

(2) Every person who has reason to believe that uranium or thorium occurs at any place in India, shall without delay, send intimation of such belief and the reasons there for to the Central Government or to any such person or authority as aforesaid.

5.   **Control over mining or concentration of substances containing uranium.**

(1) If the Central Government is satisfied that any person is mining or is about to mine any substance from which, in the opinion of the Central Government, uranium can be or may reasonably be expected to be, isolated or extracted, or is engaged or is about to be engaged in treating or concentrating by any physical, chemical or metallurgical process any substance from which, in the opinion of the Central Government, uranium can be or may reasonably be expected to be, isolated or extracted, the Central Government may by notice in writing given to that person either -

   (a) Require him in conducting the mining operations or in treating or concentrating the substance aforesaid to comply with such terms and conditions and adopt such processes as the Central Government may in the notice, or from time to time thereafter, think fit to specify, or

   (b) Totally prohibit him from conducting the mining operations or treating or concentrating the substance aforesaid.

(2) Where any terms and conditions are imposed on any person conducting any mining operations or treating or concentrating any substance under clause (a) of sub-section (1), the Central Government may, having regard to the nature of the terms and conditions, decide as to whether or not to pay any compensation to that person and the decision of the Central Government shall be final [4]; Provided that where the Central Government decides not to

---

4 IBID-37

pay any compensation, it shall record in writing a brief statement giving the reasons for such decision.

(3) Where the Central Government decides to pay any compensation under sub-section (2), the amount thereof shall be determined in accordance with section 21 but in calculating the compensation payable, no account shall be taken of the value of any uranium contained in the substance referred to in sub-section (1).

(4) Where any mining operation or any process of treatment or concentration of any substance is prohibited under clause (b) of sub-section (1), the Central Government shall pay compensation to the person conducting the mining operations or using the process of treatment or concentration and the amount of such compensation shall be determined in accordance with section 21 but in calculating the compensation payable, no account shall be taken of the value of any uranium contained in the substance.

6.   Disposal of Uranium.

(1) No minerals, concentrates and other materials which contain uranium in its natural state in excess of such proportion as may be prescribed by notification by the Central Government shall be disposed of except with the previous permission in writing of the Central Government and in accordance with such terms and conditions as it may impose.

(2)[5] The Central Government may serve notice on any person who has produced any mineral, concentrate or other material referred to in sub-section (1) that the Central Government proposes to compulsorily acquire it and upon the service of the notice, the mineral, concentrate or other material shall become the property of the Central Government and shall be delivered to the Central Government or as it may direct; Provided that in determining the compensation regard shall be had to the cost of production of such mineral, concentrate or other material and such other factors as may be relevant, but no account shall be taken of the value of uranium in its natural state contained therein.

---

5   IBID-36

(3)[6] Compensation in respect of acquisition under sub-section (2) shall be paid in accordance with section 21 and in determining such compensation regard shall be had to the cost of production of such mineral, concentrate or other material and such other factors as may be relevant, but no account shall be taken of the value of uranium in its natural state contained therein. [7],[8]

7.   Power to obtain Information regarding; Materials, Plants or Processes.

The Central Government may, by notice in writing served on any person, require him to make such periodical and other returns, or statements at such times and containing such particulars and accompanied by such plans, drawings and other documents as may be specified in the notice relating to —

(a) Any prescribed substance, specified in the notice, in his possession or under his control or present in or on any land or mine owned or occupied by him which in the opinion of the Central Government is or can be a source of any of the prescribed substances, including returns in respect of any such land or mine;

(b) Any plant in his possession or under his control designed for mining or processing of minerals so specified, or adapted for the production or use of atomic energy or research into matters connected therewith;

(c) Any contract entered into by him or any license granted by or to him relating to prospecting or mining of minerals so specified or the production or use of atomic energy or research into matters connected therewith;

(d) Any other information in his possession relating to any work carried out by him or on his behalf or under his directions, in connection with prospecting or mining of arterials so specified or the production or use of atomic energy or research into matters connected therewith.

---

6   IBID-37

7   Substituted vide the Atomic Energy (Amendment) Act 1986 (No. 59 of 1986).

8   Inserted vide the Atomic Energy (Amendment) Act 1986 (No. 59 of 1986).

8.   **Power of Entry and Inspection.**

(1)   Any person authorized by the Central Government may, on producing, if so required, a duly authenticated document showing his authority, enter any mine, premises or land —

(a)   Where he has reason to believe that work is being carried out for the purpose of or in connection with production and processing of any prescribed substances or substances from which a prescribed substance can be obtained or production, development or use of atomic energy or research into matters connected therewith, or

(b)   Where any such plant as is mentioned in clause (b) of section 7 is situated, and may inspect the mine, premises or land and any articles contained therein.

(2)   The person carrying out the inspection may make copies of or extracts from any drawing, plan or other document found in the mine, premises or land and for the purpose of making such copies or extracts, may remove any such drawing, plan or other document after giving a duly signed receipt for the same and retain possession thereof for a period not exceeding seven days.

9.   **Power to do Work for Discovering Minerals.**

(1)   The Central Government may, subject to the provisions of this section, do on, over or below the surface of any land such work as it considers necessary for the purpose of discovering whether there is present in or on the land, either in a natural state or in a deposit of waste material obtained from any underground or surface working, any substance from which in its opinion any of the prescribed substances can be obtained, and the extent to which such substance is so present.

(2)   Before any powers are exercised under sub-section (1) in relation to any land, the Central Government shall serve on every owner, lessee and occupier of the land a notice in writing specifying the nature of the work proposed to be done and the extent of the land affected, and the time, not being less than twenty-eight days, within which and the manner in which objections can be made

thereto, and no such powers shall be exercised otherwise than in pursuance of the notice or before the expiration of the time specified therein for making objections.

(3) The Central Government may, after giving the person making the objection an opportunity of appearing before and being heard by a person appointed by the Central Government for the purpose, and after considering any such objection and the report of the person so appointed, make such orders as it may deem proper but not so as to increase the extent of the land affected.

(4) Compensation shall be determined and paid in accordance with section 21 in respect of any diminution in the value of any land or property situate thereon resulting from the exercise of powers under this section.

10. Compulsory Acquisition of Rights to work Minerals.

(1) Where it appears to the Central Government that any minerals from which in its opinion any of the prescribed substances can be obtained are present in or on any land, either in a natural state or in a deposit of waste material obtained from any underground or surface working, it may by order provide for compulsorily vesting in the Central Government the exclusive right, so long as the order remains in force, to work those minerals and any other minerals which it appears to the Central Government to be necessary to work with those minerals, and may also provide, by that order or a subsequent order, for compulsorily vesting in the Central Government any other ancillary rights which appear to the Central Government to be necessary for the purpose of working the minerals aforesaid including (without prejudice to the generality of the foregoing provisions) —

(a) Right to withdraw support;

(b) Rights necessary for the purpose of access to or conveyance of the minerals aforesaid or the ventilation or drainage of the working;

(c) Rights to use and occupy the surface of any land for the purpose of erecting any necessary buildings and installing any necessary plant in connection with the working of the minerals aforesaid;

(d) Rights to use and occupy for the purpose of working the minerals aforesaid any land forming part of or used in connection with an existing mine or quarry, and to use or acquire any plant used in connection with any such mine or quarry; and

(e) Rights to obtain a supply of water for any of the purposes connected with the working of the minerals aforesaid, or to dispose of water or other liquid matter obtained in consequence of working such minerals.

(2) Notice of any order proposed to be made under this section shall be served by the Central Government —

(a) On all persons who, but for the order, would be entitled to work the minerals affected; and

(b) On every owner, lessee and occupier (except tenants for a month or for less than a month) of any land in respect of which rights are proposed to be acquired under the order.

(3) Compensation in respect of any right acquired under this section shall be paid in accordance with section 21, but in calculating the compensation payable, no account shall be taken of the value of any minerals present in or on land affected by the order, being minerals specified in the order as those from which in the opinion of the Central Government uranium or any concentrate or derivative of uranium can be obtained.

11.   Compulsory Acquisition of Prescribed Substances, Minerals and Plants.

(1) Save as otherwise provided in any other provision of this Act, the Central Government may compulsorily acquire in accordance with the provisions of this section —

(a) Any prescribed substance;

(b) Any minerals from which in the opinion of the Central Government any of the prescribed substances can be obtained;

(c) Any prescribed equipment;

(d) Any plant which is designed or adapted for the mining or processing of any minerals referred to in clause (b) or substances obtained there from or for the production or use of any prescribed substance or a radioactive substance or for the production, use or disposal of such articles as are or are likely to be required for or in connection with the production, use or disposal of atomic energy or for research into matters connected therewith.

(2) Where the Central Government acquires any plant referred to in clause (d) of subsection (1), it shall also have the right to acquire any buildings, railway sidings, tramway lines, or aerial ropeways serving such plant.

(3) Where the Central Government proposes to acquire any property under sub-section (1), it shall serve upon the person appearing to be the owner thereof, a notice in writing specifying the property to be acquired and requiring that person to make to the Central Government within the time specified in the notice a written declaration containing such particulars as may be so specified regarding the ownership of such property and any agreement or charge by virtue of which any other person has an interest in such property.

(4) Upon the service of a notice under sub-section (3), no property to which the notice relates shall be disposed of without the previous permission in writing of the Central Government.

(5) If it appears to the Central Government in consequence of any written declaration made to it in pursuance of sub-section (3) that any person other than the person on whom the notice under sub-section (3) was served is the owner of, or has any interest in, the property to which the notice relates, the Central Government shall serve a copy of the notice on that other person.

(6) A notice served under sub-section (3) shall contain a statement to the effect that an objection may be made thereto within such time and in such manner as may be specified, and if any such objection is duly made and not withdrawn, the Central Government shall

afford an opportunity to the person making the objection of appearing before and being heard by a person appointed by the Central Government for the purpose.

(7) After considering any such objection, and the report of the person appointed by it under sub-section (6), the Central Government may serve on the persons upon whom the notice under sub-section (3) or a copy thereof was served a further notice in writing either withdrawing the notice of acquisition or confirming the said notice as respects the property to which it relates or such part of the property as may be specified.

(8) Any property with respect to which a notice of acquisition is served under this section shall -

(a) If no objection is duly made to the notice, vest in the Central Government at the expiration of the time for making such objection;

(b) If such an objection is duly made and the notice is confirmed as respects the whole or any part of that property by a notice served under sub-section (7), vest accordingly in the Central Government on the service of the last mentioned notice; and shall in either case vest free from all encumbrances.

(9) Compensation in respect of acquisition under this section shall be paid in accordance with section 21.

11-A   Compulsory Acquisition not Sale *

For the removal of doubts, it is hereby declared that the compulsory acquisition of any mineral, concentrate or other material under sub-section (2) of section 6, or of any substance, minerals, equipment or plant under sub-section (1) of section 11, shall not be deemed to be a sale for any purpose whatsoever.

12.   Compensation in case of Compulsory Acquisition of a Mine.

Where the Central Government acquires, in accordance with any law, any mine or part of a mine from which in the opinion of the Central Government any of the prescribed substances can be obtained, a compensation in respect of such acquisition shall be paid in accordance with section 21; Provided that in determining the amount of such compensation, no account shall be taken of the value of uranium which may be obtained from such mine or part of a mine.

13. **Notation of Certain Contracts.**

(1) The Central Government may serve on the parties to a contract relating to prospecting or mining of any substance from which any of the prescribed substances can be obtained or to production or use of atomic energy or to research into matters connected therewith, not being a contract for the rendering of personal services, a notice in writing stating that on such date as may be specified in the notice the rights and liabilities of any of the parties to the contract specified in the notice (hereinafter referred to as the specified party) will be transferred to the Central Government, and thereupon subject to any withdrawal of the notice under the following provisions of this section, the contract shall, as regards any rights exercisable, or liabilities incurred, on or after the said date, have effect as if the Central Government were a party to the contract instead of the specified party and as if for any reference in the contract to the specified party there were substituted as reference to the Central Government.

(2) A notice served under sub-section (1) shall contain a statement to the effect that an objection may be made thereto within such time and in such manner as may be specified, and if any such objection is duly made and not withdrawn, the Central Government shall afford an opportunity to the person making the objection of appearing before and being heard by a person appointed by the Central Government for the purpose.

* This has been amended vide the Atomic Energy (Amendment) Act 1986 (No. 59 of 1986).

(3) After considering any such objection and the report of the person appointed by it under sub-section (2), the Central Government may make such order as it may deem proper.

(4) Where the rights and liabilities of a party to a contract are transferred to the Central Government under this section, there

shall be paid to that party such compensation in respect of any loss suffered by that party as may be agreed between him and the Central Government, and in default of such agreement, as may be determined by arbitration.

14.   **Control over Production and use of Atomic Energy.**

(1) The Central Government may, subject to such rules as may be made in this behalf and by order prohibit except under a license granted by it —

(i) The working of any mine or minerals specified in the order, being a mine or minerals from which in the opinion of the Central Government any of the prescribed substances can be obtained;

(ii) The acquisition, production, possession, use, disposal, export or import —

(a) Of any of the prescribed substances; or

(b) Of any minerals or other substances specified in the rules, from which in the opinion of the Central Government any of the prescribed substances can be obtained; or

(c) Of any plant designed or adopted or manufactured for the production, development and use of atomic energy or for research into matters connected therewith; or

(d) Of any prescribed equipment.

(2) Nothing in this section shall affect the authority of the Central Government to refuse a license for the purpose of this section or to include in a license such conditions as the Central Government thinks fit or to revoke a license and the Central Government may take any action as aforesaid.

(3) Without prejudice to the generality of the foregoing provisions, the rules referred to in this section may provide for —

(a) The extent to which information in the possession of, or which has been made available to, the person granted a license for purposes of this section, should be regarded as restricted information;

(b) The extent to which the area or premises under the control of the person to whom a license has been granted for purposes of this section, should be regarded as a prohibited area;

(c) The conditions and criteria for location of any installation or operation of any plant in respect of which a license has been granted or is intended to be granted for the purposes of this section including those necessary for protection against radiation and safe disposal of harmful by-products or wastes;

(d) The extent of the licensee's liability in respect of any hurt to any person or any damage to property caused by ionizing radiations or any radioactive contamination either at the plant under license or in the surrounding area;

(e) Provision by licensee either by insurance or by such other means as the Central Government may approve, of sufficient funds to be available at all times to ensure settlement of any claims in connection with the use of the site or the plant under license which have been or may be duly established against the licensee in respect of any hurt to any person or any damage to any property caused by ionizing radiations emitted at the plant under license or radioactive contamination either at the plant under license or in surrounding areas;

(f) Obligatory qualifications, security clearances, hours of employment, minimum leave and periodical medical examination of the persons employed and any other requirement or restriction or prohibition on the employer, employed persons and other persons; and

(g) Such other incidental and supplementary provisions including provisions for inspection and also for the sealing of premises and seizure, retention and disposal of any article in respect of which there are reasonable grounds for suspecting that a contravention of the rules has been committed, as the Central Government considers necessary.

(4) The Central Government may also prescribe the fees payable for issue of licenses under sub-section (1).

15.   Requisitioning of any Substance for Extracting Uranium or Plutonium

(1) The Central Government shall have the right to require that any substance which, in the opinion of the Central Government, contains uranium, plutonium or any of their isotopes, shall be delivered to it and the Central Government may extract from that substance the uranium, plutonium or any of their isotopes contained therein and return the substance to the person concerned on payment of compensation which shall be determined in accordance with section 21; Provided that such compensation shall not, in any case, exceed the cost incurred by the person in the production, mining or irradiation of the substance and in determining the same no account shall be taken of the value of uranium, plutonium or any of their isotopes extracted from the substance.

(2) Nothing in this section shall prevent the Central Government from permitting, subject to such conditions as it may deem fit to impose, the use of small quantities of natural uranium for the purpose of examination, test or analysis.

16.   Control over Radioactive Substances.

The Central Government may prohibit the manufacture, possession, use, transfer by sale or otherwise, export and import and in an emergency, transport and disposal, of any radioactive substances without its written consent.

17.   Special Provisions as to Safety.

(1) The Central Government may, as regards any class or description of premises or places, being premises or places, in which radioactive substances are manufactured, produced, mined, treated, stored or used or any radiation generating plant, equipment or appliance is used, make such provision by rules as appear to the Central Government to be necessary —

    (a) To prevent injury being caused to the health of persons employed at such premises or places or other persons either by radiations, or by the ingestion of any radioactive substance;

    (b) To secure that any radioactive waste products resulting from such manufacture, production, mining, treatment, storage, or use as aforesaid are disposed of safely;

(c) To prescribe qualifications of the persons for employment at such premises or places and the regulation of their hours of employment, minimum leave and periodical medical examination and the rules may, in particular and without prejudice to the generality of this subsection provide for imposing requirements as to the erection or structural alterations of buildings or the carrying out of works.

(2) The Central Government may, as respects the transport of any radioactive substance or any prescribed substance specified by an order issued under this Act as being dangerous to health, make such rules as appear to be necessary to prevent injury being caused by such transport to the health of persons engaged therein and other persons.

(3) Rules made under this section may provide for imposing requirements, prohibitions and restrictions on employers, employed persons and other persons.

(4) Any person authorized by the Central Government under this section, may, on producing, if so required, a duly authenticated document showing his authority, enter at all reasonable hours any premises, or any vehicle, vessel or aircraft for the purpose of ascertaining whether there has been committed, or is being committed, in or in connection with the premises, vehicle, vessel or aircraft, any contravention of the rules made under this section.

(5) In the event of any contravention of the rules made under this section, the Central Government shall have the right to take such measures as it may deem necessary to prevent further injury to persons or damage to property arising from radiation or contamination by radioactive substances including, without prejudice to the generality of the foregoing provisions, and to the right to take further action for the enforcement of penalties under section 24, the sealing of premises, vehicle, vessel, or aircraft, and the seizure of radioactive substances and contaminated equipment.

18.   **Restriction on Disclosure of Information.**

(1) The Central Government may by order restrict the disclosure of information, whether contained in a document, drawing, photograph, plan, model or in any other form whatsoever, which relates to, represents or illustrates —

(a) An existing or proposed plant used or proposed to be used for the purpose of producing, developing or using atomic energy, or

(b) The purpose or method of operation of any such existing or proposed plant or

(c) Any process operated or proposed to be operated in any such existing or proposed plant.

(2) No person shall —

(a) Disclose, or obtain or attempt to obtain any information restricted under subsection (1), or

(b) Disclose, without the authority of the Central Government, any information obtained in the discharge of any functions under this Act or in the performance of his official duties.

(3) Nothing in this section shall apply —

(i) To the disclosure of information with respect to any plant of a type in use for purposes other than the production, development or use of atomic energy, unless the information discloses that plant of that type is used or proposed to be used for the production, development or use of atomic energy or research into any matters connected therewith; or

(ii) Where any information has been made available to the general public otherwise than in contravention of this section, to any subsequent disclosure of that information.

19.   **Prevention of Entry into Prohibited Areas.**

The Central Government may by order prohibit-

(a) Entry of any person, without obtaining permission, into a prohibited area and

(b) Taking by any persons, without permission, of any photograph, sketch, pictures, drawing, map or other document from a prohibited area and any permission, if given to do these things, may be subject to stipulations which the Central Government may consider necessary.

20. Special Provision as to Inventions.

(1) As from the commencement of this Act, no patents shall be granted for inventions which in the opinion of the Central Government are useful for or relate to the production, control, use or disposal of atomic energy or the prospecting, mining, extraction, production, physical and chemical treatment, fabrication, enrichment, canning or use of any prescribed substance or radioactive substance or the ensuring of safety in atomic energy operations.

(2) The prohibition under sub-section (1) shall also apply to any invention of the nature specified in that sub-section in respect of which an application for the grant of a patent has been made to the Controller of Patents and Designs appointed under the Indian Patents and Designs Act, 1911, before the commencement of this Act and is pending with him at such commencement.

(3) The Central Government shall have the power to inspect at any time any pending patent application and specification before its acceptance and if it considers that the invention relates to atomic energy, to issue directions to the Controller of Patents and Designs to refuse the application on that ground.

(4) Any person, who has made an invention which he has reason to believe relates to atomic energy, shall communicate to the Central Government the nature and description of the invention.

(5) Any person desiring to apply for a patent abroad for an invention relating to or which he has reason to believe relates to atomic energy shall obtain prior permission from the Central Government before making the application abroad or communicating the invention to any person abroad, unless three months have elapsed since his request for permission was made to the Central Government and no reply was received by him.

(6) The Controller of Patents and Designs shall have the power to refer any application to the Central Government for direction as to whether the invention is one relating to atomic energy and the direction given by the Central Government shall be final.

(7) Any invention in the field of atomic energy conceived whether in establishments controlled by the Central Government or under any contract, sub-contract, arrangement or other relationship with the Central Government shall be deemed to have been made or conceived by the Central Government, irrespective of whether such contract, subcontract, arrangement or other relationship involves financial participation of or assistance from the Central Government.

(8) Notwithstanding anything contained in the Indian Patents and Designs Act, 1911, the decision of the Central Government on points connected with or arising out of this section shall be final.

21.   **Principles relating to Payment of Compensation.**

(1) Save as otherwise provided in this Act, where by reason of exercise of any powers under this Act, any compensation is payable, the amount of such compensation shall be determined in the manner and in accordance with the principles here in after set out, that is to say —

    (a) Where the amount of compensation is fixed by agreement, it shall be paid in accordance with such agreement;

    (b) Where no agreement is reached, the Central Government shall appoint as arbitrator a person having expert knowledge as to the nature of the right affected who shall determine the amount of compensation payable.

(2) In making his award, the arbitrator appointed under sub-section (1) shall have regard —

    (a) In the case of any compensation payable under section 9 —

    (i) To the nature of the work done;

    (ii) The manner, extent and duration of the exercise of any power under that section;

(iii) The diminution in the rent of the land and of the property situated thereon, which might reasonably be expected over any period or diminution in the market value of the land and property on the date when the exercise of powers comes to an end; and

(iv) The provisions of sub-section (1) of section 23 of the Land Acquisition Act, 1894, in so far as such provisions can be made applicable to the exercise of powers under section 9; and

(b) In the case of any compensation payable under section 11 or under section 12, to the price which the owner might reasonably have been expected to obtain on a sale of the property effected by him immediately before the date of the acquisition.

(3) An appeal shall lie to the High Court against an award of the arbitrator except in cases where the amount claimed thereof does not exceed an amount prescribed in this behalf by the Central Government.

(4) The Central Government may make rules prescribing the procedure to be followed in the arbitrations under this Act and the principles to be followed in the apportionment of the cost of proceedings before the arbitrator and on appeal.

(5) Save as provided in this Act, nothing in any law for the time being in force relating to arbitration shall apply to arbitrations under this Act.

22. **Special Provisions as to Electricity.**

(1) Notwithstanding anything contained in the Electricity (Supply) Act, 1948, the Central Government shall have authority —

(a) To develop a sound and adequate national policy in regard to atomic power, to co-ordinate such policy with the Central Electricity Authority and the State Electricity Boards constituted under sections 3 and 5 respectively of that Act and other similar statutory corporations concerned with the control and utilization of other power resources, to implement schemes for the generation of electricity in pursuance of such policy and to operate either[9] by itself or through any authority or corporation established by it or a Government Company, atomic power stations in the manner determined by it in consultation with the Boards or Corporations concerned, with whom it shall enter into agreement regarding the supply of electricity so produced;

(b) To fix rates for and regulate the supply of electricity from atomic power stations either[10] by itself or through any authority or corporation established by it or a Government Company in consultation with the Central Electricity Authority.

(c) To enter into arrangements with the Electricity Board of the State in which an atomic power station is situated either by itself or through any authority or corporation established by it or a Government Company, for the transmission of electricity to any other State; Provided that in case there is a difference of opinion between the Central Government or such authority or corporation or Government Company as the case[11] ,[12] may be, and any State Electricity Board in regard to the construction of necessary transmission lines, the matter shall be referred to the Central Electricity Authority whose decision shall be binding on the parties concerned.

(2) No provision of the Indian Electricity Act, 1910, or any rule made there under or of any instrument having effect by virtue of such law or rule shall have any effect so far as it is inconsistent with any of the provisions of this Act.

(3) Save as otherwise provided in this Act, the provisions of this Act shall be in addition to, and not in derogation of, the Indian Electricity Act, 1910, and the Electricity (Supply) Act, 1948.

23. Administration of Factories Act, 1948.

Notwithstanding anything contained in the Factories Act, 1948, the

---

9   Inserted vide the Atomic Energy (Amendment) Act 1987 (No. 29 of 1987)

10 Substituted vide the Atomic Energy (Amendment) Act 1987 (No. 29 of 1987)

11 IBID-44

12 IBID-45

authority to administer the said Act, and to do all things for the enforcement of its provisions, including the appointment of inspecting staff and the making of rules there under, shall vest in the Central Government in relation to any factory owned by the Central Government or any authority or corporation established by it or a Government Company and engaged in carrying out the purposes of this Act.

24.   **Offences and Penalties.**

(1) Whoever —

    (a) Contravenes any order made under section 14 or any condition subject to which a license is granted under that section; or

    (b) Contravenes any rules made under section 17 or any requirement, prohibition or restriction imposed under any such rule; or

    (c) Obstruct any person authorized by the Central Government under sub-section (4) of section 17 in the exercise of powers under that sub-section; or

    (d) Contravenes sub-section (2) of section 18; shall be punishable with imprisonment for a term which may extent to five years, or with fine, or both.

(2) Whoever —

    (a) Fails to comply with any notice served on him under section 5 or with any terms and conditions that may be imposed on him under that section; or

    (b) Fails to comply with any notice served on him under section 7 or knowingly makes any untrue statement in any return or statement made in pursuance of any such notice; or

    (c) Obstructs any person or authority in the exercise of powers under section 8 or 9; or

    (d) Contravenes any other provision of this Act or any order made there under; shall be punishable with imprisonment for a term which may extent to one year, or with fine, or with both.

25.   **Offences by Companies.**

(1) Where an offence under this Act has been committed by a company, every person who at the time the offence was committed was in charge of, and was responsible to, the company for the conduct of the business of the company as well as the company, shall be deemed to be guilty of the offence and shall be liable to be proceeded against and punished accordingly; Provided that nothing contained in this sub-section shall render any such person liable to any punishment, if he proves that the offence was committed without his knowledge orthat he exercised all due diligence to prevent the commission of such offence.

(2) Notwithstanding anything contained in sub-section (1), where any offence under this Act has been committed by a company and it is proved that the offence has been committed with the consent or connivance of, or is attributable to, any neglect on the part of, any director, manager, secretary or other officer of the company, such director, manager, secretary or other officer shall be deemed to be guilty of that offence and shall be liable to be proceeded against and punished accordingly.

Explanation - For the purposes of this section,

(a) "Company" means anybody corporate and includes a firm and other association of individuals; and

(b) "Director" in relation to a firm, means a partner in the firm.

26.   **Cognizance of offences**

(1) All offences under this Act shall be cognizable under the Code of Criminal Procedure, 1898, but no action shall be taken in respect of any person for any offence under this Act except on the basis of a written complaint made -

(a) In respect of contravention of section 8, 14 or 17 or any rules or order made there under, by the person authorized to exercise powers of entry and inspection;

(b) In respect of any other contravention, by a person duly authorized to make such complaints by the Central

Government.

(2) Proceedings in respect of contravention of section 18 shall not be instituted except with the consent of the Attorney General of India.

27. Delegation of powers.

The Central Government may, by order, direct that any power conferred or any duty imposed on it by this Act shall, in such circumstances and subject to such conditions as may be specified in the direction, be exercised or discharged also by —

(a) Such officer or authority subordinate to the Central Government, or

(b) Such State Government or such officer or authority subordinate to a State Government as may be specified in the direction.

28. Effect of Other Laws.

The provisions of this Act shall have effect notwithstanding anything inconsistent therewith contained in any enactment other than this Act or any other instrument having effect by virtue of any enactment other than this Act.

29. Protection of Action taken in Good Faith.

No suit, prosecution or other legal proceeding shall lie against the Government or any person or authority in respect of anything done by it or him in good faith in pursuance of this Act or of any rule or order made thereunder.

30. Power to Make Rules.

(1) The Central Government may, by notification, make rules for carrying out the purposes of this Act.

(2) In particular, and without prejudice to the generality of the foregoing powers, such rules may provide for-

(a) Declaring any information not so far published or otherwise made public as restricted information and prescribing the measures to be taken to guard against unauthorized dissemination or use thereof;

(b) Declaring any area or premises as prohibited area and prescribing the measures to be taken to provide against unauthorised entry into or departure from such prohibited area;

(c) Reporting of information relating to the discovery of uranium, thorium and other prescribed substances and for payment of rewards for such discoveries;

(d) Control over mining or concentration of substances containing uranium;

(e) Regulating by licensing and encouraging by award of concessions including rewards, floor prices and guarantees, mining of and prospecting for other prescribed substances;

(f) Compulsory acquisition of prescribed substances, minerals and plants;

(g) Regulating the production, import, export, transfer, refining, possession, ownership, sale, use or disposal of the prescribed substances and any other articles that in the opinion of the Central Government may be used for, or may result as a consequence of, the production, use or application of atomic energy;

(h) Regulating the use of prescribed equipment;

(i) Regulating the manufacture, custody, transport, transfer, sale, export, import, use or disposal of any radioactive substance;

(j) Regulating the transport of such prescribed substances as are declared dangerous to health under sub-section (2) of section 17;

(k) Developing, controlling, supervising and licensing the production, application and use of atomic energy;

(l) Tees for issue of licenses under this Act;

(m)   The manner of serving notices under this Act;

(n) Generally promoting co-operation among persons, institutions and countries in the production, use, application of atomic energy and in research and investigations in that field.

(3) Rules made under this Act may provide that a contravention of the rules shall, save as otherwise expressly provided in this Act, be punishable with fine which may extend to five hundred rupees.

(4) Every rule made under this Act shall be laid as soon as may be after it is made, before each House of Parliament while it is in session for a total period of thirty days which may be comprised in one session or in two or more successive sessions, and if before the expiry of the session in which it is so laid or the successive sessions aforesaid, both Houses agree in making any modification in the rule or both Houses agree that the rule should not be made, the rule shall thereafter have effect only in such modified form or be of no effect, as the case may be; so however that any such modification or annulment shall be without prejudice to the validity of anything previously done under that rule.

31. Act binding on Government

The provisions of this Act shall be binding on Government.

32. Repeal of Act 29 of 1948

The Atomic Energy Act, 1948, is hereby repealed.

THE ATOMIC ENERGY (AMENDMENT) ACT, 1986

(No.59 of 1986)

[23rd December, 1986]

An Act further to amend the Atomic Energy Act, 1962. Be it enacted by Parliament in the Thirty-seventh Year of the Republic of India as follows :-

Short title and commencement

1.   (1)   This Act may be called the Atomic Energy (Amendment) Act, 1986.

(2)   It shall be deemed to have come into force on the 21st day of September, 1962.

Amendment of section 6

2.   In section 6 of the Atomic Energy Act, 1962 (hereinafter referred to as the principal Act).

   (a) In sub-section (2),

      (i) For the words and figures *"proposes to acquire it and upon the service of the notice and the payment of compensation in accordance with section 21"*, the words *"proposes to compulsorily acquire it and upon the service of the notice"* shall be substituted;

      (ii) The proviso shall be omitted;

   (b) After sub-section (2), the following sub-section shall be inserted, namely :

   (3) Compensation in respect of acquisition under sub-section (2) shall be paid in accordance with section 21 and in determining such

compensation regard shall be had to the cost of production of such mineral, concentrate or other material and such other factors as may be relevant, but no account shall be taken of the value of uranium in its natural state contained therein".

Insertion of the new section 11 A

3.   After section 11 of the principal Act, the following section shall be inserted, namely -

"11 A. For the removal of doubts, it is hereby declared that the compulsory acquisition of any mineral, concentrate or other material under sub-section (2) of section 6,or of any substance, minerals, equipment or plant under sub- section (1) of section 11, shall not be deemed to be a sale for any purpose whatsoever".

C. Raman Menon,

Additional Secretary to the Govt. of India

THE ATOMIC ENERGY (AMENDMENT) ACT, 1987

[ACT NO.29 OF 1987]

[8th September, 1987]

An Act further to amend the Atomic Energy Act, 1962. Be it enacted by Parliament in the Thirty eighth year of the Republic of India as follows:-

1.   **Short title** — This Act will be called the Atomic Energy (Amendment) Act, 1987.

2.   **Amendment of section 2** — In section 2 of the Atomic Energy Act, 1962 (Hereinafter referred to as the principal Act), in sub-section (1), after clause (b), the following clause shall be inserted, namely:-

(bb) "Government company" means company in which not less than fifty-one per cent of the paid up share capital is held by the Central Government.

3.   **Amendment of section 3** — In section 3 of the principal Act -

(i)   In clause (a), after the words "atomic energy", the words "either by itself or through any authority or corporation established by it or a Government company" shall be inserted;

(ii)   For clause (b) the following clauses shall be substituted, namely—

(b) To manufacture or otherwise produce any prescribed or radioactive substance and any articles which in its opinion are, or are likely to be, required for, or in connection with, the production, development or use of atomic energy or such research as aforesaid and to dispose of such prescribed or radioactive substance or any article manufactured or otherwise produced; (bb) (i) to buy or otherwise acquire, store and transport any prescribed or radioactive

substance and any articles which in its opinion are, or are likely to be, required for, or in connection with, the production, development or use of atomic energy; and

(ii)   To dispose of such prescribed or radioactive substance or any articles bought or otherwise acquired by it, either by itself or through any authority or corporation established by it, or by a Government company".

(iii)   In clause (f), after the words "all matters incidental thereto", the words "either by itself or through any authority or corporation established by it or a Government company" shall be inserted.

4.   **Amendment of section 22** — In section (1) of S.22 of the principal Act,

(i) In clause (a), after the words "to operate" the words "either by itself or through any authority or corporation established by it or a Government company", shall be inserted.

(ii)   In clause (b), for the words "with the concurrence of", the words "either by it or through any authority or corporation" may be substituted.

An Appraisal of US- Indo Civil Nuclear Agreement

Introduction

US-Indo Civil Nuclear Agreement-2008 is a unique agreement which shows that national interests are far more important to define the relations between the countries than any other consideration. India had persistently been against signing of Non- Proliferation Treaty (NPT)[1] as she had always considered it discriminatory and is still one of the five countries which have not signed it or have withdrawn from it.

Respecting India's position on the issue, finally USA came around and offered a deal to India which is in the national interest of both the countries. While USA gets many of her strategic and economic objectives met, as far as India is concerned, this deal helps India to come out of nuclear isolation and much required technological infusion.

Chronology of the Indo-US Nuclear Deal

The process of negotiations and discussions, which finally culminated in signing of the Indo- US deal, started in 2005. It was a very detailed process, which besides other factors is a testimony to the commitment of the two leaders (the 43rd President of United States of America, George W Bush Jr and Prime Minister of India Dr Manmohan Singh) to their respective national interests and their single minded endeavours against

---

1   Treaty on the 'Non-Proliferation of Nuclear Weapons' is commonly known as the Non-Proliferation Treaty or NPT. It was opened for signature on 01 July 1968 and came into force on 05 March 1970. A total of 190 countries had signed the 'Treaty'. Out of that, Democratic Republic of Korea (North Korea) has withdrawn from the Treaty in 2003. The Treaty gives special status to five countries namely; USA, Russia (successor of erstwhile USSR), UK, France and People's Republic of China by recognizing them as 'Nuclear Weapon States'. Countries which have either not signed or have withdrawn are; India, Israel, North Korea, Pakistan and South Sudan (one of the successor state of erstwhile Sudan)

all odds to get the deal signed. The chronology of the events, in this deal was as enumerated below: -

- 18 July 2005: President Bush and Prime Minister Singh first announce their intention to enter into a nuclear agreement in Washington.

- 01 March 2006: Bush visits India for the first time.

- 03 March 2006: Bush and Singh issue a joint statement on their growing strategic partnership, emphasizing their agreement on civil nuclear cooperation.

- 26 July 2006: The US House of Representatives passes the 'Henry J Hyde United States-India Peaceful Atomic Energy Cooperation Act of 2006,' which stipulates that Washington will cooperate with New Delhi on nuclear issues and exempt it from signing the Nuclear Nonproliferation Treaty.

- 16 November 2006: The US Senate passes the 'United States-India Peaceful Atomic Energy Cooperation and US Additional Protocol Implementation Act' to "exempt from certain requirements of the Atomic Energy Act of 1954 United States exports of nuclear materials, equipment, and technology to India."

- 18 December 2006: President Bush signs into law congressional legislation on Indian atomic energy.

- 27 July 2007: Negotiations on a bilateral agreement between the United States and India conclude.

- 03 August 2007: The text of the 'Agreement for Cooperation between the Government of the United States of America and the Government of India concerning peaceful uses of nuclear energy' (123 Agreement) is released by both governments.

- 13 August 2007: Prime Minister Manmohan Singh makes a *suo moto* statement on the deal in the Indian Parliament.

- 23 April 2008: The Indian Government says it will seek the sense of the House on the 123 Agreement before it is taken up for ratification by the US Congress.

- 09 July 2008:   The draft India-specific safeguards accord with the IAEA[2] circulated to IAEA's Board of Governors for approval.

- 10 July 2008:   Prime Minister Manmohan Singh calls for a vote of confidence in Parliament.

- 18 July 2008:   Foreign Secretary Shivshankar Menon briefs the IAEA Board of Governors and some NSG countries in Vienna on the safeguards agreement.

- 22 July 2008:   The UPA government led by Manmohan Singh wins trust vote in the Loksabha in India.

- 24 July 2008:   India launches full blast lobbying among the 45-nations NSG for an exemption for nuclear commerce.

- 01 August 2008: IAEA Board of Governors adopts India- specific safeguards agreement unanimously.

- 04-06 September 2008: The NSG meets for the second time on the issue after the US comes up with a revised draft and grants waiver to India after marathon parleys.

- 11 September 2008: President Bush sends the text of the 123 Agreement to the US Congress for final approval.

- 13 September 2008: The State Department issues a fact sheet on the nuclear deal saying that the initiative would prove to be a good step to meet India's growing energy requirements and would also contribute to US efforts to strengthen the non- proliferation regime

---

2   The International Atomic Energy Agency (IAEA) is an international organization that seeks to promote the peaceful use of nuclear energy, and to inhibit its use for any military purpose, including nuclear weapons. The IAEA was established as an autonomous organization on 29 July 1957. Though established independently of the United Nations through its own international treaty, 'the IAEA Statute', it reports to both the UN General Assembly and the Security Council. With headquarters in Vienna, Austria, the IAEA has two "Regional Safeguards Offices"; at Toronto, Canada, and at Tokyo, Japan. In addition it also has two liaison offices which are located in New York, USA, and Geneva, Switzerland. IT also has three laboratories located; in Vienna & Seibersdorf, Austria, and in Monaco. The IAEA serves as an intergovernmental forum for scientific and technical cooperation in the peaceful use of nuclear technology and nuclear power worldwide. The programmes of the IAEA encourage the development of the peaceful applications of nuclear technology, provide international safeguards against misuse of nuclear technology & nuclear materials, promotes nuclear safety (including radiation protection) and nuclear security standards & their implementation.

by welcoming New Delhi into globally accepted non-proliferation standards and practices.

- 27 September 2008: House of Representatives approves the Indo-US nuclear deal. 298 members voted for the Bill while 117 voted against the Bill.

- 01 October 2008: Senate approves the Indo-US civil nuclear deal with 86 votes for the deal and 13 against it.

- 04 October 2008: White House announces that President Bush will sign the legislation on the Indo-US nuclear deal into a law on October 8.

- 08 October 2008: President Bush signs legislation to enact the landmark US-India civilian nuclear agreement.

- 10 October 2008: The 123 Agreement between India and US is finally operationalized between the two countries after the deal is signed by the External Affairs Minister Pranab Mukherjee and his counterpart; Secretary of State Condoleezza Rice in Washington DC.

Salient features of 123 Agreement between India and USA

Following are the salient features of the 123 Agreement signed between India and the US on civil nuclear energy cooperation:-

- Nuclear material, equipment and components transferred pursuant to the Agreement and nuclear material and by-product material used in/or produced through the use of any nuclear material, equipment and components so transferred should not be used by the recipient party for any nuclear device, for research on or development of any nuclear device or for any military purpose.

- The United States is willing to incorporate assurances regarding fuel supply in the bilateral India-US agreement on peaceful uses of nuclear energy which would be submitted to the US Congress.

- The United States will join India in seeking to negotiate with the IAEA an India-specific fuel supply agreement.

- The United States will support an Indian effort to develop a strategic reserve of nuclear fuel to guard against any disruption of supply in the lifetime of India's reactors.

- If despite these arrangements, a disruption of fuel supplies occurs, the US and India would jointly convene a group of friendly supplier countries, including; Russia, UK and France, to pursue measures to restore fuel supplies to India.

- An India-specific 'safeguards agreement' would be negotiated between India and the IAEA, providing for safeguards to guard against withdrawal of safeguarded nuclear material from civilian use at any time as well as providing for corrective measures that India may take to ensure uninterrupted operation of its civilian nuclear reactors in the event of disruption of foreign fuel supplies. Taking this into account, India would place its civilian nuclear facilities under India-specific safeguards in perpetuity and negotiate an appropriate safeguards agreement with the IAEA.

- The nuclear material and equipment transferred to India by the US pursuant to the agreement and any nuclear material used in or produced through the use of nuclear material, non nuclear material, equipment or components so transferred shall be subject to safeguards in perpetuity in accordance with the India-specific Safeguards Agreement between India and the IAEA and an additional protocol, when in force.

- Under the Agreement, India would establish a new national re-processing facility dedicated to re-processing safeguarded nuclear material under IAEA safeguards and the two countries will agree on arrangements and procedures under which such re-processing will take place in this new facility.

- The provisions of the agreement will not be used to interfere with the nuclear plicy or programmes for the promotion of the peaceful uses of nuclear energy including research and development.

- The agreement which remain in force for 40 years, and continue thereafter for an additional period of ten years each.

- Either country will have the right to terminate the Agreement prior to its expiration on one year's written notice to the other country. The Agreement would terminate one year from the date of the written notice. The country seeking termination would cease further cooperation if it determined that a mutually-acceptable solution of outstanding issues had not been possible or could not be achieved through consultations. If a country seeking termination, cited violation of IAEA safeguards agreement as the reason, a crucial factor would be whether the IAEA Board of Governors had found non-compliance. Following the termination, either Party would have the right to require the return of any nuclear or non-nuclear material or component through consultations. However, efforts would have to be made to resolve any dispute through negotiations.

Full text of the agreement is given at Annexure -III

Source: UNI, "Salient features of 123 agreement between India and USA", published in One India News, dated 03 August 2007 and uploaded on: http://news.oneindia.in/2007/08/03/salient-features-of-123-agreement-between-india-and-us-1186146576.html

Agreement for Cooperation between the Government of the United States of America and the Government of India Concerning Peaceful Uses of Nuclear Energy (123 Agreement)

Agreement

This agreement, supported by the United States-India Peaceful Atomic Energy Cooperation Act, concerns the two countries' conditions for civilian nuclear cooperation.

The Government of India and the Government of the United States of America, hereinafter referred to as the Parties,

RECOGNIZING the significance of civilian nuclear energy for meeting growing global energy demands in a cleaner and more efficient manner;

DESIRING to cooperate extensively in the full development and use of nuclear energy for peaceful purposes as a means of achieving energy security, on a stable, reliable and predictable basis;

WISHING to develop such cooperation on the basis of mutual respect for sovereignty, non-interference in each other's internal affairs, equality, mutual benefit, reciprocity and with due respect for each other's nuclear programmes;

DESIRING to establish the necessary legal framework and basis for cooperation concerning peaceful uses of nuclear energy;

AFFIRMING that cooperation under this Agreement is between two States possessing advanced nuclear technology, both Parties having the same benefits and advantages, both committed to preventing WMD proliferation;

NOTING the understandings expressed in the India - U.S. Joint Statement of July 18, 2005 to enable full civil nuclear energy cooperation with India covering aspects of the associated nuclear fuel cycle;

AFFIRMING their support for the objectives of the International Atomic Energy Agency (IAEA) and its safeguards system, as applicable to India and the United States of America, and its importance in ensuring that international cooperation in development and use of nuclear energy for peaceful purposes is carried out under arrangements that will not contribute to the proliferation of nuclear weapons or other nuclear explosive devices;

NOTING their respective commitments to safety and security of peaceful uses of nuclear energy, to adequate physical protection of nuclear material and effective national export controls;

MINDFUL that peaceful nuclear activities must be undertaken with a view to protecting the environment;

MINDFUL of their shared commitment to preventing the proliferation of weapons of mass destruction; and

DESIROUS of strengthening the strategic partnership between them;

Have agreed on the following:

ARTICLE 1 - DEFINITIONS

For the purposes of this Agreement:

(A) "By-product material" means any radioactive material (except special fissionable material) yielded in/or made radioactive by exposure to the radiation incident to the process of producing or utilizing special fissionable material. By-product material shall not be subject to safeguards or any other form of verification under this Agreement, unless it has been decided otherwise by prior mutual agreement in writing between the two Parties.

(B) "Component" means a component part of equipment, or other item so designated by agreement of the Parties.

(C) "Conversion" means any of the normal operations in the nuclear fuel cycle, preceding fuel fabrication and excluding enrichment, by which uranium is transformed from one chemical form to another - for example, from uranium hexafluoride (UF_6) to uranium dioxide (UO_2) or from uranium oxide to metal.

(D) "Decommissioning" means the actions taken at the end of a facility's useful life to retire the facility from service in the manner that provides adequate protection for the health and safety of the decommissioning workers and the general public, and for the environment. These actions can range from closing down the facility and a minimal removal of nuclear material coupled with continuing maintenance and surveillance, to a complete removal of residual radioactivity in excess of levels acceptable for unrestricted use of the facility and its site.

(E) "Dual-Use Item" means a nuclear related item which has a technical use in both nuclear and non-nuclear applications.

(F) "Equipment" means any equipment in nuclear operation including reactor, reactor pressure vessel, reactor fuel charging and discharging equipment, reactor control rods, reactor pressure tubes, reactor primary coolant pumps, zirconium tubing, equipment for fuel fabrication and any other item so designated by the Parties.

(G) "High enriched uranium" means uranium enriched to twenty percent or greater in the isotope 235.

(H) "Information" means any information that is not in the public domain and is transferred in any form pursuant to this Agreement and so designated and documented in hard copy or digital form by mutual agreement by the Parties that it shall be subject to this Agreement, but will cease to be information whenever the Party transferring the information or any third party legitimately releases it into the public domain.

(I) "Low enriched uranium" means uranium enriched to less than twenty percent in the isotope 235.

(J) "Major critical component" means any part or group of parts essential to the operation of a sensitive nuclear facility or heavy water production facility.

(K) "Non-nuclear material" means heavy water, or any other material suitable for use in a reactor to slow down high velocity neutrons and increase the likelihood of further fission, as may be jointly designated by the appropriate authorities of the Parties.

(L) "Nuclear material" means (1) source material and (2) special fissionable material. "Source material" means uranium containing the mixture of isotopes occurring in nature; uranium depleted in the isotope 235; thorium; any of the foregoing in the form of metal, alloy, chemical compound, or concentrate; any other material containing one or more of the foregoing in such concentration as the Board of Governors of the IAEA shall from time to time determine; and such other materials as the Board of Governors of the IAEA may determine or as may be agreed by the appropriate authorities of both Parties. "Special fissionable material" means plutonium, uranium-233, uranium enriched in the isotope 233 or 235, any substance containing one or more of the foregoing, and such other substances as the Board of Governors of the IAEA may determine or as may be agreed by the appropriate authorities of both Parties. "Special fissionable material" does not include "source material". Any determination by the Board of Governors of the IAEA under Article XX of that Agency's Statute or otherwise that amends the list of materials considered to be "source material" or "special fissionable material" shall only have effect under this Agreement when both Parties to this Agreement have informed each other in writing that they accept such amendment.

(M) "Peaceful purposes" include the use of information, nuclear material, equipment or components in such fields as research, power generation, medicine, agriculture and industry, but do not include use in, research on, or development of any nuclear explosive device or any other military purpose. Provision of power for a military base drawn from any power network, production of radioisotopes to be used for medical purposes in military environment for diagnostics, therapy and sterility assurance, and other similar purposes as may be mutually agreed by the Parties shall not be regarded as military purpose.

(N) "Person" means any individual or any entity subject to the territorial jurisdiction of either Party but does not include the Parties.

(O) "Reactor" means any apparatus, other than a nuclear weapon or other nuclear explosive device, in which a self-sustaining fission chain reaction is maintained by utilizing uranium, plutonium, or thorium or any combination thereof.

(P) "Sensitive nuclear facility" means any facility designed or used primarily for uranium enrichment, reprocessing of nuclear fuel, or fabrication of nuclear fuel containing plutonium.

(Q) "Sensitive nuclear technology" means any information that is not in the public domain and that is important to the design, construction, fabrication, operation, or maintenance of any sensitive nuclear facility, or other such information that may be so designated by agreement of the Parties.

ARTICLE 2 - SCOPE OF COOPERATION

1.   The Parties shall cooperate in the use of nuclear energy for peaceful purposes in accordance with the provisions of this Agreement. Each Party shall implement this Agreement in accordance with its respective applicable treaties, national laws, regulations, and license requirements concerning the use of nuclear energy for peaceful purposes.

2.   The purpose of the Agreement being to enable full civil nuclear energy cooperation between the Parties, the Parties may pursue cooperation in all relevant areas to include, but not limited to, the following:

   a.   Advanced nuclear energy research and development in such areas as may be agreed between the Parties;

   b.   Nuclear safety matters of mutual interest and competence, as set out in Article 3;

   c.   Facilitation of exchange of scientists for visits, meetings, symposia and collaborative research;

   d.   Full civil nuclear cooperation activities covering nuclear reactors and aspects of the associated nuclear fuel cycleincluding technology transfer on an industrial or commercial scale between the Parties or authorized persons;

   e.   Development of a strategic reserve of nuclear fuel to guard against any disruption of supply over the lifetime of India's reactors;

   f.   Advanced research and development in nuclear sciences including but not limited to biological research, medicine, agriculture and industry, environment and climate change;

   g.   Supply between the Parties, whether for use by or for the benefit of the Parties or third countries, of nuclear material;

h.   Alteration in form or content of nuclear material as provided for in Article 6;

i.   Supply between the Parties of equipment, whether for use by or for the benefit of the Parties or third countries;

j.   Controlled thermonuclear fusion including multilateral projects; and other areas of mutual interest as may be agreed by the Parties.

3.   Transfer of nuclear material, non-nuclear material, equipment, components and information under this Agreement may be undertaken directly between the Parties or through authorized persons. Such transfers shall be subject to this Agreement and to such additional terms and conditions as may be agreed by the Parties. Nuclear material, non-nuclear material, equipment, components and information transferred from the territory of one Party to the territory of the other Party, whether directly or through a third country, will be regarded as having been transferred pursuant to this Agreement only upon confirmation, by the appropriate authority of the recipient Party to the appropriate authority of the supplier Party that such items both will be subject to the Agreement and have been received by the recipient Party.

4.   The Parties affirm that the purpose of this Agreement is to provide for peaceful nuclear cooperation and not to affect the unsafeguarded nuclear activities of either Party. Accordingly, nothing in this Agreement shall be interpreted as affecting the rights of the Parties to use for their own purposes nuclear material, non-nuclear material, equipment, components, information or technology produced, acquired or developed by them independent of any nuclear material, non-nuclear material, equipment, components, information or technology transferred to them pursuant to this Agreement. This Agreement shall be implemented in a manner so as not to hinder or otherwise interfere with any other activities involving the use of nuclear material, non-nuclear material, equipment, components, information or technology and military nuclear facilities produced, acquired or developed by them independent of this Agreement for their own purposes.

ARTICLE 3 - TRANSFER OF INFORMATION

1.   Information concerning the use of nuclear energy for peaceful purposes may be transferred between the Parties. Transfers of information

may be accomplished through reports, data banks and computer programs and any other means mutually agreed to by the Parties. Fields that may be covered include, but shall not be limited to, the following:

a. Research, development, design, construction, operation, maintenance and use of reactors, reactor experiments, and decommissioning;

b. The use of nuclear material in physical, chemical, radiological and biological research, medicine, agriculture and industry;

c. Fuel cycle activities to meet future world-wide civil nuclear energy needs, including multilateral approaches to which they are parties for ensuring nuclear fuel supply and appropriate techniques for management of nuclear wastes;

d. Advanced research and development in nuclear science and technology;

e. Health, safety, and environmental considerations related to the foregoing;

f. Assessments of the role nuclear power may play in national energy plans;

g. Codes, regulations and standards for the nuclear industry;

h. Research on controlled thermonuclear fusion which would also include bilateral activities and contributions toward multilateral projects; such as the International Thermonuclear Experimental Reactor (ITER); and any other field mutually agreed to by the Parties.

2.   Cooperation pursuant to this Article may include, but is not limited to, training, exchange of personnel, meetings, exchange of samples, materials and instruments for experimental purposes and a balanced participation in joint studies and projects.

3.   This Agreement does not require the transfer of any information regarding matters outside the scope of this Agreement, or information that the Parties are not permitted under their respective treaties, national laws, or regulations to transfer.

4.   Restricted Data, as defined by each Party, shall not be transferred

under this Agreement.

ARTICLE 4 - NUCLEAR TRADE

1.　　The Parties shall facilitate nuclear trade between themselves in the mutual interests of their respective industry, utilities and consumers and also, where appropriate, trade between third countries and either Party of items obligated to the other Party. The Parties recognize that reliability of supplies is essential to ensure smooth and uninterrupted operation of nuclear facilities and that industry in both the Parties needs continuing reassurance that deliveries can be made on time in order to plan for the efficient operation of nuclear installations.

2.　　Authorizations, including export and import licenses as well as authorizations or consents to third parties, relating to trade, industrial operations or nuclear material movement should be consistent with the sound and efficient administration of this Agreement and should not be used to restrict trade. It is further agreed that if the relevant authority of the concerned Party considers that an application cannot be processed within a two month period it shall immediately, upon request, provide reasoned information to the submitting Party. In the event of a refusal to authorize an application or a delay exceeding four months from the date of the first application the Party of the submitting persons or undertakings may call for urgent consultations under Article 13 of this Agreement, which shall take place at the earliest opportunity and in any case not later than 30 days after such a request.

ARTICLE 5 - TRANSFER OF NUCLEAR MATERIAL, NON-NUCLEAR MATERIAL, EQUIPMENT, COMPONENTS AND RELATED TECHNOLOGY

1.　　Nuclear material, non-nuclear material, equipment and components may be transferred for applications consistent with this Agreement. Any special fissionable material transferred under this Agreement shall be low enriched uranium, except as provided in paragraph 5.

2.　　Sensitive nuclear technology, heavy water production technology, sensitive nuclear facilities, heavy water production facilities and major critical components of such facilities may be transferred under this Agreement pursuant to an amendment to this Agreement. Transfers of dual-use items that could be used in enrichment, reprocessing or heavy water production facilities will be subject to the Parties' respective applicable laws, regulations and license policies.

3.   Natural or low enriched uranium may be transferred for use as fuel in reactor experiments and in reactors, for conversion or fabrication, or for such other purposes as may be agreed to by the Parties.

4.   The quantity of nuclear material transferred under this Agreement shall be consistent with any of the following purposes: use in reactor experiments or the loading of reactors, the efficient and continuous conduct of such reactor experiments or operation of reactors for their lifetime, use as samples, standards, detectors, and targets, and the accomplishment of other purposes as may be agreed by the Parties.

5.   Small quantities of special fissionable material may be transferred for use as samples, standards, detectors, and targets, and for such other purposes as the Parties may agree.

6.   (a)   The United States has conveyed its commitment to the reliable supply of fuel to India. Consistent with the July 18, 2005, Joint Statement, the United States has also reaffirmed its assurance to create the necessary conditions for India to have assured and full access to fuel for its reactors. As part of its implementation of the July 18, 2005, Joint Statement the United States is committed to seeking agreement from the U.S. Congress to amend its domestic laws and to work with friends and allies to adjust the practices of the Nuclear Suppliers Group to create the necessary conditions for India to obtain full access to the international fuel market, including reliable, uninterrupted and continual access to fuel supplies from firms in several nations.

(b)   To further guard against any disruption of fuel supplies, the United States is prepared to take the following additional steps:

     (i)   The United States is willing to incorporate assurances regarding fuel supply in the bilateral U.S.-India agreement on peaceful uses of nuclear energy under Section 123 of the U.S. Atomic Energy Act, which would be submitted to the U.S. Congress.

     (ii)   The United States will join India in seeking to negotiate with the IAEA an India-specific fuel supply agreement.

     (iii)   The United States will support an Indian effort to develop a strategic reserve of nuclear fuel to guard against any disruption of supply over the lifetime of India's reactors.

(iv) If despite these arrangements, a disruption of fuel supplies to India occurs, the United States and India would jointly convene a group of friendly supplier countries to include countries such as Russia, France and the United Kingdom to pursue such measures as would restore fuel supply to India.

(c) In light of the above understandings with the United States, an India-specific safeguards agreement will be negotiated between India and the IAEA providing for safeguards to guard against withdrawal of safeguarded nuclear material from civilian use at any time as well as providing for corrective measures that India may take to ensure uninterrupted operation of its civilian nuclear reactors in the event of disruption of foreign fuel supplies. Taking this into account, India will place its civilian nuclear facilities under India-specific safeguards in perpetuity and negotiate an appropriate safeguards agreement to this end with the IAEA.

ARTICLE 6 - NUCLEAR FUEL CYCLE ACTIVITIES

In keeping with their commitment to full civil nuclear cooperation, both Parties, as they do with other states with advanced nuclear technology, may carry out the following nuclear fuel cycle activities:

(i) Within the territorial jurisdiction of either Party, enrichment up to twenty percent in the isotope 235 of uranium transferred pursuant to this Agreement, as well as of uranium used in or produced through the use of equipment so transferred, may be carried out.

(ii) Irradiation within the territorial jurisdiction of either Party of plutonium, uranium-233, high enriched uranium and irradiated nuclear material transferred pursuant to this Agreement or used in or produced through the use of non-nuclear material, nuclear material or equipment so transferred may be carried out.

(iii) With a view to implementing full civil nuclear cooperation as envisioned in the Joint Statement of the Parties of July 18, 2005, the Parties grant each other consent to reprocess or otherwise alter in form or content nuclear material transferred pursuant to this Agreement and nuclear material and by-product material used in or produced through the use of nuclear material, non-nuclear material, or equipment so transferred. To bring these rights into effect, India will establish a new national reprocessing facility dedicated to reprocessing safeguarded nuclear material under IAEA safeguards and the Parties will agree on arrangements and procedures under which such reprocessing or other alteration in form or content will take place in this new facility. Consultations on arrangements and procedures will begin within six months of a request by either Party and will be concluded within one year. The Parties agree on the application of IAEA safeguards to all facilities concerned with the above activities. These arrangements and procedures shall include provisions with respect to physical protection standards set out in Article 8, storage standards set out in Article 7, and environmental protections set forth in Article 11 of this Agreement, and such other provisions as may be agreed by the Parties. Any special fissionable material that may be separated may only be utilized in national facilities under IAEA safeguards.

(iv)   Post-irradiation examination involving chemical dissolution or separation of irradiated nuclear material transferred pursuant to this Agreement or irradiated nuclear material used in or produced through the use of non-nuclear material, nuclear material or equipment so transferred may be carried out.

ARTICLE 7 - STORAGE AND RETRANSFERS

1.   Plutonium and uranium 233 (except as either may be contained in irradiated fuel elements), and high enriched uranium, transferred pursuant to this Agreement or used in or produced through the use of material or equipment so transferred, may be stored in facilities that are at all times subject, as a minimum, to the levels of physical protection that are set out in IAEA document INFCIRC 225/REV 4 as it may be revised and accepted by the Parties. Each Party shall record such facilities on a list, made available to the other Party. A Party's list shall be held confidential if that Party so requests. Either Party may make changes to its list by notifying the other Party in writing and receiving a written acknowledgement. Such acknowledgement shall be given no later than thirty days after the receipt of the notification and shall be limited to a statement that the notification has been received. If there are grounds to believe that the provisions of this sub-Article are not being fully complied with, immediate consultations may be called for. Following upon such consultations, each Party shall ensure by means of such consultations that necessary remedial measures are taken immediately. Such measures shall be sufficient to restore the

levels of physical protection referred to above at the facility in question. However, if the Party on whose territory the nuclear material in question is stored determines that such measures are not feasible, it will shift the nuclear material to another appropriate, listed facility it identifies.

2.   Nuclear material, non-nuclear material, equipment, components, and information transferred pursuant to this Agreement and any special fissionable material produced through the use of nuclear material, non-nuclear material or equipment so transferred shall not be transferred or re-transferred to unauthorized persons or, unless the Parties agree, beyond the recipient Party's territorial jurisdiction.

ARTICLE 8 - PHYSICAL PROTECTION

1.   Adequate physical protection shall be maintained with respect to nuclear material and equipment transferred pursuant to this Agreement and nuclear material used in or produced through the use of nuclear material, non-nuclear material or equipment so transferred.

2.   To fulfill the requirement in paragraph 1, each Party shall apply measures in accordance with

(i) Levels of physical protection at least equivalent to the recommendations published in IAEA document INFCIRC/225/ Rev.4 entitled "The Physical Protection of Nuclear Material and Nuclear Facilities," and in any subsequent revisions of that document agreed to by the Parties, and

(ii) The provisions of the 1980 Convention on the Physical Protection of Nuclear Material and any amendments to the Convention that enter into force for both Parties.

3.   The Parties will keep each other informed through diplomatic channels of those agencies or authorities having responsibility for ensuring that levels of physical protection for nuclear material in their territory or under their jurisdiction or control are adequately met and having responsibility for coordinating response and recovery operations in the event of unauthorized use or handling of material subject to this Article. The Parties will also keep each other informed through diplomatic channels of the designated points of contact within their national authorities to cooperate on matters of out-of-country transportation and other matters of mutual concern.

4.   The provisions of this Article shall be implemented in such a manner as to avoid undue interference in the Parties' peaceful nuclear activities and so as to be consistent with prudent management practices required for the safe and economic conduct of their peaceful nuclear programs.

ARTICLE 9 - PEACEFUL USE

Nuclear material, equipment and components transferred pursuant to this Agreement and nuclear material and by-product material used in or produced through the use of any nuclear material, equipment, and components so transferred shall not be used by the recipient Party for any nuclear explosive device, for research on or development of any nuclear explosive device or for any military purpose.

ARTICLE 10 - IAEA SAFEGUARDS

1.   Safeguards will be maintained with respect to all nuclear materials and equipment transferred pursuant to this Agreement, and with respect to all special fissionable material used in or produced through the use of such nuclear materials and equipment, so long as the material or equipment remains under the jurisdiction or control of the cooperating Party.

2.   Taking into account Article 5.6 of this Agreement, India agrees that nuclear material and equipment transferred to India by the United States of America pursuant to this Agreement and any nuclear material used in or produced through the use of nuclear material, non-nuclear material, equipment or components so transferred shall be subject to safeguards in perpetuity in accordance with the India-specific Safeguards Agreement between India and the IAEA [identifying data] and an Additional Protocol, when in force.

3.   Nuclear material and equipment transferred to the United States of America pursuant to this Agreement and any nuclear material used in or produced through the use of any nuclear material, non-nuclear material, equipment, or components so transferred shall be subject to the Agreement between the United States of America and the IAEA for the application of safeguards in the United States of America, done at Vienna November 18, 1977, which entered into force on December 9, 1980, and an Additional Protocol, when in force.

4.   If the IAEA decides that the application of IAEA safeguards is

no longer possible, the supplier and recipient should consult and agree on appropriate verification measures.

5.   Each Party shall take such measures as are necessary to maintain and facilitate the application of IAEA safeguards in its respective territory provided for under this Article.

6.   Each Party shall establish and maintain a system of accounting for and control of nuclear material transferred pursuant to this Agreement and nuclear material used in or produced through the use of any material, equipment, or components so transferred. The procedures applicable to India shall be those set forth in the India-specific Safeguards Agreement referred to in Paragraph 2 of this Article.

7.   Upon the request of either Party, the other Party shall report or permit the IAEA to report to the requesting Party on the status of all inventories of material subject to this Agreement.

8.   The provisions of this Article shall be implemented in such a manner as to avoid hampering, delay, or undue interference in the Parties' peaceful nuclear activities and so as to be consistent with prudent management practices required for the safe and economic conduct of their peaceful nuclear programs.

ARTICLE 11 - ENVIRONMENTAL PROTECTION

The Parties shall cooperate in following the best practices for minimizing the impact on the environment from any radioactive, chemical or thermal contamination arising from peaceful nuclear activities under this Agreement and in related matters of health and safety.

ARTICLE 12 - IMPLEMENTATION OF THE AGREEMENT

1. This Agreement shall be implemented in a manner designed:

  (a) To avoid hampering or delaying the nuclear activities in the territory of either Party;

  (b) To avoid interference in such activities;

  (c) To be consistent with prudent management practices required for the safe conduct of such activities; and

  (d) To take full account of the long term requirements of the nuclear energy programs of the Parties.

2.   The provisions of this Agreement shall not be used to:

(a) Secure unfair commercial or industrial advantages or to restrict trade to the disadvantage of persons and undertakings of either Party or hamper their commercial or industrial interests, whether international or domestic;

(b) Interfere with the nuclear policy or programs for the promotion of the peaceful uses of nuclear energy including research and development; or

(c) Impede the free movement of nuclear material, non nuclear material and equipment supplied under this Agreement within the territory of the Parties.

3.   When execution of an agreement or contract pursuant to this Agreement between Indian and United States organizations requires exchanges of experts, the Parties shall facilitate entry of the experts to their territories and their stay therein consistent with national laws, regulations and practices. When other cooperation pursuant to this Agreement requires visits of experts, the Parties shall facilitate entry of the experts to their territory and their stay therein consistent with national laws, regulations and practices.

ARTICLE 13 - CONSULTATIONS

1.   The Parties undertake to consult at the request of either Party regarding the implementation of this Agreement and the development of further cooperation in the field of peaceful uses of nuclear energy on a stable, reliable and predictable basis. The Parties recognize that such consultations are between two States with advanced nuclear technology, which have agreed to assume the same responsibilities and practices and acquire the same benefits and advantages as other leading countries with advanced nuclear technology.

2.   Each Party shall endeavor to avoid taking any action that adversely affects cooperation envisaged under Article 2 of this Agreement. If either Party at any time following the entry into force of this Agreement does not comply with the provisions of this Agreement, the Parties shall promptly hold consultations with a view to resolving the matter in a way that protects the legitimate interests of both Parties, it being understood that rights of

either Party under Article 16.2 remain unaffected.

3.   Consultations under this Article may be carried out by a Joint Committee specifically established for this purpose. A Joint Technical Working Group reporting to the Joint Committee will be set up to ensure the fulfillment of the requirements of the Administrative Arrangements referred to in Article 17.

ARTICLE 14 - TERMINATION AND CESSATION OF COOPERATION

1.   Either Party shall have the right to terminate this Agreement prior to its expiration on one year's written notice to the other Party. A Party giving notice of termination shall provide the reasons for seeking such termination. The Agreement shall terminate one year from the date of the written notice, unless the notice has been withdrawn by the providing Party in writing prior to the date of termination.

2.   Before this Agreement is terminated pursuant to paragraph 1 of this Article, the Parties shall consider the relevant circumstances and promptly hold consultations, as provided in Article 13, to address the reasons cited by the Party seeking termination. The Party seeking termination has the right to cease further cooperation under this Agreement if it determines that a mutually acceptable resolution of outstanding issues has not been possible or cannot be achieved through consultations. The Parties agree to consider carefully the circumstances that may lead to termination or cessation of cooperation. They further agree to take into account whether the circumstances that may lead to termination or cessation resulted from a Party's serious concern about a changed security environment or as a response to similar actions by other States which could impact national security.

3.   If a Party seeking termination cites a violation of this Agreement as the reason for notice for seeking termination, the Parties shall consider whether the action was caused inadvertently or otherwise and whether the violation could be considered as material. No violation may be considered as being material unless corresponding to the definition of material violation or breach in the Vienna Convention on the Law of Treaties. If a Party seeking termination cites a violation of an IAEA safeguards agreement as the reason for notice for seeking termination, a crucial factor will be whether the IAEA Board of Governors has made a finding of non-compliance.

4.   Following the cessation of cooperation under this Agreement, either Party shall have the right to require the return by the other Party of any nuclear material, equipment, non-nuclear material or components transferred under this Agreement and any special fissionable material produced through their use. A notice by a Party that is invoking the right of return shall be delivered to the other Party on or before the date of termination of this Agreement. The notice shall contain a statement of the items subject to this Agreement as to which the Party is requesting return. Except as provided in provisions of Article 16.3, all other legal obligations pertaining to this Agreement shall cease to apply with respect to the nuclear items remaining on the territory of the Party concerned upon termination of this Agreement.

5.   The two Parties recognize that exercising the right of return would have profound implications for their relations. If either Party seeks to exercise its right pursuant to paragraph 4 of this Article, it shall, prior to the removal from the territory or from the control of the other Party of any nuclear items mentioned in paragraph 4, undertake consultations with the other Party. Such consultations shall give special consideration to the importance of uninterrupted operation of nuclear reactors of the Party concerned with respect to the availability of nuclear energy for peaceful purposes as a means of achieving energy security. Both Parties shall take into account the potential negative consequences of such termination on the on-going contracts and projects initiated under this Agreement of significance for the respective nuclear programmes of either Party.

6.   If either Party exercises its right of return pursuant to paragraph 4 of this Article, it shall, prior to the removal from the territory or from the control of the other Party, compensate promptly that Party for the fair market value thereof and for the costs incurred as a consequence of such removal. If the return of nuclear items is required, the Parties shall agree on methods and arrangements for the return of the items, the relevant quantity of the items to be returned, and the amount of compensation that would have to be paid by the Party exercising the right to the other Party.

7.   Prior to return of nuclear items, the Parties shall satisfy themselves that full safety, radiological and physical protection measures have been ensured in accordance with their existing national regulations and that the transfers pose no unreasonable risk to either Party, countries through which the nuclear items may transit and to the global environment and are

in accordance with existing international regulations.

8.   The Party seeking the return of nuclear items shall ensure that the timing, methods and arrangements for return of nuclear items are in accordance with paragraphs 5, 6 and 7. Accordingly, the consultations between the Parties shall address mutual commitments as contained in Article 5.6. It is not the purpose of the provisions of this Article regarding cessation of cooperation and right of return to derogate from the rights of the Parties under Article 5.6.

9.   The arrangements and procedures concluded pursuant to Article 6 (iii) shall be subject to suspension by either Party in exceptional circumstances, as defined by the Parties, after consultations have been held between the Parties aimed at reaching mutually acceptable resolution of outstanding issues, while taking into account the effects of such suspension on other aspects of cooperation under this Agreement.

ARTICLE 15 - SETTLEMENT OF DISPUTES

Any dispute concerning the interpretation or implementation of the provisions of this Agreement shall be promptly negotiated by the Parties with a view to resolving that dispute.

ARTICLE 16 - ENTRY INTO FORCE AND DURATION

1.   This Agreement shall enter into force on the date on which the Parties exchange diplomatic notes informing each other that they have completed all applicable requirements for its entry into force.

2.   This Agreement shall remain in force for a period of 40 years. It shall continue in force thereafter for additional periods of 10 years each. Each Party may, by giving 6 months written notice to the other Party, terminate this Agreement at the end of the initial 40 year period or at the end of any subsequent 10 year period.

3.   Notwithstanding the termination or expiration of this Agreement or withdrawal of a Party from this Agreement, Articles 5.6(c), 6, 7, 8, 9, 10 and 15 shall continue in effect so long as any nuclear material, non-nuclear material, by-product material, equipment or components subject to these articles remains in the territory of the Party concerned or under its jurisdiction or control anywhere, or until such time as the Parties agree that such nuclear material is no longer usable for any nuclear activity relevant

from the point of view of safeguards.

4.   This Agreement shall be implemented in good faith and in accordance with the principles of international law.

5.   The Parties may consult, at the request of either Party, on possible amendments to this Agreement. This Agreement may be amended if the Parties so agree. Any amendment shall enter into force on the date on which the Parties exchange diplomatic notes informing each other that their respective internal legal procedures necessary for the entry into force have been completed.

ARTICLE 17 - ADMINISTRATIVE ARRANGEMENT

1.   The appropriate authorities of the Parties shall establish an Administrative Arrangement in order to provide for the effective implementation of the provisions of this Agreement.

2.   The principles of fungibility and equivalence shall apply to nuclear material and non-nuclear material subject to this Agreement. Detailed provisions for applying these principles shall be set forth in the Administrative Arrangement.

3.   The Administrative Arrangement established pursuant to this Article may be amended by agreement of the appropriate authorities of the Parties.

IN WITNESS WHEREOF the undersigned, being duly authorized, have signed this Agreement.

DONE at , this day of , 200 , in duplicate.

FOR THE GOVERNMENT OF THE
UNITED STATES OF AMERICA:

FOR THE GOVERNMENT
OF INDIA:

AGREED MINUTE

During the negotiation of the Agreement for Cooperation Between the Government of the United States of America and the Government of India Concerning Peaceful Uses of Nuclear Energy ("the Agreement") signed today, the following understandings, which shall be an integral part of the Agreement, were reached.

Proportionality

For the purposes of implementing the rights specified in Articles 6 and 7 of the Agreement with respect to special fissionable material and by-product material produced through the use of nuclear material and non-nuclear material, respectively, transferred pursuant to the Agreement and not used in or produced through the use of equipment transferred pursuant to the Agreement, such rights shall in practice be applied to that proportion of special fissionable material and by-product material produced that represents the ratio of transferred nuclear material and non-nuclear material, respectively, used in the production of the special fissionable material and by-product material to the total amount of nuclear material and non-nuclear material so used, and similarly for subsequent generations.

By-product material

The Parties agree that reporting and exchanges of information on by-product material subject to the Agreement will be limited to the following:

(1)   Both Parties would comply with the provisions as contained in the IAEA document GOV/1999/19/Rev.2, with regard to by-product material subject to the Agreement.

(2)   With regard to tritium subject to the Agreement, the Parties will exchange annually information pertaining to its disposition for peaceful purposes consistent with Article 9 of this Agreement.

FOR THE GOVERNMENT OF THE
UNITED STATES OF AMERICA:

FOR THE GOVERNMENT
OF INDIA:

END TEXT

Source: Council on Foreign Relations (CFR), "Primary sources", published during August 2007 and uploaded on www.cfr.org/about/

Appendix H

MINISTRY OF LAW AND JUSTICE

(Legislative Department)

New Delhi, the 22nd September, 201 O/Bhadra 31, 1932 (Saka)

The following Act of Parliament received the assent of the President on the 21st September, 20 I0, and is hereby published for general information:-

THE CIVIL LIABILITY FOR NUCLEAR DAMAGE ACT, 2010

No. 38 OF 2010

[21st September, 2010.]

An Act to provide for civil liability for nuclear damage and prompt compensation to the victims of a nuclear incident through a no-fault liability regime channeling liability to the operator, appointment of Claims Commissioner, establishment of Nuclear Damage Claims Commission and for matters connected therewith or incidental thereto.

BE it enacted by Parliament in the Sixty-first Year of the Republic of India as follows:-

CHAPTER- I

PRELIMINARY

1. (I) This Act may be called the Civil Liability for Nuclear Damage Act, 2010.

(2) It extends to the whole of India.

(3) It also applies to nuclear damage suffered-

(a) in or over the maritime areas beyond the territorial waters of India;

(b) In or over the exclusive economic zone of India as referred to in section 7 of the Territorial Waters, Continental Shelf, Exclusive Economic Zone and Other Maritime Zones Act, 1976; 80 of 1976.

(c) On board or by a ship registered in India under section 22 of the Merchant Shipping Act, 1958 or under any other law for the time being in force; 44 of 1958.

(d) On board or by an aircraft registered in India under clause (d) of sub-section (2) of section 5 of the Aircraft Act, 1934 or under any other law for the time being in force; 22 of 1934.

(e) On or by an artificial island, installation or structure under the jurisdiction of India.

(4) It applies only to the nuclear installation owned or controlled by the Central Government either by itself or through any authority or corporation established by it or a Government company.

Explanation.-For the purposes of this sub-section, "Government Company" shall have the same meaning as assigned to it in clause (bb) of sub-section (/) of section 2 of the Atomic Energy Act, 1962. 33 of 1962

(5) It shall come into force on such date as the Central Government may, by notification, appoint; and different dates may be appointed for different provisions of this Act, and any reference in any such provision to the commencement of this Act shall be construed as a reference to the coming into force of that provision.

2.   In this Act, unless the context otherwise requires,-

(a) "Chairperson" means the Chairperson of the Commission appointed under sub-section (/) of section 20;

(b) "Claims Commissioner" means the Claims Commissioner appointed under sub-section (2) of section 9;

(c) "Commission" means the Nuclear Damage Claims Commission established under section 19;

(d) "Environment" shall have the same meaning as assigned to it in clause (a) of section 2 of the Environment (Protection) Act, 1986;

29 of 1986.

(e) "Member" means a Member of the Commission appointed under Sub-section (1) of section 20;

(f) "Notification" means a notification published in the Official Gazette and the term "notify" shall be construed accordingly;

(g) "Nuclear damage" means-

  (i)   Loss of life or personal injury (including immediate and long term health impact) to a person; or

  (ii) Loss of, or damage to, property, caused by or arising out of a nuclear incident, and includes each of the following to the extent notified by the Central Government;

  (iii)   Any economic loss, arising from the loss or damage referred to in sub-clauses (i) or (ii) and not included in the claims made under those sub-clauses, if incurred by a person entitled to claim such loss or damage;

  (iv)   costs of measures of reinstatement of impaired environment caused by a nuclear incident, unless such impairment is insignificant, if such measures are actually taken or to be taken and not included in the claims made under sub-clause (ii);

  (v)   loss of income derived from an economic interest in any use or enjoyment of the environment, incurred as a result of a significant impairment of that environment caused by a nuclear incident, and not included in the claims under sub-clause (ii);

  (vi) the costs of preventive measures, and further loss or damage caused by such measures;

  (vii)   any other economic loss, other than the one caused by impairment of the environment referred to in sub-clauses (iv) and (v), in so far as it is permitted by the general law on civil liability in force in India and not claimed under any such law, in the case of sub-clauses (i) to (v) and (vii) above, to the extent the loss or damage arises out of, or results from, ionizing radiation emitted by any source of radiation inside a nuclear installation, or emitted from nuclear fuel or radioactive products or waste in, or of, nuclear material coming from, originating in, or sent to, a nuclear installation, whether so arising from the radioactive properties of such matter, or from a combination of radioactive properties with toxic, explosive or other hazardous properties of such matter;

(h) "Nuclear fuel" means any material which is capable of producing energy by a self-sustaining chain process of nuclear fission;

(i) "Nuclear incident" means any occurrence or series of occurrences having the same origin which causes nuclear damage or, but only with respect to preventive measures, creates a grave and imminent threat of causing such damage;

(j) "Nuclear installation" means-

(A) Any nuclear reactor other than one with which a means of transport is equipped for use as a source of power, whether for propulsion thereof or for any other purpose;

(B) Any facility using nuclear fuel for the production of nuclear material, or any facility for the processing of nuclear material, including re-processing of irradiated nuclear fuel; and

(C) Any facility where nuclear material is stored (other than storage incidental to the carriage of such material).

Explanation.-For the purpose of this clause, several nuclear installations of one operator which are located at the same site shall be considered as a single nuclear installation;

(k) "Nuclear material" means and includes-

(i) Nuclear fuel (other than natural uranium or depleted uranium) capable of producing energy by a self-sustaining chain process of nuclear fission outside a nuclear reactor, either by itself or in combination with some other material; and

(ii) Radioactive products or waste;

(l) "Nuclear reactor" means any structure containing nuclear fuel in such an arrangement that a self-sustaining chain process of nuclear fission can occur therein without an additional source of neutrons;

(m) "Operator", in relation to a nuclear installation, means the Central Government or any authority or corporation established by it or a Government company who has been granted a license pursuant to the Atomic Energy Act, 1962 for the operation of that installation;

(n) "Prescribed" means prescribed by rules made under this Act;

(0) "Preventive measures" means any reasonable measures taken by a person after a nuclear incident has occurred to prevent or minimize damage referred to in sub-clauses (i) to (v) and (vii) of clause (g), subject to the approval of the Central Government;

(p) "Radioactive products or waste" means any radioactive material produced in, or any material made radioactive by exposure to, the radiation incidental to the production or utilization of nuclear fuel, but does not include radioisotopes which have reached the final stage of fabrication so as to be usable for any scientific, medical, agricultural, commercial or industrial purpose; Atomic Energy Regulatory Board to notify nuclear incident and liability of operator.

(q) "Special Drawing Rights" means Special Drawing Rights as determined by the International Monetary Fund.

CHAPTER- II

LIABILITY FOR NUCLEAR DAMAGE

3.   (1) The Atomic Energy Regulatory Board constituted under the Atomic Energy Act, 1962 shall, within a period of fifteen days from the date of occurrence of a nuclear incident, notify such nuclear incident: Provided that where the Atomic Energy Regulatory Board is satisfied that the gravity of threat and risk involved in a nuclear incident is insignificant, it shall not be required to notify such nuclear incident.

(2) The Atomic Energy Regulatory Board shall, immediately after the notification under sub-section (1) is issued, ensures that wide publicity is to be given to the occurrence of such nuclear incident,

in such manner as it may deem fit.

4. (1) The operator of the nuclear installation shall be liable for nuclear damage caused by a nuclear incident -

(a) In that nuclear installation; or

(b) Involving nuclear material coming from, or originating in, that nuclear installation and occurring before -

    (i) The liability for nuclear incident involving such nuclear material has been assumed, pursuant to a written agreement, by another operator; or

    (ii) Another operator has taken charge of such nuclear material; or

    (iii) The person duly authorized to operate a nuclear reactor has taken charge of the nuclear material intended to be used in that reactor with which means of transport is equipped for use as a source of power, whether for propulsion thereof or for any other purpose; or

    (iv) Such nuclear material has been unloaded from the means of transport by which it was sent to a person within the territory of a foreign State; or

(c) Involving nuclear material sent to that nuclear installation and occurring after-

    (i) The liability for nuclear incident involving such nuclear material has been transferred to that operator, pursuant to a written agreement, by the operator of another nuclear installation; or

    (ii) That operator has taken charge of such nuclear material; or

    (iii) That operator has taken charge of such nuclear material from a person operating a nuclear reactor with which a means of transport is equipped for use as a source of power, whether for propulsion thereof or for any other purpose; or

    (iv) Such nuclear material has been loaded, with the written consent of that operator, on the means of transport by which it is to be carried from the territory of a foreign State.

(2) Where more than one operator is liable for nuclear damage, the liability of the operators so involved shall, in so far as the damage attributable to each operator is not separable, be joint and several: Provided that the total liability of such operators shall not exceed the extent of liability specified under sub-section (2) of section 6.

(3)   Where several nuclear installations of one and the same operator are involved in a nuclear incident, such operator shall, in respect of each such nuclear installation, be liable to the extent of liability specified under sub-section (2) of section 6.

(4) The liability of the operator of the nuclear installation shall be strict and shall be based on the principle of no-fault liability.

Explanation- For the purposes of this section-

(a) Where nuclear damage is caused by a nuclear incident occurring in a nuclear installation on account of temporary storage of material-in-transit in such installation, the person responsible for transit of such material shall be deemed to be the operator;

(b) Where a nuclear damage is caused as a result of nuclear incident during the transportation' of nuclear material, the consignor shall be deemed to be the operator;

(c) Where any written agreement has been entered into between the consignor and the consignee or, as the case may be, the consignor and the carrier of nuclear material, the person liable for any nuclear damage under such agreement shall be deemed to be the operator;

(d) Where both nuclear damage and damage other than nuclear damage have been caused by a nuclear incident or, jointly by a nuclear incident and one or more other occurrences, such other damage shall, to the extent it is not separable from the nuclear damage, be deemed to be a nuclear damage caused by such nuclear incident.

5. (1) An operator shall not be liable for any nuclear damage where such damage is caused by a nuclear incident directly due to-

(i) A grave natural disaster of an exceptional character; or

(ii) An act of armed conflict, hostility, civil war, insurrection or terrorism.

(2) An operator shall not be liable for any nuclear damage caused to-

(i) The nuclear installation itself and any other nuclear installation including a nuclear installation under construction, on the site where such installation is located; and

(ii) To any property on the same site which is used or to be used in connection with any such installation; or

(iii) To the means of transport upon which the nuclear material involved was carried at the time of nuclear incident: Provided that any compensation liable to be paid by an operator for a nuclear damage shall not have the effect of reducing the amount of his liability in respect of any other claim for damage under any other law for the time being in force.

(3) Where any nuclear damage is suffered by a person on account of his own negligence or from his own acts of commission or omission, the operator shall not be liable to such person.

6. (1) The maximum amount of liability in respect of each nuclear incident shall be the rupee equivalent of three hundred million Special Drawing Rights or such higher amount as the Central Government may specify by notification: Provided that the Central Government may take additional measures, where necessary, if the compensation to be awarded under this Act exceeds the amount specified under this sub-section.

(2) The liability of an operator for each nuclear incident shall be-

(a) In respect of nuclear reactors having thermal power equal to or above ten MW, rupees one thousand five hundred crores;

(b) In respect of spent fuel reprocessing plants, rupees three hundred crores;

(c) In respect of the research reactors having thermal power below ten MW, fuel cycle facilities other than spent fuel reprocessing plants and transportation of nuclear materials, rupees one hundred crores: Provided that the Central Government may review the amount of operator's liability from time to time and specify, by notification, a higher amount under this sub-section: Provided further that the amount of liability shall not include any interest or cost of proceedings.

7. (1) The Central Government shall be liable for nuclear damage in respect of a nuclear incident,-

   (a) Where the liability exceeds the amount of liability of an operator specified under sub-section (2) of section 6, to the extent such liability exceeds such liability of the operator;

   (b) Occurring in a nuclear installation owned by it; and

   (c) Occurring on account of causes specified in clauses (i) and (ii) of sub-section (1) of section 5: Provided that the Central Government may, by notification, assume full liability for a nuclear installation not operated by it if it is of the opinion that it is necessary in public interest.

   (2) For the purpose of meeting part of its liability under clause (a) or clause (c) of sub-section (1), the Central Government may establish a fund to be called the Nuclear Liability Fund by charging such amount of levy from the operators, in such manner, as may be prescribed.

8. (1) The operator shall, before he begins operation of his nuclear installation, take out insurance policy or such other financial security or combination of both, covering his liability under sub-section (2) of section 6, in such manner as may be prescribed.

   (2) The operator shall from time to time renew the insurance policy or other financial security referred to in sub-section (1), before the expiry of the period of validity thereof.

   (3) The provisions of sub-sections (1) and (2) shall not apply to a nuclear installation owned by the Central Government.

Explanation.-For the purposes of this section, "financial security" means a contract of indemnity or guarantee, or shares or bonds or such instrument as may be prescribed or any combination thereof.

CHAPTER-III

CLAIMS COMMISSIONER

9. (I) Who ever suffers nuclear damage shall be entitled to claim compensation in accordance with the provisions of this Act.

(2) For the purposes of adjudicating upon claims for compensation in respect of nuclear damage, the Central Government shall, by notification, appoint one or more Claims Commissioners for such area, as may be specified in that notification.

10. A person shall not be qualified for appointment as a Claims Commissioner unless he-

(a) is, or has been, a District Judge; or

(b) in the service of the Central Government and has held the post not below the rank of Additional Secretary to the Government of India or any other equivalent post in the Central Government.

11. The salary and allowances payable to and other terms and conditions of service of Claims Commissioner shall be such as may be prescribed.

12. (1) For the purposes of adjudication of claims under this Act, the Claims Commissioner shall follow such procedure as may be prescribed.

(2) For the purpose of holding inquiry, the Claims Commissioner may associate with him such persons having expertise in the nuclear field or such other persons and in such manner as may be prescribed.

(3) Where any person is associated under sub-section (2), he shall be paid such remuneration, fee or allowance, as may be prescribed.

(4) The Claims Commissioner shall, for the purposes of discharging his functions under this Act, have the same powers as are vested in a civil court under the Code of Civil Procedure, 1908, while trying a suit, in respect of the following matters, namely:-

    (a) Summoning and enforcing the attendance of any person and examining him on oath;

    (b) The discovery and production of documents;

    (c) Receiving evidence on affidavits;

    (d) Requisitioning any public record or copies thereof from any court or office;

    (e) Issuing of commission for the examination of any witness;

    (f) Any other matter which may be prescribed.

(5) The Claims Commissioner shall be deemed to be a civil court for the purposes of section 195 and Chapter XXVI of the Code of Criminal Procedure, 1973.

CHAPTER- IV

CLAIMS AND AWARDS

13. After the notification of nuclear incident under sub-section (1) of section 3, the Claims Commissioner, having jurisdiction over the area, shall cause wide publicity to be given, in such manner as he deems fit, for inviting applications for claiming compensation for nuclear damage.

14. An application for compensation before the Claims Commissioner or the Commission, as the case may be, in respect of nuclear damage may be made by-

    (a) A person who has sustained injury; or

    (b) The owner of the property to which damage has been caused; or

    (c) The legal representatives of the deceased; or

    (d) Any agent duly authorized by such person or owner or legal representatives.

15. (1) Every application for compensation before the Claims Commissioner for nuclear damage shall be made in such form, containing such particulars and accompanied by such documents, as may be prescribed.

(2) Subject to the provisions of section 18, every application under sub-section (1) shall be made within a period of three years from the date of knowledge of nuclear damage by the person suffering such damage.

16. (1) On receipt of an application under sub-section (1) of section 15, the Claims Commissioner shall, after giving notice of such application to the operator and affording an opportunity of being heard to the parties, dispose of the application within a period of three months from the date of such receipt and make an award accordingly.

(2) While making an award under this section, the Claims Commissioner shall not take into consideration any benefit, reimbursement or amount received by the applicant in pursuance of contract of insurance taken by him or for members of his family or otherwise.

(3) Where an operator is likely to remove or dispose of his property with the object of evading payment by him of the amount of the award, the Claims Commissioner may, in accordance with the provisions of rules 1 to 4 of Order XXXIX of the First Schedule to the Code of Civil Procedure, 1908, grant a temporary injunction to restrain such act.

(4) The Claims Commissioner shall arrange to deliver copies of the award to the parties within a period of fifteen days from the date of the award.

(5) Every award made under sub-section (1) shall be final.

17. The operator of the nuclear installation, after paying the compensation for nuclear damage in accordance with section 6, shall have a right of recourse where-

(a) Such right is expressly provided for in a contract in writing;

(b) The nuclear incident has resulted as a consequence of an act of supplier or his employee, which includes supply of equipment or material with patent or latent defects or sub-standard services;

(c) The nuclear incident has resulted from the act of commission or omission of an individual done with the intent to cause nuclear damage.

18. The right to claim compensation for nuclear damage shall extinguish, if such claim is not made within a period of-

   (a) Ten years, in the case of damage to property;

   (b) Twenty years, in the case of personal injury to any person, from the date of occurrence of the incident notified under sub-section (1) of section 3: Provided that where a nuclear damage is caused by a nuclear incident involving nuclear material which, prior to such nuclear incident, had been stolen, lost, jettisoned or abandoned. The said period often years shall be computed from the date of such nuclear incident, but, in no case, it shall exceed a period of twenty years from the date of such theft, loss, jettison or abandonment.

CHAPTER V

NUCLEAR DAMAGE CLAIMS COMMISSION

19. Where the Central Government, having regard to the injury or damage caused by a nuclear incident, is of the opinion that it is expedient in public interest that such claims for such damage be adjudicated by the Commission instead of a Claims Commissioner, it may, by notification, establish a Commission for the purpose of this Act.

20. (1) The Commission shall consist of a Chairperson and such other Members, not exceeding six, as the Central Government may, by notification, appoint.

   (2) The Chairperson and other Members ofthe Commission shall be appointed on the recommendation of a Selection Committee consisting of three experts from amongst the persons having at least thirty years of experience in nuclear science and a retired Supreme Court Judge.

   (3) A person shall not be qualified for appointment as the Chairperson of the Commission unless he has attained the age of fifty-five years and is or has been or qualified to be a Judge of a High Court: Provided that no appointment of a sitting judge shall be made except after consultation with the Chief Justice of India,

(4) A person shall not be qualified for appointment as a Member unless he has attained the age of fifty-five years and-

(a) Has held or is holding or qualified to hold, the post of Additional Secretary to the Government of India or any other equivalent post in the Central Government and possesses special knowledge in law relating to nuclear liability arising out of nuclear incident; or

(b) Has been a Claims Commissioner for five years.

21. The Chairperson or a Member, as the case may be, shall hold office as such for a Term of term of three years from the date on which he enters upon his office and shall be eligible for office. Re-appointment for another term of three years: Provided that no person shall hold office as such Chairperson or Member after he has attained the age of sixty-seven years.

22. The salary and allowances payable to and other terms and conditions of service, including pension, gratuity and other retirement benefits, of the Chairperson and other Members shall be such as may be prescribed: Provided that no salary, allowances and other terms and conditions of service of the Chairperson or other Members shall be varied to his disadvantage after his appointment.

23. If, for reasons other than temporary absence, any vacancy occurs in the office of the Chairperson or Member, as the case may be, the Central Government shall appoint another person in accordance with the provisions of this Act to fill such vacancy and the proceedings may be continued before the Commission from the stage at which it was, before the vacancy is filled.

24. (1) The Chairperson or a Member may, by a notice in writing under his hand addressed to the Central Government, resign his office: Provided that the Chairperson or the Member shall, unless he is permitted by the Central Government to relinquish his office sooner, continue to hold office until the expiry of three months from the date of receipt of such notice or until a person duly appointed as his successor enters upon his office or until the expiry of his term of office, whichever is earlier.

(2) The Central Government shall remove from office the Chairperson or a Member who-

(a) Has been adjudged an insolvent; or

(b) Has been convicted of an offence which, in the opinion of the Central Government, involves moral turpitude; or

(c) Has become physically or mentally incapable of acting as a Member; or

(d) Has acquired such financial or other interest as is likely to affect prejudicially his functions as a Member; or

(e) Has so abused his position as to render his continuance in office detrimental to the public interest: Provided that no Member shall be removed under clause (d) or clause (e) unless he has been given an opportunity of being heard in the matter.

25.   A person who, immediately before the date of assuming office as a Chairperson or a Member, was in service of the Government, shall be deemed to have retired from service on the date on which he enters upon office as such, but his subsequent service as the Chairperson or a Member shall be reckoned as continuing approved service counting for pension in service to which he belonged.

26.   If a person who, immediately before the date of assuming office as the Chairperson or a Member was in receipt of or being eligible so to do, has opted to draw, a pension, other than a disability or wound pension, in respect of any previous service under the Central Government, his salary in respect of service as the Chairperson or a Member shall be reduced-

(a) By the amount of that pension; and

(b) If he had, before assuming office, received, in lieu of a portion of the pension due to him in respect of such previous service, the commuted value thereof, by the amount of that portion of the pension.

27.   No person shall, while holding office as a Chairperson or a Member, act as an arbitrator in any matter.

28.   On ceasing to hold office, the Chairperson or a Member shall not appear, act or plead before the Commission.

29.   The Chairperson shall have the power of superintendence in the

general administration of the Commission and exercise such powers as may be prescribed.

30. (1) The Central Government shall provide the Commission with such officers and other employees as it may deem fit.

(2) The salary and allowances payable to and the terms and other conditions of service of officers and other employees of the Commission shall be such as may be prescribed.

31. (1) Every application for compensation before the Commission for nuclear damage shall be made in such form, containing such particulars and accompanied by such documents, as may be prescribed.

(2) Subject to the provisions of section 18, every application under sub-section (1) shall be made within a period of three years from the date of knowledge of nuclear damage by the person suffering such damage.

32. (1) The Commission shall have original jurisdiction to adjudicate upon every application for compensation filed before it under sub-section (1) of section 31 or transferred to it under section 33, as the case may be.

(2) Upon transfer of cases to the Commission under section 33, the Commission shall hear such applications from the stage at which it was before such transfer.

(3) The Chairperson may constitute benches comprising of not more than three Members of the Commission for the purpose of hearing of claims and any decision thereon shall be rendered by a majority of the Members hearing such claims.

(4) The Commission shall not be bound by the procedure laid down in the Code of Civil Procedure, 1908 but shall be guided by the principles of natural justice and subject to the 5 of 1908. other provisions of this Act and of any rules made there under, the Commission shall have the power to regulate its own procedure including the places and the times at which it shall have its sittings.

(5) The Commission shall have, for the purposes of discharging its functions under this Act, the same powers as are vested in a civil

court under the Code of Civil Procedure, 1908, while trying a suit, in respect of the following matters, namely:-

(a) Summoning and enforcing the attendance of any person and examining him on oath;

(b) The discovery and production of documents;

(c) Receiving evidence on affidavits;

(d) Requisitioning any public record or copies thereof from any court or office;

(e) Issuing of commission for the examination of any witness;

(f) Any other matter which may be prescribed.

(6) The Commission shall, after giving notice of application to the operator and after affording an opportunity of being heard to the parties, dispose of such application within a period of three months from the date of such receipt and make an award accordingly.

(7)   While making an award under this section, the Commission shall not take into consideration any benefit, reimbursement or amount received by the applicant in pursuance of any contract of insurance or otherwise.

(8) Where an operator is likely to remove or dispose of his property with the object of evading payment by him of the amount of the award, the Commission may, in accordance with the provisions of rules 1 to 4 of Order XXXIX of the First Schedule to the Code of Civil Procedure, 1908, grant a temporary injunction to restrain such act.

(9) The Commission shall arrange to deliver copies of the award to the parties concerned within a period of fifteen days from the date of such award.

(10) Every award made under sub-section (6) shall be final.

33.   Every application for compensation pending before the Claims Commissioner immediately before the date of establishment of the Commission under section 19 shall stand transferred on that date to the

Commission.

34. Every proceeding before the Claims Commissioner or the Commission under this Act shall be deemed to be judicial proceeding within the meaning of sections 193, 219 and 228 45 of 1860. Of and for the purposes of; section 196 of, the Indian Penal Code.

35. Save as otherwise provided in section 46, no civil court (except the Supreme Court and a High Court exercising jurisdiction under articles 226 and 227 of the Constitution) shall have jurisdiction to entertain any suit or proceedings in respect of any matter which the Claims Commissioner or the Commission, as the case may be, is empowered to adjudicate under this Act and no injunction shall be granted by any court or other authority in respect of any action taken or to be taken in pursuance of any power conferred by or under this Act.

36. (1) When an award is made under sub-section (1) of section 16 or under subsection (6) of section 32,-

  (a) The insurer or any person, as the case may be, who under the contract of insurance or financial security under section 8 is required to pay any amount in terms of such award and to the extent of his liability under such contract, shall deposit that amount within such time and in such manner as the Claims Commissioner or the Commission, as the case may be, may direct; and

  (b) The operator shall, subject to the maximum liability specified under subsection (2) of section 6, deposit the remaining amount by which such award exceeds the amount deposited under clause (a).

 (2) Where any person referred to in sub-section (1) fails to deposit the amount of award within the period specified in the award, such amount shall be recoverable from such person as arrears of land revenue.

 (3) The amount deposited under sub-section (1) shall be disbursed to such person as may be specified in the award within a period of fifteen days from the date of such deposit.

37. The Commission shall prepare, in such form and at such time in each

financial year, as may be prescribed, an annual report giving full account of its activities during that financial year and submit a copy thereof to the Central Government which shall cause the same to be laid before each House of Parliament.

38. (1) Where the Central Government is satisfied that the purpose for which the Commission established under section 19 has served its purpose, or where the number of cases pending before such Commission is so less that it would not justify the cost of its continued function, or where it considers necessary or expedient so to do, the Central Government may, by notification, dissolve the Commission.

(2) With effect from the date of notification of dissolution of Commission under sub-section (1)-

(a) The proceeding, if any, pending before the Commission as on the date of such notification shall be transferred to the Claims Commissioner to be appointed by the Central Government under sub-section (2) of section 9;

(b) The Chairperson and all Members of the Commission shall be deemed to have vacated their offices as such and they shall not be entitled to any compensation for premature termination of their office;

(c) Officers and other employees of the Commission shall be transferred to such other authority or offices of the Central Government, in such manner, as may be prescribed: Provided that the officers and other employees so transferred, shall be entitled to the same terms and conditions of service as would have been held by them in the Commission: Provided further that where an officer or an employee of the Commission refuses to join the services in such other authority or office, he shall be deemed to have resigned and shall not be entitled to any compensation for premature termination of contract of service;

(d) All assets and liabilities of the Commission shall vest in the Central Government.

(3) Notwithstanding the dissolution of the Commission under sub-section (1), anything done or any action taken or purported to

have been done or taken including any order made or notice issued or any appointment, confirmation or declaration made or any document or instrument executed or any direction given by the Commission before such dissolution, shall be deemed to have been validly done or taken.

(4) Nothing in this section shall be construed to prevent the Central Government to establish the Commission subsequent to the dissolution of the Commission in accordance with the provisions of this Act.

CHAPTER- VI

OFFENCES AND PENALTIES

39. (1) Whoever-

    (a) contravenes any rule made or any direction issued under this Act; or

    (b) fails to comply with the provisions of section 8; or

    (c) fails to deposit the amount under section 36, shall be punishable with imprisonment for a term which may extend to five years or with fine or with both.

(2) Whoever fails to comply with any direction issued under section 43 or obstructs any authority or person in the exercise of his powers under this Act shall be punishable with imprisonment for a term which may extend to one year or with fine or with both.

40. (1) Where an offence under this Act has been committed by a company, every person who at the time the offence was committed, was directly in charge of, and was responsible to, the company for the conduct of the business of the company, as well as the company, shall be deemed to be guilty of the offence and shall be liable to be proceeded against and punished accordingly: Provided that nothing contained in this sub-section shall render any such person liable to any punishment under this Act, if he proves that the offence was committed without his knowledge or that he exercised all due diligence to prevent the commission of such offence.

(2) Notwithstanding anything contained in sub-section (1), where any

offence under this Act has been committed by a company and it is proved that the offence has been committed with the consent or connivance of, or is attributable to any neglect on the part of, any director, manager, secretary or other officer of the company, such director, manager, secretary or other officer shall also be deemed to be guilty of that offence and shall be liable to be proceeded against and punished accordingly.

Explanation. - For the purposes of this section,-

(a) *"Company" means any body corporate and includes a firm or other association of individuals;*

(b) *"Director", in relation to a firm, means a partner in the firm.*

41.   Where an offence under this Act has been committed by any Department of the Government, the Head of the Department shall be deemed to be guilty of the offence and shall be liable to be proceeded against and punished accordingly: Provided that nothing contained in this section shall render such Head of the Department liable to any punishment if he proves that the offence was committed without his knowledge or that he exercised all due diligence to prevent the commission of such offence.

42.   No court inferior to that of a Metropolitan Magistrate or a Judicial Magistrate of Cognizance the first class shall try any offence under this Act: of offences. Provided that cognizance of such offence shall not be taken except on a complaint made by the Central Government or any authority or officer authorized in this behalf by that Government.

CHAPTER-VII

MISCELLANEOUS

43. The Central Government may, in exercise of its powers and performance of its functions under this Act, issue such directions, as it may deem fit, for the purposes of this Act, to any operator, person, officer, authority or body and such operator, person, officer, authority or body shall be bound to comply with such directions.

44. The Central Government may call for such information from an operator as it may deem necessary.

45.   The Central Government may, by notification, exempt any nuclear

installation from the application of this Act where, having regard to small quantity of nuclear material, it is of the opinion that the risk involved is insignificant.

46. The provisions of this Act shall be in addition to, and not in derogation of, any other law for the time being in force, and nothing contained herein shall exempt the operator from any proceeding which might, apart from this Act, be instituted against such operator.

47. No suit, prosecution or other legal proceedings shall lie against the Central Government or the person, officer or authority in respect of anything done by it or him in good faith in pursuance of this Act or of any rule or order made, or direction issued, there under.

48. (1) The Central Government may, by notification, make rules for carrying out the purposes of this Act.

   (2) In particular, and without prejudice to the generality of the foregoing powers such rules may provide for-

   (a) the other financial security and the manner thereof under sub-section (I) of section 8;

   (b) the salary and allowances payable to and the other terms and conditions of service of Claims Commissioner under section 11;

   (c) the procedure to be followed by Claims Commissioner under sub-section (J) of section 12;

   (d) the person to be associated by Claims Commissioner and the manner thereof, under sub-section (2) of section 12;

   (e) the remuneration, fee or allowances of associated person under sub-section (3) of section 12;

   (f) any other matter under clause if) of sub-section (4) of section 12;

   (g) The form of application, the particulars it shall contain and the documents it shall accompany, under sub-section (1) of section 15;

(h) The salary and allowances payable to and other terms and conditions of service of Chairperson and other Members, under section 22;

(i) The powers of Chairperson under section 29;

(j) The salary and allowances payable to and the terms and other conditions of service of officers and other employees of the Commission, under sub-section (2) of section 30;

(k) The form of application, the particulars it shall contain and the documents it shall accompany, under sub-section (I) of section 31;

(l) Any other matter under clause (f) of sub-section (5) of section 32;

(m)   The form and the time for preparing annual report by the Commission under section 37;

(n) The manner of transfer of officers and other employees of the Commission under clause (c) of sub-section (2) of section 38.

(3) Every rule made under this Act by the Central Government shall be laid, as soon as may be after it is made, before each House of Parliament, while it is in session, for a total period of thirty days which may be comprised in one session or in two or more successive sessions, and if, before the expiry of the session immediately following the session or successive sessions aforesaid, both Houses agree in making any modification in the rule or both Houses agree that the rule-should not be made, the rule shall thereafter have effect only in such modified form or be of no effect, as the case may be; so, however, that any such modification or annulment shall be without prejudice to the validity of anything previously done under that rule.

49. (I) If any difficulty arises in giving effect to the provisions of this Act, the Central Government may, by order published in the Official Gazette, make such provisions, not inconsistent with the provisions of this Act, as appear to it to be necessary or expedient for removing the difficulty: Provided that no order shall be made under this section after the expiry of three years from the commencement of this Act.

(2) Every order made under this section shall, as soon as may be after it is made, be laid before each House of Parliament.

V.K. BHASIN,

Secy. to the Govt. of India

PRINTED BY THE GENERAL MANAGER, GOVT. OF INDIA PRESS, MINTO ROAD, NEW DELHI AND

PUBLISHED BY THE CONTROLLER OF PUBLICATIONS, DELHI-2010.

GMGIPMRND-4600GI(S3)-24-09-2010.

IT Based Energy Management System

Introduction. Long range Energy Alternatives Planning (LEAP) System, is a widely-used software tool for energy policy analysis and climate change mitigation assessment developed at the Stockholm Environment Institute.

Details of the Programme. LEAP is an integrated modeling tool that can be used to track energy consumption, production and resource extraction in all sectors of an economy. It can be used to account for both energy sector and non-energy sector green house gas (GHG) emission sources and sinks. In addition to tracking GHGs, LEAP can also be used to analyze emissions of local and regional air pollutants, making it well-suited to studies of the climate co-benefits of local air pollution reduction.

Users and Usage. LEAP has been adopted by thousands of organizations in more than 190 countries worldwide. Its users include:-

- Government agencies, academics, non-governmental organizations, consulting companies, and energy utilities.

- At many different scales ranging from cities and states to national, regional and global applications.

- By countries undertaking integrated resource planning, greenhouse gas (GHG) mitigation assessments, and Low Emission Development Strategies (LEDS) especially in the developing world. Many countries have also chosen to use LEAP as part of their commitment to report to the U.N.O.

- Framework Convention on Climate Change (UNFCCC).

Reach of the Programme.

- LEAP is not a model of a particular energy system, but rather a tool that can be used to create models of different energy systems, where each requires its own unique data structures.

- LEAP supports a wide range of different modeling methodologies: on the demand side these range from bottoms-up, end-use accounting techniques to top-down macro-economic modeling.

- LEAP also includes a range of optional specialized methodologies including stock-turnover modeling for areas such as transport planning. On the supply side, LEAP provides a range of accounting and simulation methodologies that are powerful enough for modeling electric sector generation and capacity expansion planning, but which are also sufficiently flexible and transparent to allow LEAP to easily incorporate data and results from other more specialized models.

Modeling. LEAP's modeling capabilities operate at two basic conceptual levels:-

- At one level, LEAP's built-in calculations handle all of the "non controversial" energy, emissions and cost-benefit accounting calculations.

- At the second level, users enter spreadsheet-like expressions that can be used to specify time-varying data or to create a wide variety of sophisticated multi-variable models, thus enabling econometric and simulation approaches to be embedded within LEAP's overall accounting framework.

- The newest versions of LEAP also support optimization modeling: allowing for the construction of least cost models of electric system capacity expansion and dispatch, potentially under various constraints such as limits of CO_2 or local air pollution.

Scenario Analysis. LEAP is designed around the concept of long-range scenario analysis. Scenarios are self-consistent storylines of how an energy system might evolve over a period of time. Using LEAP, policy analysts can create and then evaluate alternative scenarios by comparing their energy requirements, their social costs and benefits and their environmental impacts. The LEAP Scenario Manager (an icon on the home page of the soft ware), can be used to describe individual policy measures which can then be combined in different combinations and permutations into alternative integrated scenarios. This approach allows policy makers to assess the marginal impact of an individual policy as well as the interactions that occur when multiple policies and measures are combined. For example, the benefits of appliance efficiency standards combined with a renewable portfolio standard might be less than the sum of the benefits of the two measures considered separately. Individual measures are combined into an overall GHG Mitigation scenario containing various measures for reducing greenhouse gas emissions, While methodology is an important factor in choosing an energy model,

Conclusion. LEAP is more than just a model: it is a full decision support system (DSS) providing extensive data management and reporting capabilities. It can serve both; as a historical database showing the evolution of an energy system and a forward-looking scenario-based tool that can create forecasts of how a system might evolve or "backcasts" that examine how a society might try to meet its development goals in the energy sector. LEAP provides powerful data management tools including full importing and exporting to Microsoft Excel, Word and PowerPoint, and a rich graphical environment for visualizing data and results. LEAP has had a significant impact in shaping energy and environmental polices worldwide. For example:

- In China, the Chinese Energy Research Institute (ERI) has used LEAP to explore how China could achieve its development goals whilst also reducing its carbon intensity. These studies have helped to influence national energy policies and plans.

- In the U.S., a prominent Non-Governmental Organization, the Natural Resources Defense Council (NRDC) uses LEAP to analyze national fuel economy standards and advocate for policies that encourage clean vehicles and fuels.

- In Rhode Island, LEAP has been the main organizational tool for analyzing and monitoring the State's award-winning GHG mitigation process, in which multiple stakeholders are guiding the State's efforts to meet its GHG emission reduction goals.

- In the Philippines, LEAP is used by the Department of Energy to help develop its National Energy Plans.

Source: It is a soft ware based programme developed by Stockholm Environment Institute (Website: http://www.sei-us.org/) as part of their

Community Environment Energy Development (COMMEND) programme uploaded on http://www.energycommunity.org/default.asp?action=80

Author's Comment

This book in no way holds brief on behalf of LEAP programme. It is the considered view of the author that LEAP is only one of the many such Decision Support Systems (DSS) which can assist a decision maker to select one of those duly analyzed options which such a DSS is capable to generate based on the data which is fed into the system.

Aim to describe the LEAP programme is to highlight the issues which such a DSS should be able to address and also to centre stage the need for an integrated energy management system which can help a decision maker to take a holistic view of the energy and all related issues, which can be done only if it is done through a computer aided programme which removes any kind of subjectivity which human handling may result into.

Finally while this or any similar programme may prove to be a base programme which may stimulate the planners in India to work out a flow of events in such a way that all aspects related to energy, which are typical to India, are used as input to work out an India specific solution in terms of time periods with financial impacts, material, infrastructure, manpower, equipments needs and finally environment effect factored into the inputs in such a way that their collective effect is reflected into the output which such a system can generate.

While; it is indeed a tall order because the development of the entire process would be quite complex, however; given the state of intellectual equity of India, particularly in the field of IT, it should not be very difficult. Although it may take a while but the effort needs to start at some point in time, keeping in view the criticality of such a programme for the desired monitoring of the energy management in India. It is felt that the time for the commencement of the task is not a day too late.

Reference and Bibliography

ADB Report, published in The Economic Times, page-06 dated 29 June 2013.

Al Gore, " Our Choice", published by Rodale Books, pp-165-166, year 2009.

Anil Sasi, "India to get 510 tonnes of uranium from Kazakhstan, Russia". Hindu Business Line, dated 10 March 2010.

Annual Energy Outlook2013,"Levelized Cost of New Generation Resources in the Annual Energy Outlook 2013", published by EIA of DOE, USA dated 28 January 2013

Anshu Bharadwaj, LV Krishnan, S Rajagopal, "Nuclear Power in India: The Road Ahead",published by Centre for Study of Science, Technology & Policy (CSTEP), Bangalore dated October 2008.

Anthony Andrews, " Nuclear Fuel Reprocessing: US Policy Development", CRS Report for Congress Order code RS 22542, updated 27 March 2008.

"A Nuclear Power Renaissance", published in Scientific American, May 2008, uploaded on www.scientificamerican.com/

APJ Abdul Kalam and Srijan Pal Singh, "Nuclear Power Is Our Gateway To A Prosperous Future", Published In The Hindu, November 6, 2011.

"A Policy Brief-Challenges facing Asia: Second Thoughts about Nuclear Power, published by Lee Kuan Yew School of Public Policy, National University of Singapore, January 2011.

Ashley J Tellis, "Atoms for War?", published by Carnegie Endowment for International Peace, pp-14, year of publication 2006. Also available on http://www.carnegieendowment.org/files/atomsfor

"Atomic Reactor Makes Electricity", published in Popular Mechanics

March 1952, pp-105

Avril Ormsby; Editing by Richard Williams, "UK, India sign civil nuclear accord", Reuters Report, dated 13 February 2010. Retrieved 22 August 2010

Ayesha Rascoe, "US Approves First New Nuclear Plant in a Generation", reported by Reuters dated 09 February 2012

Bagchi, Indrani, "Keep your word, we will keep ours, India tells NSG", published in Times of India11August 2011. Retrieved 21 August 2011.

Bain, Alister S., et al, "Canada Enters the Nuclear Age: A Technical History of Atom", published by Magill Queen's University Press in 1997, pp-ix.

Dr Baldev Raj, " History and Evolution of Fast Breeder Reactor Design in India- A Saga of Challenges and Successes", published in IGC News Letter, Volume 69, July 2006.

Banerjee, Srikumar, "Thorium Utilization for Sustainable Supply of Nuclear Energy", published in Virginia Tech dated September 2010, retrieved 5 April 2012

Batra R.K., "India: water Shale Gas" dated 06 September 2013, uploaded on www.teriin.org/

BBC News Archives, "South Asia | Russia agrees India nuclear deal".. 11 February 2009. Retrieved 22 August 2010

BBC News, "India and Canada finalize conditions of nuclear deal", 06 November 2012. Retrieved 18 November 2012

BBC News, "On This Day: October 17", dated 17 October 1956

Bedi, Rahul , "Largest uranium reserves found in India", The Telegraph, dated 19 July 2011retrieved 27 April 2012

Bellona, " Nuclear icebreaker Lenin", dated 20 June 2003, uploaded on www.bellona.org/english_import_area/international/russia/civilian_ nuclear_vessels/icebreakers/30131

Benjamin K. Sovacool," Valuing the greenhouse gas emissions from nuclear power: A critical survey", published in Energy Policy Journal available online since 0 2 June 2008 on www.elsevier.com/locate/enpol

Benjamin K Sovacool, "Contesting the Future of Nuclear Power: A Critical Global Assessment of Atomic Energy", published by World Scientific during 2011.

Bernard L Cohen," Costs Of Nuclear Power Plants — What Went Wrong? As Chapter 9 as part of THE NUCLEAR ENERGY OPTION Published by Plenum Press, 1990 uploaded on www.phyast.pitt.edu/~blc/book/chapter9.html

Bernard Cohen, "The Nuclear Energy Option", published by Plenum Press, during 1990.

Benjamin K Sovacool, "The Costs of Failure: A Preliminary Assessment of Major Energy Accidents-1907-2007", published in Energy Policy, Volume 36, dated 2008, pp-1802-1820

Benjamin K Sovacool, "Contesting the Future of Nuclear Power: A Critical Global Assessment of Atomic Energy" , published in World Scientific, pp-141 dated 2011

Bibhudatta Pradhan and Archana Chaudhary / Bloomberg, "At G-8, Singh, Bush reaffirm commitment to nuclear deal"., published by livemint.com. 10 July 2008.

Bilbao y León, Sama, "Mumbai engages ADS for nuclear energy", Mumbai: CEM Courier, dated 27 March 2012, retrieved 11 April 2012.

Bhaskar Balakrishnan, "Nuclear Programme in Take-Off Stage", published IN THE HINDU BUSINESSLINE, 18 JULY 2012.

BP Statistical Review of World Energy, dated June 2012, uploaded on Web: bp.com/statistical review.

Bromby, Robin, " Thorium a safer option", pub in The Australian dated 16 Nov 2011, retrieved 5 April 2012

Bruno Comby, " the Solution for Nuclear Waste", published in the International Journal of Environmental Studies- Volume-62, Number-6, pp-72-736 dated December 2005.

B Sivakumar, " Cold Fusion Turns Hot, City to Host Meet", published in Times of India, Chennai Edition, 25 January 2011

Bucher, R.G. (January 2009), "India's Baseline Plan for Nuclear Energy self-sufficiency stage", published by Argonne National Laboratory during January 2009, retrieved 26 March 2012.

Bureau reporters, "India signs civil nuclear deal with Mongolia", published in Financial Express dated 15 September 2009.Retrieved 13 August 2011

Business Standard report, "L&T bags Rs 844 crore order for Kakrapar Atomic Power Station", dateline; Mumbai/Ahmedabad   dated 9 December 2009, retrieved 2 May 2012

Business Standard , "Slowdown not to affect India's nuclear plans", dated 21 January 2009

Business Standard, "Nuclear power generation to touch 6,000 Mw by next year". Retrieved 26 August 2010.

B Metz, OR Davidson, PR Bosch, R Dave and LA Meyer, "Climate Change 2007: Mitigation of Climate Change, IPCC Fourth Assessment Report (AR-4) published by Cambridge University Press, United Kingdom, last updated on 04 March 2013.

CEA (2010), "Status of Distribution Sector in the Country and Introduction to Accelerated Power Development and Reform Programme", New Delhi.

Chandrasekhar M, department of Earth Sciences, IIT Mumbai, "Geothermal Energy Resources of India", presented during IBC Conference on Geothermal Power-Asia2000, Manila, Philippines, dated February 2000.

Chapter-6, "Indian Programme on Reprocessing- BARC", uploaded on   http://www.barc.gov.in/publications/eb/golden/nfc/toc/Chapter percent206/6.pdf

Chatterjee, Amit Kumar, "Argentina- India's seventh nuclear destination", India – Articles, published by Institute of Peace and Conflict Studies, dated 30 October 2009. Retrieved 21 August 2011

Chaturvedi Ram, "History of Nuclear India", presented in American Physical Society's April Meeting, held from 29 Apr-02 May 2000.

compiled by Wm. Robert Johnston, "Deadliest radiation accidents and other events causing radiation casualties", part of Database of radiological incidents and related events--Johnston's Archive, last updated 23 September 2007, uploaded on www.johnstonsarchive.net/nuclear/radevents/radevents1.html

Conservation Action Trust study done Urban Emmissions under the ageis of Green Peace India, "Coal Kills: An Assessment of Death and Disease" and uploaded on http://www.greenpeace.org/india/Global/india/report/Coal_Kills.pdf

"Construction starts on 2 700 MWe PHWRs in Rajasthan", published in World Nuclear News, 18 July 2011, retrieved 3 March 2012.

David Bodansky, " the status Nuclear waste Disposal", published by Forum on Physics & Society of the American Physical Society, Volume-35, Number-1 dated January 2006.

F. David Doty, "Overview of the Energy Challenge and the Science and Engineeringof WindFuels/CARMA Economically Producing Fuels and Chemicals from CO_2 , CH_4, and Off-peak Wind, published by www.DotyEnergy.com dated August 2012.

David Fischer, "50 Years of Nuclear Energy", part of History of the International Atomic Energy Agency: The First Forty Years, IAEA, Vienna, Austria dated 1997.

David Hambling, " 'safe' Alternative to Depleted Uranium Revealed", published in New Scientist dated 30 July 2003, uploaded on www.newscientist.com/

David Martin, "Exporting Disaster: Cost of Selling Candu reactor", published by Campaign for Nuclear Phase Out, Canada, Nov 1996.

David Sclissel and Bruce Biewald, "Nuclear Power Plant Construction Costs", published Synapse, Inc dated July 2008

Department of Atomic Energy, Government of India,"Thorium Based NPP", dated 21 Mar 2012, retrieved on 05 April 2012 uploaded on www.dae.gov.in

DGH Site with IP address: http://www.dghindia.org/NonConventionalEnergy.aspx?tab=0

Dhirendra Sharma, "Politics of the Atomic Energy Act 1962" part of " India's Nuclear Estate" at pp-31, published by Lancer Publication 1983.

Diwan, Parag; Sarkar, A.N. (2009), "Energy Security", Volume 5, published by Pentagon Press during 2009.

Dharur, Suresh (22 April 2012), "AP houses one of world's largest uranium reserves", pub in Hyderabad: The Tribune, dated 22 April 2012, retrieved 27 April 2012.

Diwakar & Chidanand Rajghatta "House of Reps clears N-deal, France set to sign agreement", published in The Times of India, dated 29 September 2008.

Donald Lawson Turcotte and Gerald Schubert, "Geodynamics", published by Cambridge (U.A.), reprinted by Cambridge University Press, 2010 edition, pp-136-137, ISBN 978-0-521-66624-4.

Dr G Balachandran, "The Civil Nuclear Liability Bill", published as IDSA Brief No 26 by IDSA dated July 2010.

Dr. Baldev Raj, Director, Indira Gandhi Centre for Atomic Research, "Fast Breeder Programme : An Inevitable Option For Energy Security" part of 2004-Technology Day Speech, AIR

Dr R Chidambaram, "India's Technology Needs: Nuclear to Rural", delivered as the Second Darbari Seth Memorial Lecture, 26 August 2003, at TERI, New Delhi.

Dr R Chidambaram, "Nuclear Power Programmes: Indian & Global", lecture delivered in the Indian Embassy Auditorium organized by Science India forum, UAE, Abu Dhabi on 18 April 2013.

Dr R Chidambaram," 'Nuclear Energy: Energy Security & Climate Change", lecture delivered at Mumbai University on 02 March 2010 and reported by ZEE News, "Closed N-fuel cycle must to mitigate climate change threat" dated 03 March 2010.

Draft Policy Report by MNRE on JNNSM Phase -2; targets 10 GW of Utility solar installations dated 03 December 2012.

Duncan Clark, "Nuclear Waste Burning Reactor Moves a step closer to Reality", published by The Guardian, dated 09 July 2012.

Ed Gerstner, " The Hybrid Returns", published in Nature/ Volume-460, published by Macmillan Publishers Limited, dated 02 July 2009

Eleanor Beardsley," "France Presses Ahead with Nuclear Power", published in NPR dated May 01, 2006 and uploaded on www.npr.org/

Environmental Protection Agency (EPA) "Part II Environmental Protection Agency, 40 CFR Part 197, Public Health and Environmental Radiation Protection Standards for Yucca Mountain, Nevada; proposed Rules", part of Federal Register/Volume-70, No 161 dated 22 august 2005.

Environmental Surveillance, Education and Research Programme, Idaho National Laboratory. Archived from the original on 21 Novemebr 2008.

Executive Energy Message. Printed at the Request of Henry M. Jackson, Chairman, Committee on Interior and Insular Affairs, United States Senate.

EIA," Annual Energy Outlook, 2006". DOE/EIA-0383 (2006), Washington DC, February 2006.

EIA, "Levelized Cost of New Generation Resources in the Annual Energy Outlook 2011", November2010 uploaded on http://www.eia.gov/oiaf/ aeo/electricity_generation.html

EIA, "International Energy Outlook 2011", dated 09 September 2011, uploaded on www.eia.gov/forecasts/ieo/world.com

EIA, "Summary Status for the US" dated 21 January 2010.

EAI, Potential for Biomass Power in India uploaded on http://www.eai.in/ ref/ae/bio/pot/biomass_power_potential.html#sthash.NROgb3Bl.dpuf

EAI, uploaded on http://www.eai.in/ref/ae/geo/geo.html#sthash. uR2S4Luc.dpuf

EAI, "India Geo-thermal Energy", uploaded on http://www.eai.in/ref/ae/ geo/geo.html

Ed Crooks, "Nuclear New Dawn now seems to be limited to East", Financial Times, 12 September 2010.

Elliot Brennan & Silvia Pastorelli , "India's Shale Gas Boom: Dream or Reality? India's Shale Gas Boom: Dream or Reality?", published in The

Diplomat dated 18 June 2013

Encyclopedia.com, "Uranium (Revised)", uploaded on www.encyclopedia. com/topic/uranium.aspx dated 26 August 2013.

Eric Yep, "India's Widening Energy Deficit", published in India real time dated 09 March 2011.

EUROSTAT, "Gross Electricity Generation by Fuel Used in Power stations" dated 2006.

Fact Sheet: Oklo: Natural Nuclear reactors, published in Internet Archive Way Back Machine uploaded on web.archive.org/

Ferguson, Charles D. (1 March 2007), "Assessing the Vulnerability of the Indian Civil Nuclear Program to Military and Terrorist Attack", in Henry D. Sokolski, Gauging U.S.-India Strategic Cooperation, Army War College (U.S.). Strategic Studies Institute, dated 01 March 2007.

Fin, Al, "A Brief Overview of Thorium Energy", oilprice.com, dated 01 July 2011 retrieved 20 March 2012.

Financial Express Report, "India Signs Civil Nuclear Deal with Mangolia", dated 15 September.

Fiona Harvey, "Dramatic fall in new nuclear power stations after Fukushima", published in The Guardian (London), dated 08 March 2012.

Fred Pearce, "Are fast breeder reactors a nuclear power panacea?' published in Biodiversity business and innovation business, innovation energy, and forest science technology dated 30 July 2012, uploaded on www.e360.yale.edu/

Fuhrmann, Matthew,"Atomic Assistance: How "Atoms for Peace" Programs Cause Nuclear Insecurity", published by Texas: Cornell University Press, dated 24 July 2012.

Gagnon, Luc, Belanger, Camille, Uchiyama, Yohji, "Lifecycle assessment of electricity generation options: the status of research in year 2001. Energy Policy 30, 1267–1278" during 2002.

G. Baidya Chief Engineer (CDM–R&D), NHPC, Faridabad, "Development

Of Small Hydro", presented at Dehradun during Himalayan Small Hydropower Summit, dated October 12-13, 2006, uploaded on http://www.iitr.ac.in/departments/AH/uploads/File/hshs/Presentations/Links/Technical percent20Papers/Overview percent20of percent20SHP percent20Development/Mr percent20G percent20Baidya_Development percent20of percent20SH.pdf,

George, Nirmala "Moscow Ends Atomic Power Blockade to India", published in Indian Express. (21 June 1998). Retrieved 21 August 2011.

Glassley, William E. (2010). Geothermal Energy: Renewable Energy and the Environment, CRC Press, ISBN 9781420075700

Gordon, Sandy, "Implications of the Sale of Australian Uranium to India", Working Paper No. 410 of Canberra: Strategic and Defence Studies Centre, during September 2008, retrieved 27 March 2012

Government of India, 12th Plan Document Vol II (Table-14.5, pp-134)

Government of India Planning Commission," Integrated energy policy: Report of the Expert Committee, New Delhi, August 2006.

H. C. Greenwell, L. M. L. Laurens, R. J. Shields, R. W. Lovitt and K. J. Flynn, "Placing microalgae on the bio-fuels priority list: a review of the technological challenges", published in Interface, Journal of Royal Society, Volume 7 No 46703-726 dated 06 May 2010, uploaded on rsif.royalsocietypublishing.org/content/7/46/703.pdf

The Hindu, India, Argentina ink agreement on peaceful uses of N-energy, dated 24 September 2010.

The Hindu Business line , 22 Aug 2012.

"How Geothermal Energy Works", Published in Clean Energy uploaded on www.UCSUSA.org/clean_energy_choices/renewable-energy/how-geothermal-energy-works.html

IAEA Publication, " International Conventions and Legal Agreements: Vienna Convention on Civil Liability for Nuclear Damage", uploaded on www.iaea.org/publications/documents/conventions/liability.html

IANS Report published in Hindustan Times, "Tata Power Eyeing $ 3 Billion Nuclear Power Foray", 15 August 2008 llen Thomas (November 2004). "Clathrates: little known components of the global carbon cycle". Wesleyan University. Retrieved 13 December 2007.

International Energy Agency, "Key World Energy Statistics, 2012" uploaded on www.iea.org

India Energy Book 2012, published by Government of India.

Information with respect to Petroleum coke (Pet coke) on the website of the International Union of Pure and Applied Chemistry (IUPAC) Compendium of Chemical Terminology known as IUPAC GOLD BOOK

Integrated Energy Policy of the Government of India: Expert Committee Report-2006

Internet: Editorial, "Adieu to Nuclear Recycling", published in Nature, Volume-460, Number-152, published online 08 July 2009, uploaded on www.nature.com/

Internet: George Monbiot, "A waste of waste" dated 05 December 2011, www.monbiot.com/

Internet: www.bhavini.nic.in/project.asp

Internet: http://en.wikipedia.org/wiki/synthetic_fuel

Internet: http://en.wikipedia.org/wiki/India_three-stage_nuclear_power_ programme

Internet:http://en.wikipedia.org/wiki/India's_three-stage_nuclear_power_ programme#CITEREFWorld_Nuclear_News2010

Internet: www.npcil.nic.in/main/powerplantdisplay.aspx, "Plants Under Operation". NPCIL. Retrieved 21 August 2011

Internet: www.rediffmail.com/news/2008/jan/25france.htm dated 25 Jan 2008, "India, France agree on civil nuclear cooperation". Retrieved 22 August 2010

Internet down load: http://www.geologydata.info/petroleum_03.htm

Internet download: Emerging opportunities and challenges India Energy

Congress – 2012, 23 January 2012 uploaded on http://www.pwc.com. au/asia-practice/india/assets/publications/Opportunities-Challenges-India-2012.pdf

Internet down load: http://www.powergridindia.com

Internet down load from MNRE, Government of India, site, "BIOMASS POWER AND COGENERATION PROGRAMME. IP Address: http:// www.mnre.gov.in/

Internet download: David JC Mackay, "Sustainable Energy- without the Hot Air", uploaded on http://www.inference.phy.cam.ac.uk/ withouthotair/c24/page_168.shtml

Internet download, "Indian companies likely to benefit from nuclear deal" http://www.stockinvest.in/posts/Indian_companies_likely_to_benefit_ from_nuclear_deal

Internet download: "The Manhattan Project: Making the Atomic Bomb Part I: Physics Background, 1919-1939" on http://www.atomicarchive. com/History/mp/p1s1.shtml

Internet download, "What do you mean by Induced Radioactivity", on Thebigger.com uploaded on www.thebigger.com/chemistry/nuclear-and-radiations-chemistry/what-do-you-mean-by-induced-radioactivity-2/ retrieved on 22 June 2013

Internet download: "Neptunium" uploaded on www.vanderkrogt.net/ elements/element.php?sym=Np

Internet download: "The Manhattan Project: Making the Atomic Bomb Introduction- The Einstein Letter", uploaded on http:// www. atomicarchive.com retrieved on 22 June 2013

Internet download: "4th Generation Nuclear Power" uploaded as http:// ossfoundation.us/projects/energy/nuclear

Internet download: nageshkumar.s@thehindu.co.in

Internet download: WNA Report-"Comparison of Lifecycle Greenhouse Gas Emissions of Various Electricity Generation Sources", published by World Nuclear Association uploaded on www.world-nuclear. org/uploadedfiles/org/WNA/publications/working_Group_reports/

Comparisons_of_lifecycle.pdf

Internet download: Energy Analysis of "Nuclear Power Results-Life Cycle Assessment Harmonization" published by National Renewable Energy Laboratory dated 24 January 2013 uploaded on www.nrel.gov/analysis/ sustain_Ica_nuclear.html

Internet download: "China is Building the World's Largest Nuclear Capability", uploaded on 21cbh.com dated 21 September 2010.

Internet download: By ITER Information Service, "Beyond ITER" uploaded on http://www.iter.org/future-beyond.htm updated up to 14 August 2013.

Internet download: "50 Years of Nuclear Energy" by IAEA uploaded on http://www.iaea.org/

ITER-India uploaded on www.iter-india.org/iter-india.htm

"India Turns to Thorium As Future Reactor Fuel", Nuclear Energy Institute, 2012 Issue, retrieved 14 April 2012.

"India, Kazakhstan ink civil nuclear cooperation deal", published in The Times of India. 17 April 2011. Retrieved 21 August 2011

"India, Kazakh ink nuke and oil pacts", published in Indian Express dated 16 April 2009. Retrieved 21 August 2011

IMF Country Report No 13/37, "India 2013 Article IV Consultation" dated February 2013.

Interview of Shri BK Chaturvedi, Member Energy Planning Commission with Yogima Seth Sharma of ET dated 16 July 2013.

Internet: www.taurianresources.co.in "Indian firm acquires uranium mining rights in Niger | Uranium, Niger, Company, Bajla, Government", Retrieved 22 December 2010

Iyengar, P.K.; Prasad, A.N.; Gopalakrishnan, A.; Karnad, Bharat, "Strategic Sell-Out: Indian-US Nuclear Deal", pub by Pentagon Press, during 2009.

Jay Newton-Small, "US Energy Legislations- May be Renaissance for Nuclear Power", published in Bloomberg dated 22 June 2005 and uploaded on www.bloomberg.com/apps/news?pid=newsarchive&sid=a Xb5iuqdZoD4&refer=US

J Reece Roth, "Introduction to Fusion Energy", 1986

Jaganathan, Venkatachari, (11 May 2011), "India's new fast-breeder on track, nuclear power from September next", TNN (Chennai: Hindustan Times), dated 11 May 2011 retrieved 25 March 2012

Jayaram, K.M.V., "An Overview of World Thorium Resources, Incentives for Further Exploration and Forecasts for Thorium Requirements in the Near Future", Hyderabad: IAEA, retrieved 26 March 2012.

JB Stevens and RC Batra, "Adibatic Shear banding in Ax symmetric Impact and Penetration Problems", Virginia Polytechnic Institute and State University, uploaded on www.sv.vt.edu/research/batra-stevens/pent.html

Jeffrey St Clair, "Pools of Fire", published in Counter Punch dated 09 August 2008, uploaded in Project Censored as, "Nuclear Waste Pools in North Carolina and uploaded on www.projectcensored.org/4-nuclear-waste-pools-in-north-carolina/

John M Broder and Clifford Krauss, "A Big and Risky Energy Bet", pub in New York Times, dated 17 Dec 2012.

John Stepenson and Peter Tynan," Will the US-India Civil Nuclear Cooperation Initiative Light India?" published as chapter-2 of United States and India Strategic Cooperation, edited by hennery Sokolski, published by Nova Science Publishers, Inc. New York during 2009.

John Deutch, "The Future of Nuclear Power-An Inter disciplinary MIT Study", 29 July 2003

Jain, S.K., "Nuclear Power – An alternative", NPCIL, retrieved 4 March 2012.

Jane Nakano, David Pumphrey, Robert Price Jr, Molly A Walton, "Prospects for Shale Gas Development in Asia Examining Potential and Challenges in China and India", published by Center for Strategic and International Studies, Washington DC, during 2012, pp-10-11

James A Lakes, "Nuclear energy's Role in Responding to the Energy

Challenges of the 21st Century", presentation by Idaho National Engineering and Environmental Laboratory, uploaded on nuclear.inl. gov/docs/papers-pstns/ga_tech_woodruff_3-4.pdf

Jayan, T.V., "Fuelling Fear", published in The Telegraph, dated 21 March 2011, retrieved 2 May 2012.

John McCarthy (2006), "Facts from Cohen and Others: How Long will Nuclear Energy Last?" Progress and US Sustainability, Stanford, retrieved 09 November 2006 citing Breeder Reactors: A Renewable Energy Source published in American Journal of Physics, Volume-51, (1), January 1983.

Jon Samseth et al, "Closing and Decommissioning Nuclear Power Reactors- Another Look following the Fukushima Accident" part of UNEP year Book 2012.

J Pamela et al, "Overview of European Fusion Development Agreement (EFDA) Activities" dated 27 July 2006.

Kademani, B.S. (12 September 2006), "World literature on thorium research: A scientometric study based on Science Citation Index, Scientometrics, retrieved 13 April 2012.

Kalam, A.P.J. Abdul, "Nuclear power is our gateway to a prosperous future", published in The Hindu, dated 06 November 2011, retrieved 13 April 2012.

Kamat, Nandkumar, "Redefining Energy Security for India", Vol. 15, No. 25 published in The Navhind Times, dated 31 May 2010, retrieved 11 April 2012.

Key World Energy Statistics-2012 by IEA

Kragh, Helge , " Quantum Generations: A History of Physics in the Twentieth Century", published by Princeton NJ: Princeton University Press, pp 286, 1999

Kranti Kumar and Deepal Jayasekera, "Nuclear Supplier Group Gives India Unique waiver, but only After Row between Delhi and Beijing", published by International Committee of the Fourth International (ICFI) dated 17 september 2008 and uploaded on www.wsws.org/en/ articles/2008/09/nucl-s17.html

Krivit, Steven; Lehr, Jay H.; Kingery, Thomas B., "Nuclear Energy Encyclopedia: Science, Technology and Applications", published as part of Wiley Series on Energy, John Wiley & Sons, dated 24 June 2011.

Kurt Kleiner, "Nuclear Energy: Assessing the Emissions", published in Nature, Volume-2, pp-130-131, dated October 2008, uploaded on www.nature.com/climate/2008/0810/pdf/climate.2008.99.pdf.

Kvenvolden, K. A.; McMenamin, M. A. (1980). "Hydrates of Natural Gas: Their Geologic Occurrence". U. S. Geological Survey Circular 825

"Lazard's Levelized Cost of Energy Analysis", dated June 2011 uploaded on http://docs.google.com/file/d/0Bxo3omeSKZ7AUEpsU215M09ZcGM/edit?pli=1

Leonard Weiss, "Power Points: The US-India Nuclear Agreement is the Wrong Deal with the Wrong Energy Source.

"Life-cycle Emissions Analyses", published by Nuclear Energy Institute, uploaded on www.nei.org/issues-policy/protecting-the-environment/life-cycle-emissions-analyses, retrived on 24 August 2010.

Researched and written by Lorne Stockman with contributions from David Turnbull and Stephen Kretzmann Petroleum Coke: the coal hiding in the tar SandS Pub in OILCHANGNGE INTERNATIONAL January 2013

Lydia Powell, "$ 150 Oil Comes Back by the Backdoor" published by ORF Centre for Resource Management, Volume IX, 52 dated 11 June 2013.

Mail Today, "Nuclear Regulation in Shambles" dated 15 March 2011.

Maitra (2009), " A Future Energy Giant? India's Thorium Based Nuclear Plans", pub in Phys.org on 01 Oct 2010, uploaded on www.phys.org/news205141972.html.

Majumdar, S., "Experience of thorium fuel development in India", BARC (Vienna: IAEA), 1999retrieved 4 March 2012.

Makarand Gadgil, "Jaitapur nuclear plant work may not start before 2014", published in livemint.com (Wall Street Journal) dated 29 November 2011. Retrieved 29 November 2011

Market Analysis of Indian Refining Sector, uploaded on CHEMTECH Foundation site: http://www.chemtech-online.com/events/chemtech/2010/01/market-analysis-of-indian-refining-sector.php dated 21 January 2010

Marco Giugni (Editor), "Social Protests and Policy Change: Ecology, Anti Nuclear and Peace Movements- case study on Shoreham Nuclear Power PlantProtests", Chapter-3, pp-38, published by Rowman and Littlefield Publishers, dated 2004.

Mark Diesendorf, "Greenhouse solutions with Sustainable Energy", published by University of South Wales during 2007, PP-252.

Mark Diesendorf, "Is nuclearenergy a Possible Solution to Global Warming", published by Centre for Energy and Environmental Markets Australia, uploaded on www.ceem.unsw.edu.au/content/user Docs/ nukes social Alternatives MD.pdf.

M King Hubbert, "Nuclear Energy and the Fossil Fuels Drilling and Production Practice, published by API, pp-36.

McHugh, Liam, "India Seeks Energy Security from Thorium", pub in Australia: Future Directions International, retrieved 4 March 2012

Mathew L Wald, "Nuclear Renaissance is Short on Largess", published in 'The New York Times' dated 07 December 2010.

Michael Marshal Ice that burns could be a green fossil fuel published in New Scientist, dated   26 March 2009 and uploaded on http://www. newscientist.com/article/dn16848-ice-that-burns-could-be-a-green-fossil-fuel.html.

MI Ojovan & WE Lee, "An Introduction to Nuclear waste Immobilization", Elsevier Science Publisher BV, Amsterdam, PP-141 and 315 year 2005.

Ministry of External Affairs, Government of India, "FAQ on the India-US Agreement for Co-operation concerning Peaceful Uses of Nuclear Energy, retrieved on 26 March 2012.

"Ministry of Power". Powermin.gov.in. Retrieved 22 August 2010.

Miranda Marquit, "Is Solar Power Cheaper than Nuclear Power?', dated 09 August 2010 uploaded on phys.org/news200578033.html

Montreal Gazette Report, "Canada, India reach nuclear deal". . 29 November 2009. Retrieved 22 August 2010.

Montgomery, Scott L, "the Powers That B", published by University of Chicago Press, pp-137, year 2010.

Moti L mittal of department of environment & occupational Health, University of South Florida, Tampa, Florida, USA, Chemendra Sharma and Richa Singh of National Physical Laboratory, India, "Estimates of emission for Coal Fired thermal Power Plants in India" uploaded on www.epa.gov/ttn.chie1/conference/ei20/session5/mmmittalpdf.

Mrinalini Prasad, "Decoding India's T&D losses", published in ElectricalMonitor dated 26 November 2012 uploaded on www.electricalmonitor.com/articles

MV Ramana," Nuclear Power in Indai: Failed Past, Dubious Future," published as Chapter Three, pp-47 of United States and India strategic cooperation edited by Henry Skolaki, published by Nova Science Publishers, Inc. New York, 2009.

MV Ramana and JY Suchitra, "Costing Plutonium: Economics of Reprocessing in India", published in Int J Global Energy Issues, Volume-27, Number-4, year of publication 2007

"Nuclear Power- Nuclear Waste Plants in North and South Carolina published in NC Warn dated 21 january 2010

Nuclear Energy Agency, "Uranium Resources Sufficient to Meet Projected Nuclear Energy Requirements Long into the Future" dated 03 June 2008, uploaded on http://www.oecd-nea.org/press/2008/2008-02.html

NWT Magazine, October 2012

Office of the Press Secretary, White House," Joint Statement Between President George W. Bush and Prime Minister Manmohan Singh" dated 18 June 2005.

outlookindia.com dated 02 October 2009.

Outlookindia.com, "news.outlookindia.com".. Retrieved 22 August 2010.

"Nuclear power plant will be a big boon for Rajasthan", published in The

Hindu, with dateline Jaipur dated 10 August 2011, retrieved 3 March 2012.

NPCIL, "Nuclear Power Plants In India", uploaded on www.npcil.nic.in/main/allprojectoperationdisplay.aspx during January 2011.

Nuclear Power in India updated up to 10 April 2013, World Nuclear Association website uploaded on www.world-nuclear.org/info/country-G-N/India/#.Ud_w_EGmjdA

"Nuclear-Powered Ships | Nuclear Submarines". World-nuclear.org. Retrieved on 14 June 2013

Pallav Bagla, "UN's Nuclear watchdog: Rajasthan Reactors are among World's safest", reported by NDTV, dated 15 November 2012 and uploaded on www.ndtv.com/article/india/un-s-nuclear-watchdog-rajasthan-reactors-are-among-world-s-safest-292623

Patel, Sonal, "India Designs Thorium-Fueled Reactor for Export", pub in powermag.com, dated 01 November 2009, retrieved 20 March 2012

Paul Brown, "Shoot it at the Sun. Send it to Earth's Core. What to do with Nuclear Waste? Published in The Guardian dated 14 April 2004.

Perinaz Bhada-Tata," The Potential For Waste To Energy In India" published in the waste management world and uploaded on http://www.waste-management-world.com/articles/print/volume-11/issue-5/features/the-potential-for-waste-to-energy-in-india.html.

Peter Fairley, "Nuclear Wasteland", posted on IEEE Spectrum, dated 01 February 2007, uploaded on www.spectrum.ieee.org/

Peter Lehner, "India's Next Big Energy Source: Energy-Efficient Buildings", uploaded on switchboard.nrdc.org/blogs/plehner dated 29 May 2013.

Peter R Lavoy, "The Enduring Effectsof Atom for Peace", Dated December 2003 uploaded on www.armscontrol.org/act/2003_12/Lavoy

Pham, Lisa, "Considering an Alternative Fuel for Nuclear Energy", published in The New York Times as a Special Report, dated 20 October 2009.

PK Agarwal, BHEL, "Key Impact for Accelerated Development of Indian Power Sector for 12th Plan and Beyond" during CBIP Conclave 18th Aug 2009, Delhi

Planning Commission, "12th Five Years Plan Document", planningcommission.gov.in/plans/planrel/12thplan/pdf/vol_2.pdf

Planning Commission-2006, "Integrated Energy Policy", New Delhi.

Planning Commission-2011 (b), " Report of the High Level Panel on Financial Position of Distribution Utilities", New Delhi

Popular Mechanics, "Reactor Makes Electricity." , March 1952, p. 105

Prabir Purkayastha, "Serious Safety Audit of India's Nuclear Program or a Cosmetic Exercise?", published in Newsclick, dated March 17, 2011, uploaded on http://newsclick.in/india/serious-safety-audit-indias-nuclear-program-or-cosmetic-exercise

A report in Power Engineering Magazine, "India's nuclear plans losing steam; Anti-nuclear protests hinder plans to ramp up power generation", dated 27 February 2012.

Pranab Dhal Samanta," India, France ink nuclear deal, first after NSG waiver published in Indian Express dated 30 September 2008.

Pranab Dhal Sharma, "Post Nuclear Deal, First US Reactor is Bound for Gujarat", published in Indian Express, 10 June 2012.

Press Information Bureau, Government of India, "Availability of Thorium", dated 10 August 2011, retrieved on 21 Mar 2012.

Press Release: Joint Statement on Prime Minister's visit to Japan: Strengthening the Strategic and Global Partnership between India and Japan beyond the 60th Anniversary of Diplomatic Relations, May 29, 2013 Tokyo, Japan.

Press Trust of India, "India Leading Research on Thorium: US Official", published in The Economic Times dated 21 May 2010, retrieved on 05 April 2012.

Professor Stephen Ansolabehere et al, "The Future of Nuclear Power- An Interdisciplinary MIT Study" dated 29 July 2003 updated up to 2009, uploaded on http://mitei.mit.edu/publications/reports-studies/future-nuclear-power

Pushker A Kharecha and James E Hanen, "Prevented Mortality and Greenhouse Gas Emissions from Historical and Projected Nuclear Power", published by American Chemical Society in Environmental Science & Technology, pp-4889-4895 dated 15 March 2013.

PTI, "ONGC Videsh Q1 net jumps 72 percent to Rs 837 Crores", published by The Economic Times dated 02 September 2013.

PTI Report, "Work on thorium-based reactor to commence soon", published in Chennai edition of Business Line, dated 21 February 2012, retrieved 21 March 2012

PTI Report, "AHWR undergoes design changes to increase safety, security", reported by Mumbai: OneIndia News, 20 April 2011, retrieved 13 April 2012

PTI Report, "India eyeing 64,000 MW nuclear power capacity by 2032: NPCIL", published in The Economic Times dated 11 October 2010.

PTI Report, "India's 20th nuclear power plant goes critical", published in Hindustan Times with dateline Kaiga, 27 November 2010. Retrieved 13 March 2011.

PTI Report, "Russia Fulfills Promise, Supplies Uranium to India", published in expressindia.com uploaded on 02 Apr 2006 on http://expressindia.indianexpress.com/news/fullstory.php?newsid=65381

PTI Report, "India, Russia sign nuclear deal", published in Times of India, dated 07 December 2009. Retrieved 21 August 2011

PTI Report, "India's 20th nuclear reactor connected to power grid", The Times of India dated 19 January 2011.

PTI Report, "Kudankulam at Advanced Stage", published in The economic Times, page-2, dated 29 June 2013

PTI Report, "India, EU to cooperate in R&D in nuclear and fusion energy" part of The India-EU Joint Action Plan issued at the end of the ninth India-European Union Summit held on Sep 29, 2008" published in The Economic Times of the same date.

PTI Report, "Rel Energy, Tata Power keen to enter nuclear power business: NPCIL" Published in Hindu dated 16 Apr 2010

PTI, "India's Breeder Reactor to be Commissioned in 2013", published in Hindustan Times dated 20 February 2012.

Ramana, M.V. (1 March 2007), "Nuclear Power in India: Failed Past, Dubious Future", in Henry D. Sokolski, Gauging U.S.-India Strategic Cooperation, Army War College (U.S.). Strategic Studies Institute,

Ranjit Devraj, "Prospects Dim for India's Nuclear Power Expansion as Grassroots Uprising Spreads", published in Inside Climate News, dated 25 October 2011.

Ratan K Sinha, Distinguished Scientist and director Reactor design and development Group BARC (Presently Chairman AEC), "India's Energy Security-the role of Nuclear Energy", Guest lecture delivered at petroleum Federation of India, New Delhi on 27 May2005.

Report on Global Energy Scenario, "Energy revolution: a sustainable world Energy Outlook", published by Greenpeace International and Europeon Renewable Energy Council (EREC) dated January 2007.

Report by the Committee on Technical Bases for Yucca Mountain standards of National Research Council, " Technical Bases for Yucca Mountain Standards" published by National Academy of Science Press, USA, 1995.

Rethinaraj, T.S. Gopi (5 June 2006), U.S.-India Nuclear Deal , Washington D.C.: Lee Kuan Yew School of Public Policy, National University of Singapore, retrieved 8 April 2012.

Rahman Maseeh, "How Homi Bhabha's Vision turned India into a Nuclear R&D Leader, Published in The Guardian with dateline of Mumbai, dated 01 November 2011 and retrieved on 01 March 2012.

Rai, Ajai K., "India's Nuclear Diplomacy after Pokhran II", published by Pearson Education India, dated 01 September 2009.

Ralph EH Sims et al, "Energy Supply, Chapter-4" uploaded on http://www.ipec.ch/pdf/assessment-report/ar4/wg3/ar4-wg3-chapter4.pdf

Rebecca A McNerney, "The Changing Structure of the Electric Power

Inductry: An Update", published by EIA of DOE of the USA, December 1996.

Reuters Report, "UK, India Sign Civil Nuclear Accord", date line London, dated 13 February 2010.

Reuters Report, "Bush signs India-US nuclear deal into law - Home" published in livemint.com,dated 09 October 2008. Retrieved 22 August 2010.

Reuters, TOKYO,"Japan approves two reactor restarts". Taipei Times. 2013-06-07. Retrieved 2013-06-14.

Ruggero Bertani of End Green Power Italy, Ian Thain of Geothermal Energy Tech Services New Zealand, "Geothermal Power Generating Plant CO2 Emission Survey, Published in IGA News Quarterly No 47 for the period Jul-Sep 2002.

Ryan Wiser, Eric Lantz, Mark Bolinger, Moureen Hand, "Recent Developments in the Levelized Cost of Energy for US Wind Power Projects", published by National Renewable Energy Laboratory (Berkley Lab), funded by the Wind & Water Power Program, Office of Energy Efficiency & Renewable Energy of the US DOE, pp-16, dated February 2012.

S Kumar et al," Integrated Radioactive Waste Management from NPP, Research Reactor and Backend of Nuclear Fuel Cycle- An Indian Experience", published by IAEA-SM-357/78 uploaded on www-pub. iaea.org/MTCD/publications/PDF/csp-006c/PDF-Files/paper-38.pdf.

Samanta, Pranab Dhal, "India, France ink nuclear deal, first after NSG waiver", published in Indian Express, dated 01 October 2008. Retrieved 21 August 2011

Sanjay Dutta, TNN, "Kazakh nuclear, oil deals hang in balance", Published in The Times of India, dated 23 January 2009, Retrieved 22 August 2010

Sasi, Anil, "NPCIL to go into details with 4 reactor suppliers", published in The Hindu (Business Online), 12 October 2008, retrieved on 21 August 2011.

SK Jain, "'Nuclear Power in India — The Fourth Revolution", pub in An International Journal of Nuclear Power - Vol. 18 No. 2-3 (2004).

Science Daily dated 25 July 2013, "New Nuclear Fuel Rod Cladding could lead to Safer Power Plants".

Seema Singh, "Uranium shortage holding back India's nuclear power drive - Corporate News". Published in Live Mint & Wall Street Journal dated 30 June 2008 uploaded on livemint.com and retrieved 22 August 2010.

Sethi, Manpreet, "The Nuclear Energy Imperative", published by IDFC, retrieved 11 April 2012.

Shri Prathvi Raj Chauhan, Minister of State for Science and Technology, Earth sciences (Independent Charge) and PMO in reply to the question No 413 of Shri Pradeep Majhi on 24 february 2010 in Lok sabha and by shri V Narayan Swami, Minister of State in PMO in reply to a question No 238 of Shri S semmalai on 13 march 2013 in Lok Sabha

Siddharth Srivastava, "India's Rising Nuclear Safety Concerns", published in Asia Sentinel dated 27 October 2011.

Siddharth Vardarajan," Thirty Wordsthat saved the Day", Published in The Hindu dated 09 September 2008.

Sinha Mohnish,"Indo-Canada Nuclear Accord", published in IndiaStand, dated 06 April 2010, uploaded on www.indiastand.com/articles/indo-canada-nuclear-accord

Srikanth, "80 percent of work on fast breeder reactor at Kalpakkam over", published in The Hindu, dateline: Kalpakkam dated 27 November 2011, retrieved 2 March 2012.

Srinivas Laxman, "India and South Korea Sign Civil Nuclear agreement", published in Asian Scientist, dated 26 July 2011 uploaded on www.asianscientist.com/topnews/india-soth-korea-sign-civil-nuclear-agreement/

Srinivasan G, KV Suresh Kumar, PV Ramlingam, " Two Decades of Operating Experience with the FBTR", uploaded on www.pub.iaea.org/MTCD/publications/PDF/P1360_ICRR_2007_CD/papers/S percentGopala.pdf

Staff reporters, "India signs N-pact with Argentina", uploaded on OneIndia (online), dated 14 October 2009. Retrieved on 21 August 2011.

Staff Report, "From Obninsk Beyond: Nuclear Power Conference Looks to Future Pub by IAEA Journal dated 24 June 2004 up loaded on http://www.iaea.org/newscenter/news/2004/obninsk.html

Staff Report, "India Safeguards Agreement Signed" published in IAEA News Letter dated 02 February 2009

Staff Report, "IAEA Board Approves India-Safeguards Agreement" Published in IAEA, News Letter dated 01 August 2008.

Stephenson, John; Tynan, Peter, "Will the U.S.-India Civil Nuclear Cooperation Initiative Light India?", in Henry D. Sokolski, Gauging U.S.-India Strategic Cooperation, Army War College (U.S.). Strategic Studies Institute, dated 01 March 2007.

Stephanie Cooke, "In Mortal hands: A Cautionary History of the Nuclear Age", published by Bloomberg bury, pp488, during 2009.

Steve Kidd, "New Nuclear Build- Sufficient Supply Capability", published in Nuclear Engineering International dated 03 March 2009 uploaded on www.neimagazine.com/opinion/opinionnew-nuclear-build-sufficient-supply-capability

Sue Sturgis, "Investigations: Revelations about Three Mile Island Disaster raise Doubts over Nuclear Plant Safety", published in Facing South, Institute of Southern Studies dated 04 February 2009

"Submarine Thermal Reactors (STR) in Reactors Designed by Argonne National Laboratory: Light Water Reactors' Technical Development", pub by Argonne National Laboratory, Nuclear Engineering Division of the US Department of Energy during 2012

Subramaniam, Kandula, "Now, fuel crunch takes toll on Kalpakkam unit", published in The Indian Express, New Delhi edition, dated 11 June 2008, retrieved 2 May 2012.

Subramanian, T.S., "Total self-sufficiency in PHWR programme", Volume 24, May 2007 Issue

The Asahi Shim Bun, "Atomic Agency Plans to Restart Monju Prototype Fast Breeder Reactor" dated 09 November 2012, uploaded on ajw.asahi.com/

T Hamacher and AM Bradshaw, "Fusion as a Future Power Source: Recent Achievements and Prospects" paper presented during 18th Congress at World Energy Council, October 2001.

T. S. SUBRAMANIAN, Massive uranium deposits found in Andhra Pradesh, published in The Hindu dated 20 March 2011.

taragana.com". "India, Namibia sign uranium supply deal", published in Republikein Online dated 02 September 2009. Retrieved 21 August 2011

Tarjane Risto, Kivisto Aija, "Comparison of Electricity Generation Costs", Table-1, pp-6, pyblished by Lappeenranta University of Technology, during 2008

Tongia, Rahul; Arunachalam, V.S., "India's Nuclear Breeders: Technology, Viability and Options", published in Pittsburgh: Current Science, pages: 549-558 dated 15 December 1997, retrieved on 9 April 2012.

Tellis, Ashley J., "Atoms for War? U.S.-Indian Civil Nuclear Cooperation and India's Nuclear Arsenal", published by Carnegie Endowment for International Peace during 2006, retrieved 7 April 2012.

The Economic Times Report quoting Prime Minister of India dated 06 July 2006.

Times of India Report, "Development work on 300 MW advanced heavy water reactor at advanced stage", TNN (Chennai: The Times of India), 20 December 2008, retrieved 26 March 2012.

The Times of India Report, "India, South Korea ink civil nuclear deal", dated 25 July 2011.

The Times of India-India Times Report, "Kovvada Nuclear Plant to Enhance its Capacity" up loaded on timesofindia.indiatimes.com/topic/nuclear-power-plant-at-kovvada

The Hindu, "India's fast breeder reactor nears second milestone", Chennai edition, dated 16 June 2009.

UDAILY, "UD-led team sets solar cell record, joins DuPont on $100 million project", published by University of Delware, dated 23 July 2007 and uploaded on http://www.udel.edu/PR/UDaily/2008/jul/

solar072307.html

UNSCEAR-2008 Report to General Assembly with scientific annexes, Volume-1, "Sources and Effects of Ionizing Radiation United Nations Scientific Committee on the Effects of Atomic Radiation, published during 2010.

US Energy Information Administration, Press Release during November 2011,"Levelized Cost of New Generation Resources in the Annual Energy Outlook-2011.

United States Nuclear Regulatory Commission, 1983. The Price-Anderson Act: the Third Decade, NUREG-0957.

Vandenbosch 200, p-21.

Verma, Nidhi,. "Westinghouse, AREVA eye India nuclear plants-paper". published by Reuters, 18 August 2008..

Victor, David G.," the India Nuclear Deal Implications for Global climate Change," Testimony before the US Senatr Committee on Energy and National Resources, 18 July 2006, available at: www.cfr.org/publication/11123/india_nuclear_deal.html

Vinay Shukla, Russia & India Report, 15 October 2013.

Vito A. Stagliano, "A policy of Discontent The Making Energy Strategy",pub by PennWell Corporation, Oklahoma USA, 2001, P-8-9 , 21, 22

Voorgelê deur Republikein,"India, Namibia sign uranium supply deal", dated 02 September 2009 uploaded on http://www.republikein.com.na/die-mark/india-namibia-sign-uranium-supply-deal.92293.php

Woddi, Paul; Charlton, William S.; Nelson (September 2009), India's nuclear fuel cycle: Unraveling the impact of the US-India nuclear accord, Synthesis Lectures on Nuclear Technology and Society, Morgan & Claypool Publishers, PP-7, 8.

WDI-2012, "World Development Indicators", World Bank, uploaded on http://databank.worldbank.org

World Energy Council, 2001: Living in One World

World Nuclear Association, " Nuclear Power in India", March 2012, retrieved 05 April 2012

World Nuclear Association, "Advanced Nuclear Power Reactors", updated up to June 2013.

WNA updated up to July 2013, "Renewable Energy & Electricity".

World Nuclear Association, "Nuclear Power in Russia", dated 24 July 2013.

World Nuclear Association, "Nuclear Power in China", dated 10 December 2010.

World Nuclear Association, "Plans for New Reactors ", dated March 2013

World Nuclear Association, "Thorium" updated up to June 2013, uploaded on www.world-nuclear.org/info/

World Nuclear Association, "Processing of Used Nuclear Fuel", updated up to June 2013, uploaded on www.world-nuclear.org/

World Nuclear Association, "Nuclear Power in the USA", dated 31 July 2013.

World Nuclear Association, " radioactive waste Management", updated up to April 2012, www.world-nuclear.org/

World Nuclear News, "Large Fast Reactor Approved for Beloyarsk" dated 27 June 2012, uploaded on www.world-nuclear-news.org/

World Nuclear News, "Sodium Coolant Arrives at Fast Reactor" dated 24 January 2013, uploaded on www.world-nuclear-news.org/

"World Nuclear Power Reactors 2007-08 and Uranium Requirements". World Nuclear Association. 2008-06-09. Archived from the original on March 3, 2008. Retrieved 2008-06-21

"What is Nuclear Power Plant - How Nuclear Power Plants work | What is Nuclear Power Reactor - Types of Nuclear Power Reactors". EngineersGarage. Retrieved 2013-06-14.

"Worldwide First Reactor to Start Up in 2013, in China - World Nuclear Industry Status Report". Worldnuclearreport.org. Retrieved 2013-06-14

Xinhua English News, "China Makes Nuclear Power Development", dated 31 October 2012.

Yep, Eric & Jagota, Mukesh, "AREVA and NPCIL Sign Nuclear Agreement", published in The Wall Street Journal - Business (online), dated 06 December 2010. Retrieved 21 August 2011

Yoshifumi Takemoto and Allan Katz, "Samurai-Sword Maker's Reactor Monopoly may Cool Nuclear Revival", published in Bloomberg dated 12 March 2008.

ZeeNews, "India's first PFBR to go critical early 2013", dateline: IANS, Chennai, dated 21 January 2012, retrieved 5 April 2012

ZeeNews, "India designs new version of AHWR for thorium use", dateline Mumbai, dated 16 September 2009, retrieved 13 April 2012

Index